CRIMINAL LAW

CRIMINAL LAW

HISTORY · PHILOSOPHY · ENFORCEMENT ·

EDWARD ELDEFONSO
ALAN R. COFFEY

1817

HARPER & ROW, PUBLISHERS, New York

Cambridge, Hagerstown, Philadelphia, San Francisco,
London, Mexico City, São Paulo, Sydney

Sponsoring Editor: John L. Michel
Project Editor: Karla Billups Philip
Designer: T. R. Funderburk
Production Manager: Marion A. Palen
Compositor: Maryland Linotype Composition Co., Inc.
Printed and Binder: The Book Press
Art Studio: Vantage Art Inc.

CRIMINAL LAW: HISTORY, PHILOSOPHY, ENFORCEMENT

Library of Congress Cataloging in Publication Data

Eldefonso, Edward
  Criminal law—history, philosophy, enforcement.

  Includes bibliographical references and index.
    1. Criminal law—United States. 2. Law enforce-
ment—United States. I. Coffey, Alan, joint author.
II. Title.
KF9219.E43   345.73   80–16177
ISBN 0–06–041879–6

CONTENTS

CONTENTS
IN DETAIL

PREFACE

THE OBVIOUS RELATIONSHIP BETWEEN THE police and criminal law has generated far more questions than answers. The wide diversity of police practice from one jurisdiction to another accounts for some of the difficulty in clarifying criminal law in terms of the police function and variations in the law itself, compounded by shifting judicial interpretation, account for still more confusion.

Criminal Law: History, Philosophy, and Enforcement seeks to provide some answers to the many questions raised about the police function and criminal law, and because this is an introductory text, answers will be provided, in part, by an exploration of the general nature of criminal law and law enforcement. Still other answers will be considered within the framework of the criminal justice system as a process that includes arrest, prosecution, and defense—all of which require an awareness of search and seizure, evidence, confessions, offense elements, the arraignment process, and countless technical matters. Of course, all the subjects pertinent to the field of criminal law—or those that educators consider germane to the study of criminal law—could not be included. Although some material was excluded, the ultimate selection of material covered in this textbook was guided by a resolve to discuss only areas pertinent to the *enforcement* of law. The authors have tried to clarify some of the pragmatic and specific (and oftentimes confusing) aspects of American criminal law as they relate to law enforcement in a rapidly changing society and to present, at the same time, an overview of the entire problem of criminal law and its impact on the agencies of law enforcement, specifically, the practitioner in the field—the working cop.

We have divided *Criminal Law* into two parts. Part One presents the historical aspects of criminal law, its *basic* rudiments, and its impact on the enforcers of the law, the police. The philosophy of Part One, then, is quite simple: To provide a *general overview* of criminal law and the justice processes and show how they relate to law enforcement. In an effort to introduce the reader to police and the criminal law, Part One is based on the premise that an elementary description of criminal law (and attempts by police to enforce it) is necessary.

The material in Part One, as in Part Two, is destinctively descriptive. The authors have taken great care to *describe* (as opposed to theorize or philosophize) the principles and objectives prevalent in criminal law. To this end, illustrative aides (charts, figures, and tables) are utilized to improve comprehension. And, in keeping with this pedagogy, at the conclusion of each chapter are selected annotated references that specifically address themselves to the material previously discussed; hopefully, the annotated references will generate motivation in those students who want to research a particular area further. Instructors will also find the references helpful in assigning supplementary reading in specific areas of criminal law. At the conclusion of each chapter, also, is a list of questions compiled by the authors to test the reader's knowledge of the covered material.

Part Two of *Criminal Law* offers an in-depth exploration of substantive criminal law, and although the material presented is pragmatic in nature, the authors have retained the initial philosophical approach by maintaining a nontechnical *descriptive* examination of the laws of arrest. Part Two not only presents substantive law *as it is* throughout the United States, but also analyzes, interprets, and intertwines the concept of intent—as presented in Part One—as a method of narrowing the definitions of crime in the United States. In discussing crimes against the person and crimes against property, we point out that discussions of *crimes* will depend heavily upon the concept of *intent*. All this is technically appropriate because the definitions of *crime* in this country are based on *mens rea*, using *intent* as the *only* conceivable point on which discussions of crime in the United States can be meaningful.

Another concept, not previously mentioned in Part One, is introduced in Part Two's interpretation of crimes against the person and crimes against property. This concept of *public tolerance* is the very reason that so much variation exists in law between jurisdictions. In spite of the strength of the argument that there is variation in what can be "tolerated" by various jurisdictions, there are certain activities that are universely illegal and *generally* not tolerated. In the introduction to Part Two, the authors offer an analogy of horse-stealing to amplify the concept of *tolerance*.

In keeping with our tutorial *modus operandi* of distinctive description, supplementary material has been appended at the conclusion of this book. These appendies, the "Criminal Process and Court Structure," the "Purpose of the District Attorney's Office," and a "Glossary of Legal Terms," are quite relevant to the study of criminal law.

Criminal Law: History, Philosophy, and Enforcement will be useful in several ways: (1) the book can be used as a *primary source* for a class introducing the complexities of American criminal law; (2) the text may be utilized, along with supporting lectures and material (i.e., state penal code), as the *basic text* or it may be used to supplement *classroom reading* assignments; and (3) it can serve as a supplementary text in criminal law offering rich material for discussion. The material in this text is easily adaptable to one-quarter or single-semester courses in the field of criminal law; those readers who have a general interest in the field of criminal law will also find it rewarding.

Finally, the authors do not pretend to know all the answers. In this book we have strived to make the learning of the nature of criminal law and the law of arrest as palatable as possible. As previously stated, the authors have not attempted to treat criminal law in its entirety; that is, all the problems, all the issues, and all the relevant Supreme Court decisions. Much more could be said, of course, about each of these areas, but the authors have selected only those areas considered important to a student *entering* the study of a complex discipline. We hope that *Criminal Law* will be the starting point for a successful career in criminal law or the enforcement of criminal law.

Edward Eldefonso
Alan R. Coffey

THE NATURE OF CRIMINAL LAW

Human relationships shape criminal law and procedure; human beings are concurrently the accuser and the accused. Concomitantly, the reciprocal relations between the accused person and the society of which he is part emanate from that body of law. Human articulations formulate the communicable descriptions of the forbidden behavior, conduct standards and criminal sanctions. To be continually cognizant of that factor is an indispensable requirement for treating the subject of substantive criminal law and criminal sanctions.

W. L. Clark and W. Marshall,
A Treatise on the Law of Crimes

PART ONE WILL PRESENT THE HISTORICAL development of law enforcement from prehistoric man through twentieth-century man. The influences of the ancient Middle East, the Roman Empire, and the Feudal Era are the background for the British impact on American law enforcement in general, and of Sir Robert Peel (1788–1850) in particular. Variations in the political aspects of the development of American law enforcement are attributable to the simultaneous growth of frontier, rural, urban, and federal police functions, as well the major background differences in the population of American townships.

The specific philosophy of American law enforcement, as we shall see, includes providing personal safety and property security and yet makes the fundamental distinction between enforcing laws by apprehending violators (police function) and enforcing laws by punishing violators (court function). Law and order philosophy become the product of the combined functions of the American police and courts when the society in general shares the broad and basic responsibility of preventing law violations.

Chapter 1 will undertake the presentation of both the philosophy and history of law enforcement. The law enforcement philosophy expressed in Part One is that individuals conforming to society's regulations are entitled to personal safety. This philosophy also entitles the conformer to property security but only to the degree that a given society permits the individual to acquire property rights. In this regard, we will note that the task of enforcing the law becomes more complex when the individual is permitted to acquire property rights.

In the area of criminal law, the designation of a particular act as a crime by legislative action within a particular state is more than a matter of applying an official label; it is a social process of far-reaching significance. This particular social process is discussed in Chapter 1 under the heading "The Influence of Justice on Law and Its Enforcement."

Crime is defined in Chapter 2, at least for the purposes of this text, as "an intentional act or admission in violation of criminal law (statutory and case law), committed without defense of justification and sanctioned by the state as a felony or misdemeanor." Chapter 2 also concerns itself with the essential elements of criminal law. A true definition of criminal law is made up of three parts: (1) a *term*, (2) a *genus*, and (3) the *differentia*. These terms, as well as the principles of criminal laws, are extensively discussed in Chapter 2.

The reader will note that the discussion of enforcement and criminal law is inappropriate without considering the common law system. The common law system, as pointed out in Part One, is a process of continuously developing law by reference to precedent. As such, the development of common law is the result of judicial decisions so its distinguishing characteristics have been compared to tort or civil injury. Accordingly, the principles of criminal law, initially developed in England, will be explored. As indicated in Chapter 2, criminal law is concerned with crimes—wrongs committed against society as a whole. Criminal law does not take into consideration those offenses against a moral order unless such acts are prohibited by statutes as well. A tort or civil injury is a private wrong done by another to one's person, property, or reputation. This is also discussed in detail in Chapter 2.

The "sources of law," as well as an examination of the Constitution—a basic law for any state—are also analyzed in Chapter 2. Although the courts do not make laws (this right is reserved for legislative body), they may influence the interpretation of a given statute and this interpretation will, if given an appellate review, constitute the basis upon which the populace conducts its activities.

An area that is extremely important—and one that serves as a springboard for Part Two, a discussion of substantive criminal law—is the classifications of crime. It will be pointed out that a crime is composed of two elements: the criminal act and the criminal intent—there must be concurrence of both to establish criminal responsibility.

Moving into a specific area of law enforcement, the authors discuss in Chapter 3 the legal procedures that must be strictly adhered to it any arrest and the various techniques of taking a suspect into custody—aspects that are extremely vital to every police officer sworn to enforce the law equally among citizens. Along these lines, police discretion is of extreme importance and is probably the only tool that causes a great deal of consternation among law enforcement personnel. Whether or not to subject an individual to the processes of the criminal justice system is an extremely important decision that the arresting officer must make in the field, usually without assistance from supervising personnel. These are important aspects of police work, and the authors attempt to explore, in nontechnical language, the legalities of taking a person into custody.

The constitutional rights underscored by recent Supreme Court rulings that effect police work relating to search and seizure are analyzed in Chapter 3. The law enforcement philosophy expressed in Chapter 1 recognized a general distinction between apprehending law violators and punishing law violators. Although both the police and the courts share a mutual responsibility for preventing law violations, the police apprehend the *offenders* and the courts *punish* or otherwise dispose of cases involving accused persons. Much of the basis of the increase in Supreme Court assessment of police practice is the Fourth Amendment to the Constitutional and to some degree the Ninth Amendment. The implications of the Fourth Amendment to the police function have received more than adequate concern in the literature, however, Chapter 3 intertwines these amendments with highlights of the more significant court decisions that may serve to clarify them.

In Chapter 4 the areas of evidence, logical evidence and proof, enough evidence for a particular proof, and circumstantial evidence are explored. The authors utilize pedagogical tools that will assist the reader in comprehending the legal ramifications of gathering and perserving evidence. The Supreme Court decisions relating to *Gideon, Escobedo*, and *Miranda* are thoroughly examined as to the impact on police practices in interrogation. The reader will note that there *is* a difference between the *Escobedo* guidelines and the *Miranda* requirements, and these differences are categorized and analyzed.

The latter part of Chapter 4 is concerned with the right to counsel, discussed along with the due process clause of the Fourteenth Amendment. Finally, demonstrative evidence and entrapment is covered in the light of past court decisions. The reader will note that court decisions play a significant part in both Parts One and Two.

Chapter 5, which completes Part One, concerns itself with criminal law and the judiciary process. The process after arrest—arraignment, preliminary examination, trial, juries, and the use of the prosecutor and defense counsel is detailed. Also, in discussing the court process, the authors analyze the role of the judge and the powers of his or her office.

The first five chapters in Part One, the authors feel, will provide the reader with a solid foundation for an intelligent examination of Part Two dealing with substantive law.

Chapter 1

CRIMINAL LAW: HISTORY AND PHILOSOPHY OF ENFORCEMENT

LEARNING OBJECTIVES

The learning objectives of this chapter are:
1. To develop an understanding of the historical perspective of criminal law.
2. To explore the major divisions in American law and its heritage.
3. To recognize the concept of criminal law in terms of a relationship to law enforcement (police).
4. To analyze the nature of criminal law in terms of two distinctive systems: the *common* and the *civil* law.
5. To examine the transcendence of common-law accusatorial practices over the ecclesiastical courts' inquisitional system.

WHY POLICE INTEREST IN THE NATURE of criminal law? Why should law officers have an extensive knowledge of the complex legalities that help to clog court calendars?

It has been argued that police have little need for the working attorney's legal knowledge in their job of providing personal safety and property security. This argument readily led law-and-order proponents to question the value of extensive legal knowledge in general. Properly presented, the argument viewed the tangled nuances of civil, probate, corporate, appeal, and even some criminal law as outside the sphere of the peace officer's activities and, indeed, outside the peace officer's concern. But even the supporters of this view now admit that the enforcement of laws in a rapidly changing democracy demands a more thorough knowledge of federal constitutional law as well as state statutes. In the last 10 years, decisions by the United States Supreme Court emphasized the need for expertise in criminal law:

> In the last decade, the U.S. Supreme Court has made more changes
> in criminal procedure than had been made by the Court in the
> previous 170 years of its existence. Critics of the Court have charged
> bitterly that these changes have "coddled criminals" and have reflected
> an undesirable attitude of permissiveness toward bad conduct. A
> fair-minded review of what the Court has actually done will show that
> these contentions are not true. The Court has not created any new
> rights for criminals; it therefore cannot have coddled criminals or been
> permissive of their evil ways. *What the Court has done is to equalize
> the rights of rich suspects and poor suspects.* The Court has not created
> any new rights, but it has extended to the poor, illiterate, and ignorant
> accused those rights which have long been known and enjoyed by the
> middle- or upper-class defendant. The *Miranda* decision created not
> one right or privilege that was not known and used by defendants
> who were either experienced or sufficiently affluent to hire good counsel
> promptly.[1]

This chapter, along with chapters to follow, attempts to provide the legalities that directly and indirectly impact on police work. But before moving into substantive law, a foundation must be developed. Thus, a review of criminal law in general appears to be the most logical point of embarkation into the nuances of a rapidly changing discipline.

CRIMINAL LAW

There are actually two major divisions in American law: the *common law,* derived first from the Germanic regions and then from England, and the *civil law,* derived first from Roman influences and then from France. The common-law system is a process of developing law "continuously" by reference to precedents, whereas civil law is based on specific codes that are written and legislated. Put another way, common law seeks to "remain common" by using past court rulings from similar cases as a guide for current dispositions. Civil law, on the other hand, concerns itself with the precise interpretation of an appropriate, but legislated, statute. A further distinction might be made in the "accusatorial" (whereby the law did not take the responsibility of the accused into consideration) nature of common law and the "inquisitional" (the mere fact that the person is accused of the act does not make him or her guilty) nature of civil law.[2] But technical distinctions between common law and civil law are no longer crucial, since American courts have come to function under a combination of both systems. In this combination there is what some consider excessive dependence on precedent and constitutionally dictated due process that tends to relate more to common law than to civil law. Nevertheless, American jurisprudence, particularly the criminal law, combines both law forms.

Although American criminal law, in general, combines both law forms, American police find themselves necessarily more concerned with the civil law of the codified statutes. Some of the codified statutes, known as *substantive criminal law,* are of particular concern to police, because it is through substantive law that society prohibits homicide, rape, assault, robbery, and similar crimes against personal safety or property security. The two major categories of substantive-law violations police must deal with are *felonies* and *misdemeanors*—both categories to be discussed in depth in Chapter 2. Although it is agreed that felonies are serious crimes and misdemeanors are less serious, the various state laws differ widely in where they draw the line. More often than not, the penalty for the offense determines the classification, felonies being punished by prison and misdemeanors by jail or fines.

As a matter of interest, the notion of using the punishment to determine whether the crime is a felony or a misdemeanor relates to the concept of criminal liability. Under this concept, not only is the criminal liable, but also those who conspire with, or abet, the offender are similarly subject to judicial sanction. The phrase "accessory before or after the fact" stems from this concept.

But regardless of the manner in which felons or misdemeanants are distinguished, the apprehension of these offenders introduces police to the nature of criminal law. In the case of misdemeanants (particularly traffic violators), the policeman's introduction to criminal law is often direct. Frequently he not only arrests an alleged violator but directly participates in the court process. In the case of felons, his introduction to criminal law is frequently superficial. Following the arrest, his direct involvement in the court process becomes a frequent enough adjunct to police investigations and arrest responsibilities to require rather comprehensive understanding of the nature of criminal law— a criminal law increasingly relevant in an era marked by turmoil over individual rights.

AMERICAN CRIMINAL LAW

The nature of American criminal law is shaped by the requirements that definitions of crimes and their punishments flow from the appropriate legislature of the jurisdiction involved. The most salient feature of the American system is that the legislative decision is to be guided by the common law itself; this, in effect, combines common and civil law (statute).

> When the English colonists first came to North America they brought with them, in addition to their material possessions, a cultural heritage not the least part of which was English law, especially the Common Law. The development of the Common Law started under the Norman and Angevin kings during the eleventh and twelfth centuries. It replaced earlier tribal and feudal law in which justice had been in the hands of popular assemblies known as folk-moots. As feudalism developed, folk-moots evolved eventually into shire-moots, local courts whose membership included the elite of the feudal society: large landowners, bishops, lords, and shire-reeves. The first step in the nationalization of these courts was taken when William the Conqueror attempted to consolidate his power by sending his own representatives of the local shire-moots. William also separated lay from ecclesiastical courts, so that two distinct legal systems emerged: state law and canon law. State law came to be called Common Law, was judge-made (as opposed to king-made, or parliament-made), and was common to all England in the same way that canon law (church law) was common to all Christendom. The law was also "common" because it had been derived by the royal justices from the customary practices of the realm.[3]

When the English monarch Queen Victoria chartered the first settlers to the New World in June of 1853, she took care to ensure that all prospective colonists were afforded the rights and privileges of every English citizen. Although this initial effort at establishing rights in the New World failed, it nevertheless was the policy that prevailed insofar as the judicial systems of later colonies were concerned.

The rights and liberties of the Magna Carta were included in the first charter of the Virginia Company in 1606. While the Jamestown colony, founded by Sir Walter Raleigh, proved a temporary, arbitrary-rule exception initially, assumption of control of that colony by Captain John Smith ultimately returned the settlement to common-law practice.

The American colonies prospered and grew steadily more self-reliant during the first century of their existence. The necessity of becoming self-reliant was, no doubt, accentuated by the chaotic political conditions that existed for nearly a hundred years following the establishment of a colonial economy in England. Whatever the reasons, American colonies were no longer inclined to accept arbitrary direction from the monarch by the time political stability returned to England. Gross resentment of royal revenue measures, especially import-export taxes, was symbolized by the famous slogan "Taxation Without Representation Is Tyranny."

This deprivation of the colonists' rights to be represented before being taxed was, of course, interpreted as impinging on the rights inherent in the Magna Carta—a prospect so threatening that it no doubt underlay many of the deep-seated motives for the revolution. But well before the revolution itself, an attempt was made by the colonies to reconcile their differences with their monarch when the First Continental Congress issued the Declaration and Resolves in 1774. Claiming the right to "life, liberty and property," the colonists went on to demand the right of trial by peers pursuant to the common law. Scholars concerned with the current impact of the judiciary on law enforcement can scarcely ignore this extremely salient landmark in the evolution of American criminal law.

American criminal law was still further shaped by Benjamin Franklin's Articles of Confederation, drafted in 1775, which provided for local determination of "laws, customs, rights and privileges." The famous Declaration of Independence, which followed in 1776, elaborated numerous complaints against the English monarch, not the least of which was his obstruction of justice by making judges dependent on his will instead of authorizing the passage of local laws. The United States Constitution, adopted some three years later, not surprisingly specified that the right of habeas corpus could not be suspended and that the trial of all crimes should be by jury. The first 10 Amendments to the Constitution, known as the Bill of Rights, were drafted and adopted within two years of the Constitution and clearly delineated a number of specific rights, including freedom from unreasonable search and seizure, the right to a speedy trial, and freedom of self-incrimination.

Congressional legislation prior to the adoption of the Constitution also had a great impact on the development of American criminal law. Congress passed a bill to apply to the territory northwest of the Ohio River; this was the Northwest Ordinance, and it was to become the legal system for all the western territories later admitted to the Union. Since the Constitution had not been ratified at the time the ordinance was passed, the Articles of Confederation formed the framework from which it was produced. The Northwest Ordinance predated the Constitution and the Bill of Rights, yet it contained all the essential guarantees incorporated by these two later documents. The inclusion of the Constitutional guarantees in an ordinance geared for territories rather than for the colonies ensured the relatively uniform evolution of American criminal law—the sometimes confusing combination of common law and "civil law" nothwithstanding.

The significance of the Northwest Ordinance[4] for American criminal law is reflected in the fact that virtually one-third of the total population was admitted to the union in states with judicial systems established under the ordinance. If this third of the population brought with them a tradition other than that framed in the Constitution and the Bill of Rights, the additional complexities of criminal law would have been scarcely ponderable.

All has not been smooth in the evolution of American criminal law. Early American criminal law, like early American Puritan–Pilgrim philosophy, reflected the Calvinistic belief that man was born in sin and remained essentially sinful unless he made strenuous efforts toward salvation. In the middle eighteenth century, Jean Jacques Rousseau postulated that man was like all other animals, born neither good nor bad.[5] Rousseau popularized the notion that society, particularly industry and property, had stripped men of their essential equality, and that law, especially criminal law, merely reflected oppressive power. Rousseau's reasoning is frequently cited as the rationale for social revolutions. It might also be conceived of as a significant historical root for twentieth-century social challenges to traditional "law and order." The following chapter will deal specifically with the sociological rationale for governmental regulation of human conduct, but Rousseau's philosophy constitutes a major disruption in what had been a relatively ordered evolution of criminal law.

THE PHILOSOPHY OF CRIMINAL LAW ENFORCEMENT

The eighteenth-century Swedish naturalist Linnaeus expressed the belief that a small child isolated from human society would be likely to grow into a hairy creature walking on all fours without an intelligible language. There has since been occasional corroboration for this view.[6] But whether it is true or not, in terms of criminal law enforcement the human being must be thought of as basically a member of society, depending on society and its law and order for survival.

Entire volumes have been devoted to the many ways in which the individual depends on society for survival. One of the more obvious ways has to do with regulating human behavior. When primitive *Homo sapiens* had advanced sufficiently to acquire the rudiments of language, the necessity of regulating behavior was not long in developing—at least not long by historical standards. This is not to say that with language came civilization. Nevertheless, following the acquisition of language, primitive human beings did contrive methods of regulating human behavior, probably as a matter of survival.

One might suppose that Neanderthals and Cro-Magnons probably found their struggle for survival and personal safety complicated by the process of growing older. Killing a saber-toothed tiger for protection and for food and clothing was a young man's activity. If women, children, and older men were to survive, they would have to depend on society. Recognition of the combat wisdom of older survivors of earlier tiger fights motivated society to provide personal safety for the elders by regulating the behavior of younger men. Prehistoric society no doubt evolved rules requiring older men to offer leadership and share survival secrets in exchange for protection, skins, food, and women obtained by younger "cavemen."

The biblical Cain's assault on his brother, Abel, signaled (at least from Abel's viewpoint) a need for society to regulate behavior. The absence of such regulation proved grossly unfortunate for Abel, to say the least. Without deliberate and concrete efforts to regulate behavior, man has historically demonstrated an inclination to foster his own survival and well-being at the expense of his fellow man.

An individual's relationship to society, then, is one of dependence.[7] In exchange for permitting one's own behavior to be regulated, one expects society to provide personal safety. In this context society is or should be an enforcer. Because human beings vary so much in their willingness to be regulated (in spite of the personal-safety motive), the enforcement function of society is basic to society's existence. The enforcement problems of the Atomic Age are considerably more complicated than they were among prehistoric people, and our society's dependence on behavior regulation is certainly no less real.

Another consideration in regulating human behavior is the freedom permitted to the individual by his society. All societies provide for the personal safety of individuals who permit their own behavior to be regulated (although some such regulations at times appear virtually impossible to observe).[8] In societies that permit great personal freedom, the individual is usually permitted property rights. Societies permitting individual property rights obviously differ from societies in which the state retains the rights to all property. But, of course, no society actually permits individuals to have complete property rights with complete freedom; nor does any state deny all individual rights. In either direction, it is simply a matter of relevance and degree.

Property rights and freedom relate to enforcement of society's rules for many reasons, the most obvious of which are the complications of enforcing behavior regulation in a "free society." Unlike societies in which the state retains all property rights, in a "free society" there are as many potential property violations as there are property owners—and as many prospective property owners as there are society members. Standards of enforcement increase in complexity accordingly. On closer examination, this observation actually suggests a method for distinguishing between a "free" society and a society that is "not free." To the degree that the individual is free to acquire property rights and to expect society to protect these rights, to that degree is the society "free." Also, to that same degree is the enforcement of behavior regulation far more complicated.

Whether or not a society is free, the individual depends on his society for personal safety. But the free society is further obligated to provide property security along with personal safety for individuals permitting their behavior to be regulated. As a result, the rules regulating behavior, like the enforcement of these rules, obviously become still more complex.

Early societal rules that ultimately become criminal law can be thought of as society's formal regulation of human behavior. To be enforced effectively, criminal law must be enforced impartially. If the individual remains willing to permit his behavior to be regulated, he must also believe that he gains personal safety and (in a free society) property security. He must also believe that this gain is predictable and consistent.

In terms of individual freedom, criminal law restricts behavior either to protect the freedom of others or to control the individual. In either case, impartiality is necessary to convince the individual that there is a definite relationship between conformity and personal safety (as well as property security for free societies). Also, in either case, the main function of criminal law is to maintain an orderly society. Systematizing the approach to this function, perforce, becomes crucial.

With the goal of an orderly society, enforcement of criminal law must take into consideration the relationship between society's power and the power of man's will. Most of what is called "the wisdom of the ages" probably deals with this relationship in one way or another.

The term *enforcement* suggests power. It also suggests punishment.

Criminal laws that regulate behavior customarily specify sanctions that are intended to be punishing. Of course, the punishing aspects of legally specified sanctions differ from the punishment involved in arrest per se. A sanction is designed to be punishing, whereas apprehension or arrest (however punishing the process might be) is merely a requisite part of initiating "justice." It nevertheless remains worthy of note that arrest can be at least as punishing as certain specified sanctions.[9]

Since society must be stable to function properly, it might be said that punishing the failure to perform is necessary to maintain society, and that the only danger is in failing to administer punishment impartially—further evidence of a demand for a systematized approach to justice. Even in "very free societies," there must be punishment for behavior that threatens the stability of society, particularly when the personal safety or property security of conforming society members is threatened. Were this not so, society could not provide individuals with a motive for permitting their own behavior to be regulated.

Although law and order remain the philosophical basis of society's sanctions, the particular goals of criminal law can vary. Society can seek, through punishment, any or all of the following: retribution (retaliation); justice; deterrents (by example); or rehabilitation (treatment). Modern American criminal law, particularly as it is designed for the maintenance of an orderly American society, must increasingly assume responsibility for threats to the personal safety and property security of all who permit their own behavior to be regulated. From this philosophical viewpoint, *all* regulated behavior, from family activities to vehicle speed, are functions of contemporary criminal law enforcement.[10]

As the history of law enforcement continues to unfold, its philosophy remains relatively simple. As in the case of prehistoric society, our permitting society to regulate our behavior continues to entitle us to expect personal safety and property security from society. But criminal law enforcement, in our grossly complicated, urbanized society, increasingly demands that personal safety and property security include positive efforts to maintain a systematic approach to such enforcement—aimed at redirecting social forces tending to jeopardize the personal safety and property security of individuals who permit their behavior to be regulated. Unrestricted force is not (and probably never was) a feasible alternative to a rational system of regulating behavior by law.[11]

Whether or not unrestricted force has ever been an available alternative, there is value in examining the earliest human efforts to enforce societal rules and in making this examination much as we did with the background of common-law influences.

ENFORCEMENT IN HISTORICAL PERSPECTIVE

Various college subjects, such as psychology and sociology, are sometimes said to have "long pasts but short histories." That is, there seems to be evidence that these subjects were studied through many phases of history, even though the actual collection of related information is comparatively new. Criminal law enforcement is, to some degree, in a similar historical position. Unlike other college subjects, however, the enforcement of criminal law can draw on history not only to show a considerable amount of study down through the ages but also to demonstrate a considerable amount of law-enforcing activity as well.

Archaeologists and anthropologists provide little information on the ancient and prehistoric past of criminal law enforcement. Yet in spite of this historical weakness, there remain broad areas highly susceptible to speculative interpretation.

As an example, earliest prehistoric people have been pictured as members of small family groups, remaining together for mutual protection from the environment.[12] These family groups merged into tribes, which appointed those they considered the most reliable to protect the interests of the clan. Their tribal duties may have included waging war with hostile clans, but if so they also included the duty of enforcing various regulations developed by the tribe itself. This merger of military and police functions tended to relegate the violator of tribal law to the unfortunate position of "enemy of the clan," which may account for the brutal criminal sanctions devised by early man.

Another view, of equal validity, pictures the head of the clan as delegating police functions to clansmen in general, rather than to a particular group.[13] Without a specific police force, the clan as a group administered justice in the case of a rule violation. The military function, dealing with hostile tribes or clans, also remained a group responsibility.

Still another view believes that primitive man began by attributing violations of tribal rules to the influence of evil spirits—evil spirits which, in turn, were the object of placation and tribal ritualistic punishment of the alleged offender.[14] Social revenge evolved from this practice. Many feel the practice lent itself to the later, contradictory view of rule violations as voluntary and willful acts against the tribe, defined as *crimes*, rather than *sins*. Blood feuds between tribes removed rule violations still further from the domain of evil spirits with the development of the *lex talionis*, the "eye for an eye and tooth for a tooth" principle—also enforceable by the entire clan.[15]

Perhaps all three notions of prehistoric criminal-law enforcement are valid roots of traditional police work. However, the earliest indication that many clans felt a need to organize and standardize the control of human behavior was not recorded until a few thousand years before Christ. In about 2370 B.C., a Sumerian king, Ura-Ka-Gina, handed down several key inscriptions describing his efforts to curb oppression of the poor by certain kingdom officials. Within two centuries, another ruler, Gudea, recorded the suspension of court proceeding in at least one instance that many believed to be of considerable influence on the Babylonians' effort to organize and standardize control of human behavior.

A further historical gain in the standardization of society's enforcement of rules occurred in 2130 B.C., when King Nammu issued a somewhat fragmented but nevertheless organized code of laws. Most Babylonian rulers of the first Amorite dynasty attempted both to implement and supplement these rules during the centuries that followed, and there evolved a virtual "common law" not unlike the English common law mentioned earlier. The Sumerian kings, Lipit-Ish-Tar and Eshnunna, finally standardized what actually constituted an offense (or crime), and less than 200 years later a Babylonian king, Hammurabi, issued what many historians consider the most significant contribution of all time to the rule of society by law.[16]

In the great Code of Hammurabi, the offenses were codified, and accompanying penalties for each offense were also spelled out. Although the penalties remained as brutal as those specified by the unwritten *lex talionis*, the very fact that the relationship between offense and penalty had been standardized is considered historically significant by many criminologists.[17] It is also noteworthy that the Mosaic Code, which embodied the *lex talionis* as well (Exodus 21: 23–25), was still over 1000 years in the future when the Code of Hammurabi was written.

Enforcement of the criminal segment of Hammurabi's Code became the function of officials appointed by the kings who followed Hammurabi. Such enforcement operated within limits the king might impose, and it was, therefore, several hundred years before anything resembling what is known today evolved in the enforcement of societal law. Nevertheless, the laws enforced by appointed officials during this period probably represent the embryo of the complex criminal codes of the twentieth century. Egyptian statutes that evolved during this period incorporated penalties for offenses bearing greater resemblance to modern criminal law than the penalties embodied in the ancient *lex talionis*.

The practice of codifying the offense and the penalty on the Hammurabian model approximated western civilization's approach to criminal law until the mid-eighteenth century,[18] when there evolved a "classical school of criminology." Criminologists credit Cesare di Beccaria of Italy and Jermy Bentham of England with developing much of the classical school, which in essence held that the punishment must "completely fit the crime."[19] A more serious offense would then require a more serious penalty, which, in turn, would "deter" crime. Actually, the underlying philosophy of the ancient *lex talionis*, created some 4000 years earlier, draws on a similar rationale—lacking only what Beccaria and Bentham conceived of as sophisticated application. For that matter, hundreds of years before the Roman emperors, Plato considered punitive sanctions to serve far more purpose than simple retaliation. In any event, the classical school, in proposing "calculus for punishment," tended to further standardize the enforcement of criminal law.

One other historically significant influence on enforcement of criminal law was the decision of the Roman emperor Augustus to relieve an elite segment of his army from military duties and assign them the task of protecting his property and personal safety.[20] The Praetorian Guards, in many respects, bear considerable resemblance to traditional police organizations currently functioning in western civilization. In fact, there are many similarities in enforcement policy.

After the decline of the Roman Empire, the enforcement of criminal law appears to have lost historical pattern—at least until the era associated with the feudal system, during which the common law of England developed. Developments in France in the same period have a definite bearing on the history of criminal law enforcement, but it is to feudal England that the enforcement as well as the nature of American criminal law traces its heritage.

Early Influences of England

The law enforcement influence of feudal England can be traced through an examination of three eras: (1) before 1829; (2) the three decades following the Metropolitan Police Act of 1829; and (3) the era following the Obligatory Act of 1856.[21]

The first era referred to includes the early Anglo-Saxon period, when England was divided into four countries known as *shires*. A group of ten families was known as a *shiretything*, and ten *tythings* understandably were known as a *hundred*. The present-day English cities in many cases were, at one time, *tuns* (now known as towns), formed by combination of certain *hundreds*.

In each shire, the king appointed an individual to maintain law and order under the title *reeve*, which eventually became known as *shire-reeve*, and still later as *sheriff*.

Although the shire-reeve was responsible for enforcing the king's law in general, each man living in the shire was charged with explicit responsibility for enforcing the king's law—a responsibility carried to the point of equal punishment for not reporting the crimes of one's neighbor.

To avoid the hardships inherent in this type of responsibility, many shires adopted a system of annually assigning specific individuals to enforce the king's law. These individuals could, in turn, hire substitutes. This practice evolved into the tradition of paying for police services and, in 1737, led to King George II's levying taxes for this purpose. In 1777 King George III began standardizing the practice of establishing prescribed wages and equipment for police.

The invasion of England by William the Conqueror in A.D. 1066 was followed by a reduction in the law-enforcing responsibility of the shire-reeve and led ultimately to a clear division between judicial and police functions.[22]

Major mob violence, requiring the use of military force, led to crystallization of the traditional police function through the Metropolitan Police Act of 1829.[23] This historically significant act formally introduced the concept that each community should have its own police force. Sir Robert Peel was instrumental in persuading Parliament to adopt this concept. He was also responsible for a number of organizational suggestions that continue to influence the police function in western civilization.

The "Peelian" era was followed by the Obligatory Act of 1856, which required every county in England to create its own police force. Although this ensured police protection for every community, it also intensified a law enforcement problem that has plagued America far more than England—the problem of standardizing police practices (that is, implementing laws relating to arrest and to search and seizure, as well as laws guaranteed by state and federal Constitution).

American police, unlike the English, cope with major laws of 50 jurisdictions, some spread over areas that dwarf England. Thus far, only the federal governments of the two countries have been able to standardize police practices, evidenced by the similarity between the FBI and Scotland Yard.

DEVELOPMENT OF CRIMINAL LAW ENFORCEMENT IN AMERICA

Less than three years after the 1620 arrival of the pilgrims in Massachusetts, a large concern known as the Dutch West India Company set up operation in Nieuw Amsterdam—a city later to become known as New York. By 1629, the need for law enforcement led the Dutch West India Company to appoint a peace officer, identified in the

Dutch language as a "schout-fiscal." The city of Boston soon followed this example and appointed a peace officer with six assistants to be responsible for law enforcement after sundown. Settlements throughout New England soon followed suit, and the American police tradition was under way—a tradition developed along British lines.

The state of Massachusetts, in the late 1600s, began appointing justices of the peace with judicial powers and law enforcement responsibility.

Soon after the appointment of justices of the peace in New England, the city of Philadelphia established a significant system known then as the "watch and ward," which introduced the concept of both day *and* night enforcement of the law.

The significance of the Philadelphia innovation was underscored by the growth of American cities—growth that was accompanied by major problems in enforcing the law. Systems using only night watches proved inadequate to cope with day problems. Motivation to deal with the emerging problems was lacking because of low pay and even lower prestige for the "professional" watchman.

Responding to these problems, Boston divided the city into police districts in 1807 in order to centralize the police function. Although Boston failed to establish both day and night police activities until 1838, the effort to centralize functions ultimately proved to be useful and was adopted by New York and Philadelphia. Public support for such efforts, as well as concern for police problems in general, was not evident, however, until the 1884 "native-born versus immigrant" riots that raged totally out of control for extended periods of time.

Even before these riots, similar disorders, reflecting economic unrest, had swept the country. A riot involving 15,000 people shook Boston in 1837, and Philadelphia experienced a series of racial riots a few years later. Philadelphia also experienced labor difficulties, known at the time as the Weaver riots.

But the "native-born riots," continuing uninterrupted for some three months in New York City, focused public attention on the enforcement of law as nothing else had.

In 1844 New York established a law requiring "day and night police" —eliminating the loosely structured watchman system. The development of American law enforcement since this 1844 milestone has regrettably been blighted from time to time by corruption, brutality, and ineffectiveness. The practice of appointing police on the basis of political considerations by no means eased the impact of these blights.

Throughout the country in the 1850s, various laws were passed requiring the *election* of law enforcement administrators. This tended to weaken the political spoils system, but it complicated police efficiency by placing politicians in charge of police affairs. In terms of enforcement and the criminal law, this very problem may continue to this day. Comparisons between urban and rural law enforcement usually highlight this problem. The rural law enforcement officer is well known by the community he serves. He is elected (or selected) for his expertise as an enforcer of the law—not political astuteness. This is not to say that some understanding of the political "network" is not important, it is. However, it goes hand in hand with ability. The opposite is often true in an urban community where polemics is often confused with expertise.

Compounding the difficulty of American law enforcement was the continued, simultaneous development of Peelian English metropolitan functions, rural constabulary, frontier law enforcers, and an increasingly complicated federal law enforcement system.

Another factor in the development of American law enforcement was the difference in cultural backgrounds of the immigrants making up the population. What these various peoples expected in terms of law and order no doubt varied. Consider the now mythical western sheriff attempting to bring his skill in outwitting rustlers to bear on the violence of San Francisco's early Chinatown, or on New York's 1884 immigration riots, or consider the federal government's concern with interstate prostitution.

THE INFLUENCE OF JUSTICE ON
LAW AND ITS ENFORCEMENT

A chapter dealing with enforcement and criminal law requires at least some mention of the influences of the consequences of law violation —"consequences" frequently serving as a limited definition of "justice."

In the nineteenth century the trend in penology shifted from punishing the individual to reforming the individual. Reformers in the past two centuries have evolved the reformatory and, ultimately, the notion of parole.[24]

England, the United States, and parts of the rest of the world have come a long way from the early tradition of transporting criminals to the American colonies and to Australia as punishment and are approaching what appears to be an era of rehabilitation that virtually excludes the concept of punishment.

Although parole, pardons, restoration of prisoners' rights, and probation appear to have little direct effect on enforcing criminal law, collectively these processes influence grossly the interpretation of the laws to be enforced. Throughout this volume, it will be noted that in addition to the frequent conflicts between codes and statutes are conflicts of interpretation—conflicts often pivoting on the consequences of law violation rather than on the codified violation itself.

The chapters that follow provide a framework within which these interpretational difficulties, and the complexity of law itself, can be integrated with a general understanding of the roll of enforcement in criminal law.

DUE PROCESS

Throughout this book, we will refer to constitutional cases and, more specifically, to the due process clause of the Fourteenth Amendment. It is, therefore, necessary to analyze due process before we attempt to analyze the criminal constitutional problems that have been partially answered over the last decade by the Supreme Court.

In serving community needs, the Supreme Court cannot close its eyes to the archaic methods employed in the administration of justice. The courts must guarantee the protections that stem from the Constitution and specifically the Bill of Rights. Constitutional protections are not static. The community does not require unwavering standards and guidelines, which restrict rather than guarantee the rights of the accused. Ideally, in seeking justice we seek the truth. If standards and procedures must be violated to achieve such a result, the courts must forge ahead toward a system of perfect justice by disregarding such standards. Throughout history, and especially in the 1960s, the United States Supreme Court has opened the door for protection of the criminally accused, a protection that has been long overdue.

The importance of understanding criminal-procedural law cannot be overemphasized. A case may be dismissed just as easily for violation of *procedural* due process as for violation of *substantive* due process.[25]

Inherent in the Constitution and the Bill of Rights are certain substantive guarantees that protect the criminally accused against excessive governmental power and restrictions. As early as 1833 the Supreme Court decided that the Bill of Rights (consisting of the first 10 Amendments) was originally enacted to protect people against actions of the federal government only.[26]

Today, through the application of the Bill of Rights in the Fourteenth Amendment, the individual is protected against actions of the state government as well. The Fourteenth Amendment provides in part: "No state shall make or enforce any law which shall abridge the privileges or immunities of citizens of the United States; nor shall any state deprive any person of life, liberty, or property without due process of law; nor deny to any person within its jurisdiction the equal protection of the laws."

The critical question facing the courts in modern times is the extent to which the Fourteenth Amendment's *due process clause* incorporates the Bill of Rights.[27] The courts are in disagreement over this question.

Arguments have been advanced that the Bill of Rights should be incorporated entirely to protect the individual against state infringement.[28] However, the Supreme Court ultimately followed *the doctrine of selective incorporation.* Under this doctrine, the restrictions contained in the Bill of Rights limit state infringement *only* on a selective basis. In *Bloom* v. *Illinois,* the court held that the Bill of Rights is incorporated by the Fourteenth Amendment due process clause only on a limited basis.[29] The Supreme Court has determined that the guarantees and protections under the Bill of Rights are so fundamental and inherent to the basic rights of the individual that they should be protected against infringement by either federal or state interference.

A question arises as to how the court determines what protection is of such a fundamental nature and must be guaranteed against governmental infringement. The court reviews such rights on a case-by-case basis and has defined these rights under only the most general of terms: "those principles implicit in the concept of order or liberty,"[30] of "the principles of justice so rooted in the traditions and conscience of our people as to be ranked fundamental."[31] It is a simple task to give a definition in such broad terms, but it is difficult to apply that definition to any particular situation. Intangible guidelines cause confusion and apprehension.

Justice Frankfurter, in *Rochin* v. *California,*[32] recognized the lack of concrete guidelines when he stated:

> Formal exactitude of fixity of meaning in the due process clause because words being symbols do not speak without a gloss. A gloss of some of the verbal symbols of the constitution does not give them a fixed technical context, but it exacts a continuing process of application. . . .
>
> In each case "due process of law" requires an evaluation based on a disinterested inquiry pursued in the spirit of science, on a balanced order of facts exactly and fairly stated, on a detailed consideration of conflicting claims. . . .

Violations of constitutional rights that result in the denial of life, liberty, and property have caused the Supreme Court to look not only at the *due process clause* but also at the *equal protection clauses*[33] of the Fourteenth Amendment in order to guarantee fully the rights of the criminally accused. However, we must limit our discussion to the due process clause.

In the *Rochin* case, Justice Black, in a concurring opinion, held that the Supreme Court must measure the validity of state action not only by the justice's own personal reason or by the traditions of the legal profession but also by the "community sense of fair play and decency."[34]

Not only must we contend with the doctrine of selective incorporation, the court has begun to broaden the concept of due process to include not only the Bill of Rights but also fundamental rights not explicitly included in the first 10 Amendments.

The leading case is *Griswold* v. *Connecticut*.[35] Connecticut had a state law that made it a crime to aid or abet married persons in using contraceptive devices. The Supreme Court invalidated the state law, and used a number of theories in arriving at the result. Some of the justices held that the marriage relationship was a fundamental right and was within a "zone of privacy" that exempted it from any state infringement. The Court readily admitted that the Bill of Rights was *not* the basis on which this decision turned. However, the Court, in essence, held that freedom from state infringement comes within the penumbra, or "shades," of fundamental rights derived from the basic freedoms found in the Bill of Rights.

Other justices held that marital privacy is guaranteed by the Ninth Amendment, while some held marital privacy is one of the fundamental and substantive rights implicitly protected and guaranteed by the concept of "liberty" in the due process clause of the Fourteenth Amendment.

Result

The law enforcement officer must now look not only to the Constitution and the Bill of Rights for protection of the individual, but to the penumbras, or shades, of the Bill of Rights as well to guide his or her actions in order to guarantee the rights of the criminally accused. And students cannot limit themselves to cases decided up to now that have established guidelines and safeguards for the criminally accused. They must also search their own consciences for the "fundamental fairness essential to the very concept of justice."[36] We can no longer adjudicate the guilt or innocence of an individual without assuring that individual the rights guaranteed by the Constitution. It is necessary for the law enforcement officer to understand the difficulties surrounding marginal cases when facts must be tested against such nebulous and flexible guidelines as those discussed above. The only certainty is that change is inevitable, but individual rights cannot be disregarded during that change.

Reflection

During the 1960s, the "Warren Court" restructured and clarified the major areas in the field of criminal procedure. As a result, federal and state courts were made aware of constitutional limitations and, more important, of *the constitutional rights, protections, and privileges of the individual.* The most important question facing law enforcement agencies today is whether recent decisions of the Supreme Court have hindered law enforcement officials in their investigation and pretrial procedures.

The Supreme Court has, in essence, concluded that the constitutional rights of the individual can only be protected when all federal and state officials comply with the constitutional protections called for in the cases we shall refer to through the rest of this text. Before *Mapp* v. *Ohio*,[37] the police officer, as an agent of the state, could obtain evidence that would be excluded in the *federal* court system but was admissible in *state* court. As a result, the defendant preparing for his execution or serving his sentence in a state penitentiary had the right (not a very gratifying privilege) to sue the state law enforcement agency because of misconduct that might have amounted to trespass, assault, battery, false imprisonment, or some other type of constitutionally prohibited state actions.

The court sought to extend the protections against illicit federal action to the states. This was accomplished through a broad interpretation of the due process clause of the Fourteenth Amendment.

Unfortunately, there is a great gap between the rights afforded the criminal defendant and the reality of unlawful police practices. Only when the defendant is protected by court processes do these rights become a reality. The need to study and understand basic constitutional limitations imposed on police officials cannot be underestimated.

Whenever the Supreme Court renders a decision that imposes more restrictive limitations on law enforcement agencies in arresting and convicting defendants, peace officers typically feel indignant. They feel these limitations frustrate and impede the utopian goal of peace and tranquility. Without question, constitutional limitations make working conditions for the peace officer more difficult. The late Justice Black, on a national television interview show, stated emphatically that the police officer's role *should be a difficult* one to fulfill. The ultimate answer is a proper balance of interests. Can law enforcement agencies be burdened with the duty of preventing crime and, at the same time, be effectively restrained from obtaining evidence with which to prosecute the criminal defendant?

The duty of the peace officer is to arrest, not to prosecute and convict criminals. He cannot be given an independent forum to carry out those goals. In order to protect the rights of the individual against the minority of police officers who violate constitutional guarantees, the Supreme Court recognizes the need for preventive rather than retributive control of law enforcement agencies.[38]

The student may well conclude that peace officers are restricted in their duties and hampered in their goal of bringing about law and order. However, the opposite is true, especially with respect to enforcement of minor statutes. It is a strange horse society rides when the greatest latitude and discretion is given to officials located in the most insignificant branch of a complex bureaucracy. This book cannot presume to cover every criminal statute in every state. However, the enforcement of these "minor" statutes lies almost totally within the discretion of the lowest-ranking police officer.[39] Social values, backgrounds, formal education, and religious training vary from one police officer to the next. The unfortunate result is unequal enforcement of minor statutes, not only from county to county but from police officer to police officer.

The decision to arrest without a warrant is in the hands of the police officer. If she bases her action on conduct that she believes transgresses her own personal values, she may decide to arrest an individual after a breach of some minor statute. It is doubtful if prosecution or ultimate conviction will result if she does not act, because her failure to make the original arrest usually terminates further investigation. In making such a valid judgment, the police officer has assumed the role of prosecutor, public defender, judge, jury, and legislature. Because of this discretion, the officer's awareness must be clothed in due process reasoning.

SUMMARY

The concept of criminal law in terms of a relationship to law enforcement was introduced by examining the nature of American criminal law. It was noted that law enforcement seeks to provide personal safety and property security in the context of the chapter that follows. But it was further noted that police are increasingly expected to "understand" the law that is to be enforced—an understanding that begins, perhaps, with the nature of criminal law.

The nature of criminal law as analyzed here "combines" two distinctive systems: the common law, which develops continuously by interpreting precedents, and the civil law, based on specific codes that are written and legislated. An additional distinction noted was that common law is generally accusational (accusatorial), whereas civil law tends historically to function inquisitionally.

Chapter 1 also points out that the "accusatorial" nature of common (responsibility of accused not taken into consideration by law) and the "inquisitional" nature of civil law (mere fact that person is accused of act does not make him guilty) are not crucial since American laws have come to use both systems. American police, the chapter points out, find themselves more concerned with the civil law of codified statutes. These statutes, known as substantive criminal law, are important to law enforcement because these are the laws society excepts to be enforced (i.e., rape, murder, robbery, burglary, and similar crimes against personal safety and property security).

The concept of criminal liability was clarified. It was pointed out that the punishment concept determines whether an offense is a felony or misdemeanor. Under the aforementioned concept, it was pointed out, those who conspire with or abet the offender are also liable to be charged.

The combination of economic and political influences on criminal law during and after the American Revolution was dealt with, noting in particular the abortive effort of the English monarch to deprive the colonists of individual rights inherent in the common law. The similarity of the United State Constitution, the Bill of Rights, and their predecessor, the Northwest Ordinance, was highlighted as a probable source of continuity in the nature of criminal law during the transition of territories into states.

NOTES

1. A. B. Smith and H. Pollack, *Crime and Justice in a Mass Society* (Lexington, Mass.: Xerox College Publishing, 1973), pp. 215–216.
2. R. Paulsen and K. Kadish, *Criminal Law and Its Processes* (Boston: Little, Brown, 1972), pp. 993–1007.
3. Smith and Pollack, *Crime and Justice in a Mass Society*, pp. 9–10.
4. Lewis Mayers, *The American Legal System*, rev. ed. (New York: Harper & Row, 1969), pp. 4–6.
5. See Rousseau (*Social Contract*) for a discussion of sovereign power. L. Lloyd, *Introduction to Jurisprudence* (New York: Praeger, 1965), p. 126.
6. K. Davis, *Human Society* (New York: Macmillan, 1969), pp. 204–208.
7. *Ibid.*
8. H. E. Russell and Allan Beigel, *Understanding Human Behavior for Effective Police Work* (New York: Basic Books, 1975), p. 336.
9. J. Lacy, "Yugoslavia: Practice and Procedure in a Communist Country," 43 *Oregon Law Review* 1 (1963): 28–30.
10. L. Selynick, "Legal Institutions and Social Control," 17 *Vanderbilt Law Review* 79 (1963).
11. C. Westley, "Violence and the Police," *American Journal of Sociology* 59 (1963).
12. J. S. Sullivan, *Introduction to Police Science*, 3d ed. (New York: McGraw-Hill, 1977), p. 123.
13. A. C. Germann, F. D. Day, and R. R. Gallati, *Introduction to Law Enforcement*, 5th ed. (Springfield, Ill.: Thomas, 1977), p. 37. See also P. J. Stead, *Pioneers in Policing* (Montclair, N.J.: Patterson Smith, 1978).

14. H. Hoebel, *The Law of Primitive Man* (Cambridge, Mass.: Harvard University Press, 1969), p. 32.
15. Selynick, "Legal Institutions and Social Control," p. 79.
16. R. Seagle, *The History of Law* (New York: Tudor, 1951), pp. 104–122.
17. T. Hoebel, *Law of Primitive Man* (Cambridge: Harvard University Press, 1959), pp. 51–52.
18. P. Tappan, *Crime, Justice and Correction*, 3d ed. (New York: McGraw-Hill, 1966), p. 536.
19. *Ibid.*, pp. 16–17, 278–280.
20. Germann, Day, and Gallati, *Introduction to Law Enforcement*, p. 38.
21. E. Eldefonso, A. Coffey, and R. C. Grace, *Principles of Law Enforcement*, 2d ed. (New York: Wiley, 1974), pp. 42–50.
22. *Ibid.*, pp. 79–80.
23. *Ibid.*, pp. 43–45.
24. P. Bean, *Rehabilitation and Deviance* (Boston: Routledge and Kegan, 1976), p. 168.
25. See 16 *American Jurist* 2d (Const. Law), Sec. 550–552, for an explanation of the difference between procedural and substantive due process of law.
26. *Barron v. Baltimore*, 7 Pet. 243 (1833).
27. 19 L. Ed. 2d 1388.
28. *Adamson v. California*, 332 U.S. 46 (1947).
29. *Bloom v. Illinois*, 391 U.S. 194 (1968).
30. *Palko v. Connecticut*, 302 U.S. 319.
31. *Snyder v. Massachusetts*, 291 U.S. 97.
32. 342 U.S. 165.
33. For a definition of equal protection, see 16 *American Jurist* 2d (Const. Law), Sec. 486, 487.
34. *Rochin v. California*, 342 U.S. 165.
35. 381 U.S. 479 (1965).
36. *Lisenba v. California*, 314 U.S. 219 (1941).
37. 367 U.S. 643 (1961).
38. J. H. Skolnick, *Justice Without Trial*, (New York: Wiley, 1966), pp. 224–229.
39. J. Wilson, *Varieties of Police Behavior* (Cambridge, Mass.: Harvard University Press, 1968), pp. 7–8.

PRACTICAL EXERCISES

1. What is the right of habeas corpus?
2. Define *common law*.
3. Define *civil law*.
4. How does the inquisitional system differ from the accusational (accusatorial) system?

ANNOTATED REFERENCES

Chamelin, N. C., and Evans, K. R. *Criminal Law for Policemen.* Englewood Cliffs, N.J.: Prentice-Hall, 1976. A particularly cogent commentary on the formative era of American law. See also, by the same authors (with Vernon B. Fox and Paul M. Whisenand), *Introduction to Criminal Justice* (Englewood Cliffs, N.J.: Prentice-Hall, 1975).

Coffey, A., and Eldefonso, E. *Process and Impact of Justice.* Encino, Calif.: Glencoe Press, 1976. A paperback covering much of the information discussed in this chapter.

Klotter, J. C. *Legal Guide for Police: Detention, Arrest, Search and Seizure, Questioning, Identification.* Cincinnati: Anderson, 1977. An ideal collection of readings relevant to the nature of law in general and to the matters presented in this chapter.

LaFave, W. R. *Principles of Criminal Law: Cases, Comments and Questions.* St. Paul, Minn.: West, 1977. An excellent discussion of criminal law principles and codification, along with solid examples in case studies.

Perkins, R. M. *Criminal Law.* Mineola, N.Y.: Foundation Press, 1969. An enlightening discussion of common law and the significance of the phrase *common law.*

Chapter 2

CRIME: DEFINITION AND ESSENTIAL ELEMENTS

LEARNING OBJECTIVES

The learning objectives of this chapter are:
1. To understand that there are many different definitions, legal and social, of *crime* and the *criminal*.
2. To learn the *legal* definition of *crime* presented in this chapter, which serves as the "springboard" to a discussion of the essential elements of crime.
3. To attain a clear understanding of the nature and scope of criminal intent, capacity to commit crime, *motive* as distinguished from *intent*, corpus delicti, *mens rea* (and offenses *not* requiring *mens rea*), and parties to crime.
4. To become familiar with the classification of crimes: treason, felony, and misdemeanor.

Attempts to go beyond arbitrary statutes and define *crime* and *criminal* have tended, in some measure, to limit the reasonableness of our ideas about the purposes of law, police, courts, and correction.

The development of criminal law—from the *lex talionis* rule of retributive justice, under which it was acceptable to revenge oneself, to the present day, when taking the law into one's own hands is unacceptable—is one of the more interesting developments in the philosophy of government.

Definitions of *crime* cannot be stated in abstract adjectives and nouns—which render them so loose as to be meaningless—nor can they be rooted in judgments or prejudice. In a system aimed at equal justice under law, *crime* must be precisely defined, with explicit limitations and legislative formulations. This definition cannot include all behavior that is antisocial, or even all conduct that should be made criminal.

THE COMMON-LAW SYSTEM

It would be difficult, if not impossible, to discuss the essential elements of crime without reference to common law.* Thus, at the risk of repeating some facts already mentioned in Chapter 1, a review of this system will be presented in order to help you grasp the significance of a thoroughly integrated code of laws.

As previously stated, our criminal law is inherited in part from the common law originated in the Germanic regions and expanded in England. The principles of the common law of England are still applied in some of our states, except to the extent they have been changed by statute or modified by the interpretations of our own courts. The common law is a process of developing law continuously by reference to precedent. The development of common law is the result of judicial decisions; certain accepted principles or combinations of principles are thus more fully developed, qualified, and expanded by the magistrates.

According to Blackstone (*Blackstone's Commentaries*, 1760), common law evolves because

---

* In most jurisdictions, no act can be considered a crime unless defined as such by statute.

30

through usage and custom certain rules come to be accepted both for settling ordinary disputes or controversies between man and man and for dealing with those who commit serious crimes. Thus, there develops a complicated set of rules, principles, concepts and standards which are enforced by the courts, although they have never been [cemented or] adopted by legislative action.

Blackstone further states that the authority of these doctrines rests entirely on general reception and usage. The only method of proving that this or that maxim is a rule of common law is by showing that it has always been the custom to observe it.

But the common law has gone through stages of development, as R. M. Perkins shows us clearly:

> This, however, pictures its beginning rather than its later stages. In its maturity, the development of the common law is largely, if not wholly, the result of judicial decisions. Somehow, no one can say precisely how, certain principles came to be accepted as the law of the land. The judges held themselves bound to decide the cases which came before them according to those principles, and as new combinations of circumstances threw light on the way in which they were operated, the principles were in such cases more and more fully developed and qualified.[1]

It was fairly obvious that laws developed in this manner were inadequate and unsatisfactory—they were not meeting the demands of a rapidly changing American culture, producing a cultural lag. It was, therefore, necessary to make additions or changes by legislative enactment.

> Legislation itself, however, became a new source of common growth. In cases applying the words of the statute to a multitude of widely varying factual situations, there came to be a body of authoritative material not found in the statutes themselves but only in judicial decisions, and this is also regarded as part of the common law.[2]

Keeping the eminent Blackstone's definition in mind, we might properly say that all the authoritative instruments used to control, guide, and direct the judiciary and the administrative machinery of the state in carrying out those of its official tasks that lack the "blessing" of legislative enactment (or embodiment in a written constitution) can be referred to as the *common law*.[3]

CRIME DEFINED

What, then, is the legal definition of *crime* as it has been employed in practice, not only in our courts of law but in criminology as well?

"Crime is an intentional act or omission in violation of criminal law [statutory and case law], committed without defense or justification and sanctioned by the state as a felony or misdemeanor."[4]

The criminal law does not represent the final moral judgment of society. It does, however, restrict and regulate behavior—social behavior in the heat of passing emotions and in cool rationality, sometimes in the realm of what most people find morally reprehensible and sometimes subject to bitter dispute.[5] Criminal law usually strives to protect the safety and welfare of the community as a whole. On occasion, it serves a limited-interest group. It should not surprise us that a crime—a violation of these rules—is complex and difficult to explain.[6]

It is important to note that the legal definition given above assumes the violation of a previously existing law to warrant public prosecution. This principle of *nullum crimen sin lege, or nullum poena sin lege* (the coordinate principle) prohibits sanctions in the absence of penal law and implies that penal statutes should be precisely construed.

As indicated by its legal definition, crime concerns transgressions against the public order rather than against moral or private orders. It will be seen that mere criminal intent is not punishable,[7] although it is believed to be punishable under the general theory of Christian morality. Even an act, or an omission to act, accompanied by criminal intent is still not a crime unless it offends the general public rather than a private person.[8]

In considering the definition given above and similar definitions of *crime*, Clark and Marshall write: "Other definitions lacking some of its integral parts are fallacious because of inaccuracy or insufficiently extensive. Blackstone's definition—'An act committed or omitted in violation of a public law, either forbidding or commanding it,' although frequently quoted with approval, is inaccurate."[9] Clark and Marshall further contend that it is not the "act omitted" that constitutes a crime but the failure (omission) to act, and furthermore, the term "public law" is too broad, for it includes many other laws besides those that define and punish crimes. An act "is not necessarily a crime because it is prohibited by a public law. It is necessary to look further and ascertain the ground upon which the act is punished and by whom the punishment is imposed. To constitute a crime, it must be punished to protect the public, and it must be punished by the state or other sovereign power."[10]

Legal and Social Components in the Definition of *Crime*

A criminal, as previously indicated, is one who has committed an act punishable by law.* However, there are other factors to be taken into

---

* Crimes must be defined with appropriate definiteness in order to avoid a "due process of law" defense of lack of certainty.

consideration before a person may be treated as a criminal. Summarized, these factors are:

1. Regardless of his act, he must be of *competent age*. Under English common law, a child under seven could not commit a crime because he was not capable of *mens rea* (criminal intent) and so was not responsible. (According to the principle of *mens rea*, which will be further explained as the chapter progresses, an act and intent must concurrently exist in a particular criminal offense.) In the United States, the age of criminal responsibility is fixed by statute, or Constitution considerably above the *common* law limit. Very young children may, of course, be dealt with in juvenile courts. They may be punished or treated constructively under the philosophical tenet that the court acts in *loco parentis* (as a parent would act) and in the best interests of the child.

2. Criminal acts must also be *voluntary* and engaged in without compulsion. Compulsion, as defined by courts, must be evident and immediately related to a particular criminal act. Compulsion toward a life of crime may explain why a child becomes a criminal. It may have extended over a long period of time in the form of influence by parents, associates, or the environment. In their totality, such influences may make a life of crime a very natural—some would say inevitable—consequence. But such indirect influences, however compelling, will not be recognized in court as destroying the voluntary nature of acts essential to criminal behavior.

3. Especially in the case of serious crimes, the criminal must be shown to have had *criminal intent*. He must have meant to do wrong. Usually, criminal intent is tested in terms of his knowledge of the nature and consequences of his behavior. If it can be shown that a man who killed another did not know that it was wrong to kill, or did not know that when one pulls the trigger, death may result, he will be judged irresponsible, since he lacks *mens rea*. Other tests of insanity are used in some states, but the ultimate is generally a knowledge test even when delusions or "irresistible" impulses are recognized as proving lack of criminal responsibility.

4. Our criminal law often recognizes *degrees* of intent necessary to constitute particular crimes. To carry a heavy penalty, an assault may have to be shown to have been perpetrated "maliciously" or "wantonly," or a personal injury to have resulted from negligence. Clearly, such degrees of responsibility are extremely difficult to prove, since they require an estimate of the accused's mental processes and attitudes at the time of the crime.

5. Finally, to constitute a crime, an act must be classed legally as *an injury to the state* and not merely as a private injury, or tort. In ancient societies, acts now defined as crimes were considered only

private injuries to be avenged by the injured party or by his family or friends. Even murder, robbery, and rape were once considered to be of no concern of the state. But as society became more complex, a large number of acts once considered torts became crimes. It is increasingly difficult to discover acts without general social consequences.[11]

These components represent the legal point of view. Such a view reveals the nature of acts that may be punished as crimes. There is also a social definition of crime, which, although interesting, is outside the scope of this book.[12]

PRINCIPLES OF CRIMINAL LAW

Despite the ultimate influence of cultural change, law is, in fact, more conservative than some other forms of social control. There has been frequent criticism of "lags" in legal standards. Such conservatism is generally characteristic of the common law, since it is based on judicial decisions and on state and federal constitutions, which express well-established rules of social policy.[13] It is possible, in the Anglo-American system of criminal justice, to distinguish certain so-called principles of criminal law that stand out as evidence of conservatism. These have remained fairly constant for many decades but are still considered, nevertheless, essential to a fair system of law.[14]

Tappan and Taft have written extensively about conservatism and the principles of criminal law. The following is a summation of their writings.

1. The doctrine of *nullum crimen sine lege* (no crime without a law) or no *ex post facto* (retroactive) legislation still exists. There can be no crime without a statute that quite specifically forbids the behavior involved. It is considered a basic right that acts that are forbidden and can lead to retribution shall be *known*, and that no person may be punished at at later date for behavior that was not criminal when committed.
2. A person is presumed to have some knowledge of the law. However, whether or not he is familiar with the statutes—within a system of justice according to law—the individual must be held accountable for violations. In fairness, however, the rules must be reasonable, stable, and clear as guides to conformity. This principle, pertaining mainly to statutory law, is strengthened by the common-law rule of precedent that guides court decisions, the doctrine of *stare decisis* (let decisions stand and do not disturb settled things).[15]
3. The principle of *equality before the law* is intended to eliminate discrimination based on race, religion, and social class.

4. *Extenuating circumstances:* There are certain obvious situations or circumstances that directly relate to the violation that may be considered by the court and influence its disposition of a case.
5. An *attempt to commit crime* is viewed (all circumstances being equal) as less serious than a crime consummated. Therefore, punishment for an attempt is not as severe.
6. *Complicity:* Although an accomplice may be as guilty of the law violation as the principal party, certain specific relationships are essential to complicity.
7. In sentencing a criminal who has been involved in a multitude of offenses prior to his arrest, it is usually customary to punish him for the most serious one of which he is convicted. *Recidivism* (repeat convictions) may, however, under the "habitual criminal" acts, result in punishment of greater severity.
8. Finally, the principle of the *statute of limitations* has remained fairly constant for many years. In essence, the "limitation statute" in criminal law provides that, except for serious crimes (murder or other capital offenses), prosecution may not be initiated after a certain specified period (usually dictated by law) has elapsed.

SOURCES OF LAW

In the United States there is a specific separation of powers that emanates from the federal Constitution. The separation-of-powers doctrine prescribes the duties of each major branch of government. The *legislative branch* makes the law; the *judicial branch* interprets the law; the *executive branch* enforces the law. Whenever the law must be changed because of the changing desires or needs of society, the machinery for change is readily available through the representation of the populace by federal and state legislators. If the law is not changed when society demands it, the populace may either take the law into its own hands or totally disregard the law. However, law is the only basis upon which an orderly society may be built.

The basic law of the United States is the federal Constitution. Congress enacts statutes, which provide guidelines and/or sanctions for activities that involve federal crimes and other activities that directly or indirectly affect areas over which the government has jurisdiction. This authority and power stems from the Constitution. The basis for any *state law* is its constitution. Unfortunately, some constitutions are overburdened with provisions that should be codified rather than placed at the constitutional level.

The legislature of each state has the power and authority to enact statutes. Probably the most difficult task of any legislature is to codify the laws into separate headings. Thousands of laws flow from the floor of the legislature every year to be recorded and printed as matters of public record. Codification is the procedure by which statutes are placed into codes. These codes represent most of the written law in any given state. Aside from the written law, judges make "new law" by interpreting statutes when deciding cases. Actually, the court does not make law. That power and authority is reserved for the legislative body. However, the court may announce its interpretation of a given statute, and that interpretation will, if given at the appellate level, constitute the basis on which the populace may conduct its activities.

Stare Decisis

Stare decisis is the rule that requires a judge to follow precedent. Otherwise the defendant in a civil or criminal case would never know whether or not his activities were lawful. However, the time may come when the demand for change requires a reversal or modification of prior case law. In those instances, the appellate courts have overruled prior decisions.

Administrative Law

Other types of law exist that stem from administrative agencies. *An administrative agency is a unique body that makes, interprets, and enforces the law.* Most of these agencies are subject to judicial review. If an administrative body feels the need to make a ruling, it will give public notice of its intention to make the proposed change or addition. After public hearings, the administrative body adopts the rule. The administrative body may also make police decisions, not normally subject to judicial review, establishing health or safety standards or minimum working rights. After the administrative body has made either type of law, it acts as a court in interpreting and applying its own law. After interpretation of the law by the administrative body, the same body may enforce the law by contempt citations, which carry as much weight as a formal court proceeding.

CLASSIFICATION OF CRIME

The common law of England divided crime into three major groups: treason, felony, and misdemeanor. Treason, in turn, has been divided into high treason and petty treason.

High treason, in the words of Blackstone, is a term applied when "loyalty rears its crest to attack even majesty itself." In the ancient common law, it consisted of killing the king, promoting revolt in the kingdom or the armed forces, or counterfeiting the great seal. A tendency to enlarge the scope of the offense by analogy led to such uncertainty that an act of Parliament was required to define it. The Senate of Treason, enacted in 1350, specified exactly what should constitute high treason, including among certain other wrongs a manifested intent to kill the king, queen, or prince; levying war against the king; or adhering to his enemies, giving them aid and comfort. The punishment for treason was death.

Petty treason was based upon grave breach of an inferior allegiance. Examples would have been malicious homicide, such as killing a husband or wife, a servant killing a master or mistress, or a clergyman killing a prelate. The purpose of distinguishing this offense from high treason was to evoke a particularly brutal punishment, such as maiming. Petty treason, however, was abolished in England in 1828.

Felony, in the general adaptation of English law, comprised every species of crime that occasioned the forfeiture of land and goods. Under the theory of English common law, a felon had forfeited life and member and all that he had. But, says Wechsler, "it is better to define a felony in terms of an offense punishable by forfeiture." Although the list of felonies recognized by the English common law was very small, it was greatly enlarged by statute. And although the true criteria of a felony was forfeiture, enlargements by acts of Parliament in the early days tended to emphasize capital punishment as the chief punishment of felony.

Misdemeanor was the label ultimately applied to all offenses other than treason or felony. Acts *malum in se* (wrong in themselves, or according to natural law) included, in addition to all felonies, all branches of public order, injuries to persons and property, outrages concerning public decency and morals, and breaches of official duty when done willingly and corruptly. Acts *mala prohibita* included any matter forbidden or commanded by statute but not otherwise wrong.

Two comments are in order at this point: First, this distinction is limited to the misdemeanor group and has no application to treason or felony. Second, an offense *malum prohibitum* does not represent social harm that has been defined and made punishable by law, but rather is forbidden even though it is not otherwise wrong. It represents a situation in which a regulation was deemed wise and a penalty was imposed for purpose of enforcement.

Statutes in the United States today currently divide crimes into two classes: felonies and misdemeanors. Usually the detriment is the nature of the penalty that may be imposed. Distinguishing felony from misdemeanor generally follows one of two patterns: the distinction is based upon either type of institution in which the offender may be incarcerated or the length of term that may be imposed.

THE LIMITS OF EFFECTIVE LAW ENFORCEMENT

Criminal law does more than prohibit conduct involving major injuries to persons, property, and institutions. Not all crimes involve assaults, homicide, kidnapping, arson, burglary, theft, bribery, perjury, and the like. How, and to what extent, criminal law is the appropriate vehicle for dealing with such conduct as gambling, public drunkenness, disorderly conduct, and vagrancy should receive closer examination.

In many instances, legislators have responded to difficult problems of social control by making undesired conduct criminal. Many people are prepared to argue that if the legislature does not include a criminal penalty as a means of enforcement, it is not really serious about the matter.

Criminal law is not the sole, or even the primary, method relied on by society to ensure compliance with its rules. Laws are effectively enforced when they represent the moral consensus of the society. When there is a general lack of agreement, effective law enforcement is unlikely. The classic illustration of this principle was the Eighteenth Amendment, which made it illegal to manufacture, sell, or transport alcoholic beverages in the United States. Needless to say, this particular law did not reflect the mores of most citizens—moral consensus was lacking. Liquor was considered by the majority to be an important part of our society, and it was not difficult to locate a source of supply.

Of course, no law ever requires universal compliance. There are rebels, criminals, reformers, and subverters in every society. Although a law with *no* moral backing would almost certainly fail from lack of enforcement, a law can be enforced with far less than unanimous moral support if the dedication of its supporters exceeds that of its evaders.

The community depends on a broad spectrum of sanctions to control conduct. Civil liability, administrative regulations, licensing, and noncriminal penalties carry the brunt of the regulatory job in many very important fields, with a little additional force contributed by infrequently used criminal provisions that may appear in statute books. Internal moral compunctions and family, group, and community pressures are some of the various informal sanction that are often more effective than the prohibitions of the criminal law.

BASIC ELEMENTS OF A CRIME

It is a basic principle of the American system, as well as of most other systems of criminal justice, that every crime is composed of two elements, *a criminal act* and *criminal intent* (Figure 2.1). Neither an act alone nor intent alone is sufficient to constitute a crime. As indicated in

Figure 2.1, act *(actus reus)* and criminal intent *(mens rea)*, must concur to establish criminal responsibility. It would be futile and dangerous for the state to attempt to punish individuals merely for a subjective state of mind, which is impossible to determine with certainty anyway, or for conduct engaged in by mistake.[16]

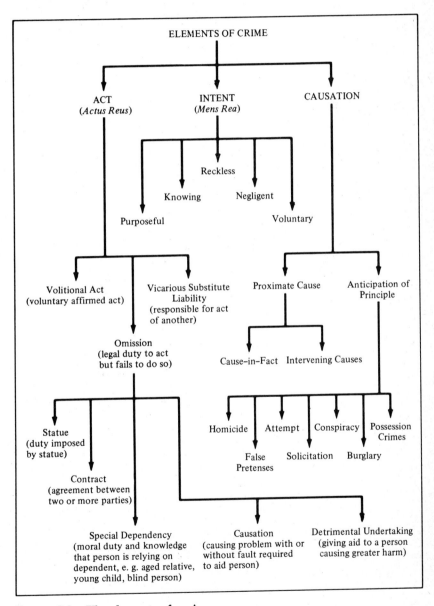

FIGURE 2.1   The elements of a crime.

"Act," or *actus reus*, is interpreted, however, to include a failure to act where there is a positive duty, as in criminal negligence of a parent or physician. American law has not gone so far as that of some countries in establishing such duty lest criminality be imputed for nonfeasance (the failure to do something one ought to do) in cases where many honest and reasonable men would hesitate to act.[17]

"Intent," or *mens rea*, refers to the so-called "guilty mind" *(mens rea)* or intention (criminal intent) to commit an injury.* *Mens rea* has been broadly interpreted to apply to behavior that is deeply imbedded in one's mind as acceptable and subject to approval by the group to which one belongs (see treatment of "mental states" in Chapter 5). According to a basic principle of criminal law, this intention must be present before we can say a crime has been committed. With few exceptions, an individual cannot be held criminally accountable for behavior that he has not willed, or intended. Thus, the law seldom holds a person accountable if he has acted unconsciously or involuntarily or has been so completely without control of his mental or physical faculties that he could not have formed a criminal intention.

Mens Rea Defined

Mens rea is too often used as though it were a synonym for criminal intent. To preserve the integrity of any definition of *mens rea*, it seems more prudent to say that *mens rea* is the nonphysical element that, combined with the act of the accused, makes up the crime charged (see Figure 2.2).[18]† Most frequently, it is criminal intent, or a guilty mind; but since it may be supplied by criminal negligence, which is often directly contrary to the intention of the actor, the term *intent* is not sufficiently inclusive. Courts and writers who identify *mens rea* with criminal intention frequently provide for unintended acts by classifying them under the anomalous term *constructive intent*.

The term *constructive intent* is used when a person commonly engaged in an unlawful act commits another, unintended, unlawful act.[19] His intent to commit the first act is carried over to the act actually committed. For example, A shoots at B but hits C. In this case, the intent A had when he shot at B carries over to the act actually committed. Thus, if A's intent was felonious and C dies, A will be held for murder or manslaughter. Conversely, if A is shooting at B, who is

---

* It has been suggested that the requirement of a mental element in crime probably developed as a result of ecclesiastical influence. The principle that resulted was expressed in the phrase *actus non facit reum nisi mens rea*. According to this principle, an act does not make a person guilty unless his intention be guilty also. In short, it is thought that one should not be punished in the absence of moral guilt.
† Some crimes by definition require *specific* intent.

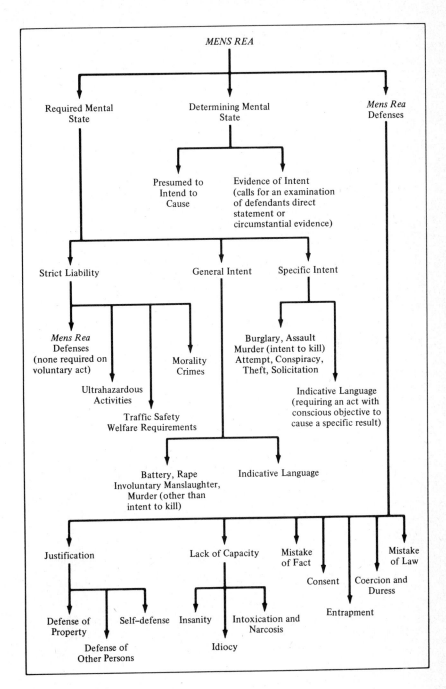

FIGURE 2.2   *Mens rea.*

an escaping felon, and C, an innocent bystander, is struck, A is not criminally liable. A did not shoot at B with felonious intent.

Certain types of crimes require only an intent to do the specific act involved (or intent not to do something that should have been done), even without awareness that such an act or omission is against the law. Such offenses are referred to as "absolute-liability," or "strict-liability," crimes. They are punishable without proof of the kind of criminal intent that is usually required. According to Michael and Wechsler:

> In crimes involving moral turpitude, criminal intent or guilty
> knowledge is, of course, generally recognized as an essential element.
> This is true whether the offense be one of common law or by statute.
> Society has so developed and extended that it has become necessary,
> in order to protect it, to pass many laws forbidding things to be done
> or commanding things to be done, the neglect to do or the doing
> whereof had theretofore been regarded as innocent and permissible.
> Most crimes falling under this head are designated as *malum*
> *prohibitum* in contradistinction to those crimes that are bad in
> themselves [*malum in se*] and in which criminal intent or guilty
> knowledge is essential.[20]

The purpose of the legislature in passing any given piece of legislation is the controlling factor.* Criminal intent or guilty knowledge as necessary ingredients of a statutory offense are determined by legislative construction. In other words, whether criminal intent or guilty knowledge is a necessary element of a statutory offense is a matter to be determined by the language of the statute in view of its manifest purpose and design.[21]

> There are many instances in recent times where the legislature in the
> exercise of police power has prohibited, under penalty, the performance
> of a specific act. The doing of the inhibited act constitutes the crime,
> and the moral or purity of the motive by which it was prompted and
> knowledge or ignorance of its criminal character are immaterial
> circumstances in the question of guilt. The only fact to be determined
> in these cases is whether the defendant did the act. In the interest of
> the public, the burden is placed upon the actor of ascertaining at his
> peril whether his deed is within the prohibition of any criminal
> statute.[22]

A fairly clear idea of the sort of crimes punishable *without mens rea* can be gained from a study of actual decisions handed down during the past half-century. These have, in the main, been violations of regu-

---

* The legislature has the power to declare some acts criminal regardless of the actor's intent.

latory statutes involving light monetary fines rather than imprisonment. Many of them are of such a nature that evidence of the defendant's actual state of mind would be peculiarly difficult, if not impossible, to obtain. Sometimes they involve enforcement against such armies of offenders that to require proof of each individual's intent would be virtually to prevent adequate enforcement.

The offenses not requiring *mens rea* fall roughly within the following groups:

1. Illegal sales of intoxicating liquor
   a. Sales of prohibited beverage
   b. Sales to minors
   c. Sales by methods prohibited by law
2. Sales of impure or adulterated food or drugs
   a. Sales of adulterated or impure milk
   b. Sales of adulterated butter or margarine
3. Sales of misbranded articles
4. Violations of antinarcotic acts
5. Criminal nuisances
   a. Annoyances or injuries to the public health, safety, repose, or conduct
   b. Obstructions of highways
6. Violations of traffic regulations
7. Violations of motor vehicle laws
8. Violations of general police regulations passed for the safety, health, or well-being of the community

NATURE AND SCOPE OF CRIMINAL INTENT

In discussing the definition and nature of crime, we have left out one component of critical importance. Thus far, we have spoken of a criminal act—overt behavior prohibited by the state and subject to penal sanctions. The simple legal definition of *crime* mentioned above requires some elaboration, for its terms have special technical implications. Its *elements* will be considered below.

Concurrence of Act and Intent

There must be a definite relationship between the act of the accused and the prohibited result (the crime). This causal relationship exists when the act of the accused is the proximate cause of injury.* To be

* The rules of proximate and direct causation for criminal law are similar to tort law, which is beyond the scope of this book.

proximate, the act of the accused need only be a contributing factor, as in the case when two persons act concurrently with common designs (e.g., two individuals stealing an automobile). In some cases this is true when the acts are concurrent, even though independent of each other (e.g., conspiring to steal an automobile). Many rules for determining proximate cause have been proposed. The following is a suggested approach: Determine whether the alleged act of the accused was the cause-in-fact of the injury to the victim. In order to ascertain cause-in-fact, apply the "but for" rule. "But for" the act, would injury not have resulted?

If there is a cause-in-fact, it must be determined whether that cause-in-fact was the proximate cause of the injury. Thus, proximate cause is merely a species of cause-in-fact. If the act of the accused was direct, it is always proximate. A *direct cause is a force that produces the result without any intervening force.*[22] It is immaterial that the results of the accused are interrupted by automatic acts of human beings or animals, caused by the subject's act; or by forces of nature set in motion by this act; by bacterial action; or by existing conditions.

EXAMPLE

Thus, if A has been mortally wounded by B, and, before the death of A, C inflicts another mortal would upon A, C is guilty of homicide although he merely hastened a death that was already bound to happen. B is also guilty of homicide.

As a further example, if the wound cause by B is not of itself mortal, and the wound caused by C is not of itself mortal, but if taken together the wounds are mortal, both are guilty of homicide.

The above examples are commonly referred to as the Substantial Factor Test. The act of the accused is called the proximate cause of the injury, though it was sufficient in itself to produce the injury, if it causes an intervening force to operate or if it sets in motion other forces, such as the negligence of the victim or of a physician. This type of intervening force is a "dependent" cause—a normal or involuntary result of the offender's act. The accused cannot base his defense on the mere fact that his victim neglected or refused to obtain medical aid, or that the victim could have recovered had he been treated under proper medical procedure. The accused is liable for his act when the act does not directly cause injury but rather sets up an intervening disease that does cause the injury.

Criminal Act—A Necessity

Generally speaking, in order for there to be a crime, there must be a criminal act as well as criminal intent.* The law does not punish mere intent to accomplish a criminal act.† There is sufficient act, however,

1. when a person solicits another to commit a felony, or in some jurisdictions, a misdemeanor, though the other may not do so.
2. when a person attempts to commit a crime, though he may not succeed in accomplishing his purpose.
3. when two or more agree or conspire to commit a crime or do any other unlawful act, although no attempt may be made to carry out the conspiracy.[24]

Capacity to Commit Crime

An analysis of criminal intent reveals that criminal law recognizes a number of situations in which the individual may *lack* criminal intent, and thus be exempt from criminal responsibility, namely:

1. It may be argued that the accused was suffering from a form of *insanity* that rendered him or her incapable of entertaining criminal intent. Intoxication, which is voluntary, does not excuse the accused. If, however, drunkenness has produced insanity (as defined in criminal law), there is an exception on the grounds of insanity.
   a. Intoxication may prevent the specific intent necessary to some crimes if the intoxication has rendered the accused incapable of forming that intent.
   b. Intoxication may be evidence of provocation and thus reduce the degree of crime (as sometimes applies to homicides).
2. An act committed in *ignorance*‡ or *mistake of fact,* under circumstances that disprove criminal intent, is not a crime.

EXAMPLE

A customer in a restaurant is not guilty of theft when, intending to take his own coat, and acting under an honest mistake of fact, he takes a coat similar to, and hanging near, his own garment.

---

* If a statute proscribes some action but does not prescribe a penalty, the act is not a crime.
† Laws defining specific modes of life as crimes have been declared unconstitutional, particularly alcoholism.
‡ Common-law rules: infants under 7 years of age *conclusively* presumed incapable of committting crime; between 7 and 14, rebuttably presumed incapable; 14 and over, presumably capable.

Mistake of fact is not a defense when the accused intends to commit a criminal offense and the result of his act produces a result different from that intended but which is also a criminal act.

EXAMPLE

An accused committing arson by setting fire to a building that he believes to be empty but that, in fact, contains a person, who is killed by the fire, is guilty of murder. There is a difference between assuming a state of fact exists when investigation discloses that no such state of fact exists and mistaking or misinterpreting facts known to the person who committed the act.

3. *Duress and coercion.* Unless a crime is punishable by death, when it is committed under threats sufficient to make the accused reasonably believe his life is in danger, the law considers the accused incapable of committing the crime. Fear of death must be not only reasonable but immediate. Fear of a mere future danger does not relieve an individual of responsibility. For a crime punishable by death, no amount of threat or coercion will relieve the accused of liability.

4. The accused may claim that the wrongful act occurred by *accident,* and if the accused was acting with due care and engaged in a lawful act, he is absolved.

5. In many states, there are statutory provisions that deny the possibility of criminal intent below a certain *age* (often about 16 years) and persons below that age are therefore incapable of committing a crime. The juvenile court must assume jurisdiction of those cases.

6. The accused may claim that he acted in *self-defense* when threatened with serious bodily harm.

These denials of criminal responsibility—sometimes known as *defenses to crimes*—are hedged about with numerous qualifications and refinements, but in general they all point to the same idea. Before the state can inflict punishment on the individual who has committed a a wrongful act, it must be shown that the act was a voluntary attempt to violate the criminal law.

Motive

Motive can be distinguished from intent (sometimes, however, only with difficulty). Motive is "reason," or "moving" cause; intent is "purpose," or "resolve" to do an act.† Thus, a bad motive will not make an act a crime, nor will a good motive prevent an act from being a crime. For example, the father of a child who is dying and in extreme pain willfully kills that child and hastens the death by a moment; although the father has acted out of compassion for his child (a good motive), he is nevertheless guilty of murder. Conversely, a woman who obtains goods from another by making representations that she believes false (a bad motive) but that are in fact true commits no crime because the element of fraud is absent.

Motive, of course, is often important in offering proof of the existence of the essential elements of crime.

Corpus Delicti

Corpus delicti, the essential elements of a crime, sometimes referred to as the "body of the crime," is often mistakenly thought to be the actual body in a murder case. This error has lead to the belief that you cannot have a case of murder or manslaughter unless the body of the deceased is produced, but a homicide may be proved by circumstantial evidence without producing the dead body.

PARTIES TO CRIME

A *principal in the first degree* is the one who actually commits the crime, either by his or her own hand, by an inanimate agent, or by an innocent human agent. A *principal in the second degree* (often referred to in most states as "accomplished law") is one who is present when a felony is committed by another and who aids or abets in its commission (both "principals" differ from "accessory before the fact" in that a crime has been committed). For someone to be a principal in the second degree, (1) there must be a guilty principal in the first degree; (2) the principal in the second degree must be present when the offense is committed but his presence must be "constructive" in that he must (3) aid or abet in the commission of the offense. Some participation is necessary, though it need not be active. Mere knowledge of the offense and mental approval is not enough.

Furthermore, when one has counseled and advised the commission

† Proof of motive does not establish guilt, nor does absence of motive prove innocence. Re: *Peterson, 15 Utah 2d 27.*

of a crime, his responsibility will not cease unless, while there is still time to prevent commission of the contemplated act, he has done everything to prevent its consummation. It is not enough that he may have changed his mind and tried, when it was too late, to avoid responsibility.[25] He will be liable if he fails to let the other party know of his withdrawal soon enough and does not do everything in his power to prevent commission of the crime.

Accessories After the Fact

Accessories after the fact are "every person, who after a felony has been committed, harbors, conceals or aids the principal in such felony with the intent that said principal may avoid or escape from arrest, trial, conviction or punishment, having the knowledge that such a principal has committed such felony or has been charged with such felony or convicted thereof."[26] Accessories after the fact are specifically defined in most states, and it is clearly pointed out that *charge* means more than accusation. It means an indictment, information, or complaint has been filed, or at least that the principal has been placed under arrest on a felony charge. *Concealed* means more than merely withholding knowledge or remaining silent—there must be an act of concealment or hiding. There are no accessories before the fact in California. Under the California Penal Code, persons who might elsewhere be accessories before the fact are treated as principals. The following cases are examples of crimes involving accessories.

CASES

A. Defendants admitted commission of the crime of murder while engaged in robbing the victim, but each sought to exonerate himself by contending that the other wielded the deadly instrument. It was immaterial which one struck the death blow, since each was equally guilty.

B. When a conspiracy to defraud a city existed, each of the conspirators was liable for all acts performed in furtherance of the conspiracy.

C. A defendant who participated as a principal in a crime in which a dangerous or deadly weapon was used is liable to the same penalties that are imposed upon a codefendant who actually possessed the weapon.

D. Three defendants were acting together to commit a burglary when one of them armed himself with a gun. The consequences of his act were visited equally upon his associates, who were aiding and abetting him in the crime.

E. Evidence that the defendant aided and abetted in commission of a robbery, although he did not strike the blows with the rolled-up kit of automobile tools, justified his conviction as a principal in the crime.

F. The evidence justified the conclusion that one defendant aided and abetted in the commission of the crime of keeping a room for receiving bets on horses when he was arrested a short distance from the room in an automobile after making a bet on a horse race and after he admitted that he was employed by his codefendant.

ATTEMPTS TO COMMIT CRIMES

Mere intention to commit an act defined as a crime is not punishable. There is a point, however, somewhere between formation of the intent and actual commission of the crime at which the criminal taking overt action toward the accomplishment of the intended crime has gone so far in carrying out his purpose that he is guilty of an attempt to commit the crime. As Figure 2.3 points out, an attempt must include a specific intent to commit an overt (sufficient) act.

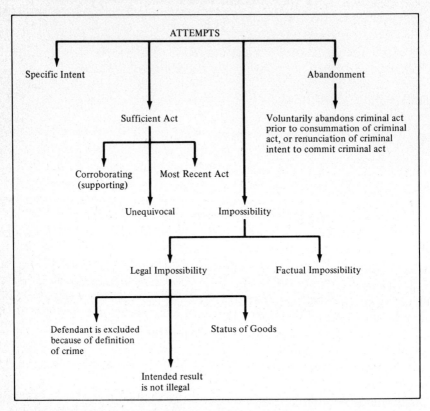

FIGURE 2.3   Attempts to commit crimes.

Acts of mere preparation, before, or unaccompanied by, an overt act toward actual commission of the intended crime, are not attempts.

An attempt consists of an *overt act* toward commission of a crime following preparation for it and amounting to commencement of the actual perpetration, which would end in consummation of the crime if not interrupted or stayed. The act must be one that immediately and directly tends to the execution of the principal crime and must be committed by the criminal under such circumstances that he has the power of carrying his intentions into execution and would do so but for some intervening cause. (With conspiracy, the overt act may merely be an act of preparation).

INABILITY IN LAW TO COMMIT THE CRIME

When the crime attempted is one that, as a matter of law, could not be committed because, by reason of the law, an essential element of the corpus delicti cannot exist, and the intended crime is therefore a legal impossibility, there can be no attempt to commit such a crime. For example, the California Penal Code, Section 288 (Crimes Against Children: Lewd or Lascivious Acts), pertains to children under 14 years of age. Since a violation of Section 288 can be committed only on a person under the age of 14 years, there can be no attempt to commit that crime on a minor over that age.

SUMMARY

Crime is defined as a intentional act or omission in violation of criminal law (statutory and case law), committed without defense or justification, and prohibited by the state as a felony or misdemeanor.

Although a criminal is one who has committed an act punishable by law, there are other factors that must be taken into consideration before a person may be treated as a criminal. The factors as listed and discussed in this chapter may be summarized as follows: (1) regardless of his act, the accused must be of competent age; (2) criminal acts must be voluntary and engaged in without compulsion; (3) especially in the case of serious crimes, the accused must be shown to have had criminal intent; (4) our criminal law recognizes degrees of intent necessary for the commission of crimes; (5) finally, to constitute a crime, an act must be classed legally as an injury to the state and not merely as a private injury, or tort.

In general, a crime consists of two elements: (1) the criminal act or omission and (2) the mental element. The requirement of a mental element—generally understood to be a "guilty mind"—is referred to in legal terminology as *mens rea*. According to the *mens rea* concept, the law seldom holds a person accountable if he has acted unconsciously or involuntarily or has been so completely without control of his mental or physical faculties that he could not have formed a criminal intention.

It is noted, however, that certain types of crimes require only intent to do or omit the specific act (or omission) involved even without awareness that the act is against the law. Further discussion of these acts involving "strict" liability (proof of criminal intent unnecessary) is included in this chapter.

In some states, various categories of persons are considered incapable of forming a criminal intent; or certain circumstances negate the intent even though the capacity exists. These categories—insanity, accident, ignorance or mistake of fact, age, self-defense, duress, and coercion—are important when discussing capacity to commit a crime.

Motive, which is not an essential element of crime, is distinguished from intent. Motive is a "reason" or a "moving cause." Intent is "purpose" or "resolve" to do an act. Motive, of course, is often important in offering proof of the existence of the essential elements of the crime. *Corpus delicti* means the essential elements of a crime—sometimes referred to as the "body of the crime."

There are three types of criminal intent: general intent, specific intent, and constructive intent. All three are defined and discussed in this chapter.

There must be a causal relationship between the act of the accused and the prohibited result that constitutes a crime. In other words, the act and intent must be concurrent. This relationship exists when the act of the accused is the proximate cause of the injury involved.

In California, there are no accessories before the fact. Such people are treated as principals in the first degree. California law does recognize, however, accessories *after* the fact.

NOTES

1. R. M. Perkins, *Criminal Law* (Mineola, N.Y.: Foundation Press, 1969), p. 23.
2. *Ibid.*
3. *Ibid.*
4. P. Tappan, *Crime and Correction*, 3d ed. (New York: McGraw-Hill, 1966), p. 10.
5. G. Sykes, *Crime and Society* (New York: Random House, 1966), p. 21. See also S. McCabe and F. Sutcliffe, *Defining Crime* (Oxford: Basil Blackwell, 1978).
6. Sykes, *Crime and Society.*
7. *Badders* v. *United States*, 240 U.S. 391.
8. M. E. Wolfgang, L. Savitz, and N. Johnston, eds., *Sociology of Crime and Delinquency* (New York: Wiley, 1972), p. 14.
9. W. L. Clark and W. Marshall, *A Treatise on the Law of Crimes*, 7th ed. revised by M. Q. Barnes (Mundelein, Ill.: Callaghan, 1967), pp. 1–13.
10. *Ibid.*
11. D. R. Taft, *Criminology*, 5th ed. (New York: Macmillan, 1966), pp. 6–8.
12. For an extensive treatment of the social definition of crime, see E. H. Johnson, *Crime, Correction and Society*, 3d ed. (Homewood, Ill.: Dorsey Press, 1977), p. 13.
13. L. Radzwowicz and M. E. Wolfgang, *Crime and Justice: The Criminal in Society*, 2d ed. (New York: Basic Books, 1977), p. 621.
14. Taft, *Criminology*, pp. 377–378.
15. Tappan, *Crime, Justice and Correction*, p. 23.
16. Wolfgang, Savitz, and N. Johnson, *Sociology of Crime and Delinquency*, p. 18.
17. *Ibid.*
18. *Ibid.*
19. See *People* v. *Wells*, 33 Cal. 2d 330.
20. J. Michael and H. Wechsler, *Criminal Law and Its Administration*

(Mineola, N.Y.: Foundation Press, 1940), p. 777 (material in brackets added).
21. *Ibid.*, p. 778.
22. *Ibid.*
23. *Actus non facit reum, misi menus sit rea* (act and intent). See *Black's Law Dictionary*, 2d ed.
24. Wolfgang, Savitz, and N. Johnston, *Sociology of Crime and Delinquency*, p. 18.
25. *Karnes* v. *State*, 159 Ark. 240.
26. *State* v. *Young*, 7 Ohio App. 2d 194.

PRACTICAL EXERCISES

1. Define *mens rea.*
2. List the items relevant to *capacity to commit crime.*
3. Define *motive.*
4. Define *corpus delicti.*

ANNOTATED REFERENCES

Benson, James C. *The Criminal Justice System: An Introduction,* Boston, Houghton Mifflin, 1976. Part IV, on courts, introduces the student to legal terminology and discusses criminal law in a clear and concise fashion.

Cook, P. J., and Pye, K. K. *Law and Contemporary Problems.* Special Issue: "Criminal Process in the Seventies." Durham, N.C.: Duke University Press, 1977. Excellent coverage of criminal procedures and innovations.

Inbau, F. E., and Thompson, J. R. *Criminal Law and Its Administration,* 2d ed. Mineola, N.Y.: Foundation Press, 1970. Excellent overview of criminal law.

Johnson, E. H. *Crime, Correction and Society,* 3d ed. Homewood, Ill.: Dorsey Press, 1977. This book draws on theory to promote an understanding of crime causation, the modes of societal responses to crime, and the relationships between crime and patterns of legitimate society.

McNamara, D. E. J., and Sgarin, E. *Sex, Crime and the Law.* New York: Macmillan, 1977. Detailed coverage of the subject title.

Perkins, R. M. *Criminal Law,* 3d ed. Mineola, N.Y.: Foundation Press, 1969. Chapter 1, "Scope, Purpose, Definition and Classification," is a classic introduction to the field of criminal law. See also Sachar, Edward J. "Behavior Science and Criminal Law." *Scientific American,* November 1963, pp. 40–41.

Senna, J. J., and Siegel, L. J. *Introduction to Criminal Justice,* St. Paul, Minn.: 1978. Crime definitions and basic elements of crime are discussed in the non technical text. This volume also elaborates on some of the physiological theories of crime causes briefly discussed in this chapter.

Skolnick, J. H. *Justice Without Trial.* New York: Wiley, 1966. This discussion of democratic order and the rule of law provides an excellent background for the concept of criminal defense.

Westbrook, J. E. "Mens Rea in the Juvenile Court." *Journal of Family Law* 5 (1965): 121–29. This article discusses *mens rea* in its historical perspective and introduces the reader to the concept of free will.

Chapter 3

ARREST, SEARCH, AND SEIZURE

LEARNING OBJECTIVES

The learning objectives of this chapter are:

1. To understand the laws of arrest and proper arrest procedure, which is a significant part of police work.
2. To become thoroughly familiar with the responsibilities in effecting an arrest, with a great deal of emphasis on the *elements* of arrest (i.e., the intention to arrest, the cause of the arrest, and the authority to make the arrest); *exemptions* from arrest; arrest *with* or *without* a warrant; *probable cause* for arrest; use of *force* in arresting; and arrests by *private persons*.
3. To examine carefully the subject of "search and seizure"—which is indirectly related to arrest (evidence secured)—paying particular attention to "search incident to arrest."
4. To understand each of the court cases presented in the chapter.

IN THIS CHAPTER WE WILL SURVEY THE principal constitutional limitations on law enforcement activity. Decisions of appellate courts are presented on occasion, to help the reader better understand the material discussed.

It is most important, we feel, to stress at the outset what this chapter will *not* cover. We will simply provide an overview of arrest and of search and seizure. No attempt will be made to explain or fully justify any of the legal principles involved. That would be a task for a more definitive volume. Nor does this chapter attempt to consider any of the arguments for and against these legal limitations. That, too, is beyond the scope of this chapter.

Preceding chapters in this volume suggest that the prosecution begins when a suspect is arrested. If the report of a crime is not accompanied by any identification of the criminal, investigation is usually being carried out until an arrest is effected or until the investigation process reaches a stalemate. Obviously, police officers must know when they have the power to make a legal arrest. It should also be pointed out that many persons besides police officers have arrest powers. In some states, such as New York, there is a distinction between police officers and peace officers in terms of arrest powers.[1] Although an invalid arrest will not void an otherwise valid conviction, the validity of the arrest is important for two principal reasons: first, only a valid arrest will justify a search for evidence incident to the arrest; and second, an officer can be sued for damages for making an illegal or false arrest. Therefore, the law of arrest seems an appropriate place to begin our survey of the relevant areas of criminal procedure.

We will cover the subject in three sections: first, arrest procedures; second, federal limitations on the power of arrest; and third, the law of search and seizure and federal Constitutional limitations that have provoked current controversies.

But, first, a brief word about police officers' decisions *not* to set the criminal justice process in motion.

POLICE DISCRETION

Occasionally, a police officer may decide to use his or her discretion in effecting an arrest, particularly when the offender is a juvenile. The frequency and type of arrests to be made are questions of priorities, which are established by local law enforcement officials. It is obvious that police officers do not arrest all people who commit offenses. Why? Because, at the grass roots level, the police officer is the party with discretion to decide whether or not to arrest an individual.

The police officer's job cannot be summarized as simply enforcement of the law. He is placed on the street for the purpose of preventing crime. Although the arresting officer, like any other citizen, is biased and prejudiced by his religious, ethnic, and social background, he must draw the line between morality and law in an objective manner. When the officer takes the stand under oath, he must be able to say at what point he believed he had probable cause to make an arrest. What facts and circumstances led him to believe there was probable cause to make the arrest? The police officer, then, is an interpreter not only of *local* policy but also of *constitutional* law that protects the criminal defendant. This discretion is never more evident than in domestic squabbles. Physical and emotional restraint must be exercised during riots and insurrections. The police officer must weigh his right to arrest a trespasser against the possibility of such an arrest causing the death or injury of numerous persons.

ARREST PROCEDURES

Who may make an arrest? How should the arrest be made? Who is exempt from arrest? In this section the answers to these questions will be given and some other aspects of arrest, such as arrests with or without a warrant, will be discussed.[2]

The position of the law enforcement officer, in the light of many recent Supreme Court decisions about arrest and search and seizure, has changed immeasurably, and his task has been made more difficult. The officer may not make an arrest without "reasonable" and "probable" cause for believing that the person being arrested is guilty of committing a violation.[3]

Throughout the world, an arrest is considered to be the taking of a person into official custody in the manner authorized by law (see Figure 3.1). This same definition is used throughout the United States for police officers and citizens alike. The term *arrest* is derived from the French word *arrêter*, which means "to stop." Two well-known definitions might prove helpful: *Cochran's Law Lexicon* says an arrest is the seizing of a person and detaining him in custody by lawful authority; *Black's Law Dictionary* defines it as depriving a person of his liberty by legal authority. The general definition in most penal codes is the "taking of a person *into custody* that he may be forthcoming to answer for the commission of any offense."[4] When an arrest is being

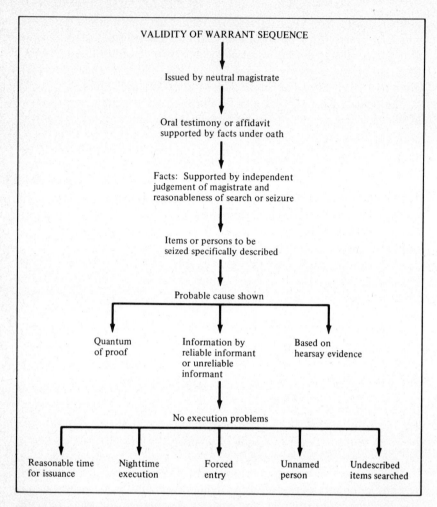

FIGURE 3.1 Sequence of validity of warrant.

made, words alone are not sufficient. There must be some actual restraint of the accused, or she must submit to the custody of the arresting officer. An arrest may be the opening move in criminal prosecution. On the other hand, it may follow the filing of an indictment, information, or complaint.

Distinction Between the Rules of Arrest and the Rules of Search and Seizure

In any discussion of the law of arrest, a fundamental and critical distinction must be made between the rules of arrest and the rules of search and seizure. The well-settled rule that a police officer must have probable cause for making an arrest has led to countless court decisions attempting to apply this rule. The following contrasting cases are good examples.

CASE

State v. Pickens, 160 So. 2d 577 (La. 1964). The defendants were convicted of simple burglary. On appeal, the defendants contended that the trial court erred in refusing to grant their motions to suppress illegally seized evidence and in overruling their motion for a new trial on the same grounds. The Supreme Court of Louisiana *affirmed* their conviction, holding that when police officers investigating a very recent burglary noticed the defendants, whom they did not recognize as "local boys," driving a car 3 to 5 miles per hour in an alley behind the burglarized premises, and upon hailing the defendants' car to a halt, noticed a box on the front seat that one defendant, in answer to an officer's questions, said contained "nothing," the officers had probable cause to believe defendants had committed the burglary under investigation and thus probable cause to arrest defendants without a warrant. The search of the defendants' car, which yielded merchandise taken during the burglary, was lawful as incidental to the arrest; and consequently the trial court properly received in evidence the goods complained of, since they were seized as the result of a lawful search. (The arresting officer's testimony shows, however, that no arrest was made until after a search of the box and car revealed stolen property.)

CASE

People v. Frank, 37 Cal. Rptr. 202 (Dist. Ct. App., 1964). Defendant was convicted of possession of marijuana. On appeal, defendant contended the marijuana was obtained through an unlawful search and seizure. The California District Court of Appeal *reversed* the conviction, holding that since before the search of defendant's room without a warrant the officer did not have probable cause to arrest him for possession of marijuana, the admissibility of the marijuana depended upon whether effective consent was given to the search of defendant's room. The trial court erred in finding that the defendant's landlady's consent to the search, given while defendant was present, made the search valid. Defendant's constitutional right of privacy was not so under the landlady's control that he could not personally assert it under the circumstances. Having erroneously relied on the landlady's consent to validate the search, the trial court failed to determine the crucial issue (upon which the evidence was in substantial conflict) of whether defendant himself consented.

Even if probable cause exists, that is, even if an arrest is lawful, it does not follow that any and all searches conducted along with the arrest are lawful. The validity of the arrest is only the first step; the lawfulness of the search that follows the arrest may still be questioned.

EXAMPLE

Police officers receive reliable information that X is dealing in narcotics. Personal observation confirms the information. As X drives up to a house and parks his car in front, police arrest him. The defendant shouts a name. A woman opens the door of a house and observes the scene. A search of the car reveals narcotics. A search of the house also reveals narcotics. Are these searches lawful?

The arrests are lawful because they have been made upon probable cause (information received from a reliable informant). The following case may help to clarify this:

CASE

Irby v. United States, 314 F. 2d 251 (C.A.D.C., 1963). The defendant appealed from the District Court's ruling that the search warrant authorizing a search that yielded narcotics was valid. Defendant contended that the affidavits upon which the warrant was issued failed to set forth probable cause for belief that criminal acts were being committed on the premises in question. The Court of Appeals for the District of Columbia Circuit affirmed. Since the affidavit set forth (1) the direct knowledge of affiants (experienced narcotics squad officers) that on one occasion seven known narcotics addicts were in front of the premises, which were

occupied by a convicted narcotics seller, and (2) statements made
to the affiants on another occasion by a "special employee"
(informer) that the informer had purchased drugs on the premises
and had been told that the drug peddler who lived there had been
away "capping" heroin, the facts set forth in the affidavit constituted
probable cause for an experienced narcotics squad officer to believe
that illegal narcotics were concealed on the premises. Consequently,
the warrant was properly issued. One judge dissented because the
policemen waited over six weeks after the first incident and eight
days after the second before obtaining the warrant.

The lawfulness of each search is tested by the following rule: A search
may be *incidental* to an arrest (Figure 3.2). A search is incidental to
an arrest if it is limited to the area directly under the suspect's control, and is reasonable in scope.

Taking into consideration *Irby* v. *United States*, the search of the
defendant's person and car in the previous example were clearly
proper. The search of the house was unlawful because the defendant
was not arrested on the premises searched. Evidence seized in the house
is inadmissible.[5]

The United States Constitution is of great importance to law enforcement officers not only because it sets out general standards and
protects personal liberties but also because a misunderstanding of its
separate parts will hinder the law enforcement officer's proper performance of her duty. Nowhere is this more evident than in the area
of search and seizure. The rules and procedures in this area, which
have developed from the Fourth and Fifth Amendments, require careful study to ensure that the individual's rights are protected while the
criminal is denied the opportunity to evade or escape conviction because
of a technical mistake. With the ever-improving competence of law
officers throughout the country, there should be fewer instances of
criminals being set free because of a technical error in law enforcement.

The purpose of this section is to develop some understanding of
the constitutional protections against illegal search and seizures. The
Fourth Amendment states:

The right of the people to be secure in their persons, houses, papers,
and effects, against unreasonable searches and seizures, shall not be
violated, and no warrants shall be issued, but upon probable cause,
supported by oaths or affirmation, and particularly describing the
place to be searched, and the persons or things being seized.

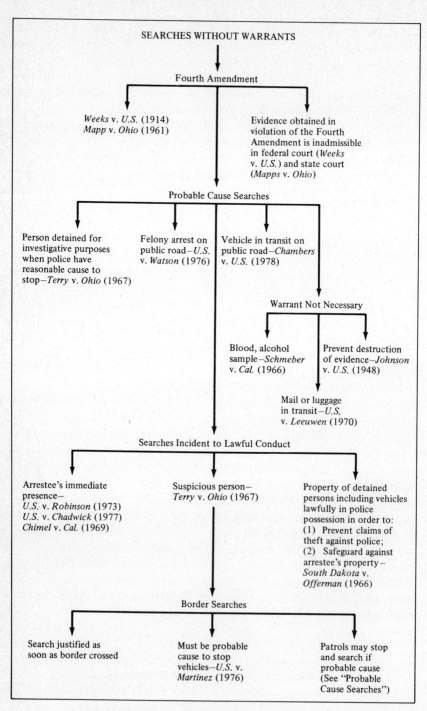

FIGURE 3.2   Searches without warrants.

Clearly, the Fourth Amendment is designed for the protection of the individual's privacy. This means security for both one's person and one's property. The amendment allows one to conceal oneself and one's property from the view of one's government—local, state, and federal. However, the framers of the Constitution recognized that this right must, at times, give way to other needs of society. The three words or phrases that are most important for police officers are *unreasonable*, *probable cause*, and *particularly*. It is around these terms that most cases and problems arise.

The Fourth Amendment prohibits "unreasonable" searches and seizures, not *all* searches and seizures. The problem is in deciding what is reasonable. While the search is usually deemed reasonable if a valid search warrant is first obtained, the courts have allowed searches without a warrant when consent was given by the subject, when the search was incident to a lawful arrest, and when only vehicles were searched. Such tests are, at best, general, and there are many facets to each type of search. It is these difficult factors that determine the validity of the search.

"Probable cause" raises further problems for law enforcement officers. While determinations as to the reasonableness of a search can be categorized to some extent, according to the methods officers use, whether there is probable cause to justify a search must ultimately be decided on the basis of each specific set of facts.

The standard for determining whether there is probable cause to justify a search has been established by the Supreme Court of the United States. The Court defined probable cause as: "A reasonable ground of suspicion, supported by circumstances sufficiently strong in themselves to warrant a cautious man in the belief that the party is guilty of the offense with which he is charged."

Further, the Court has viewed probable cause as a nontechnical standard. It has judged the problem in the light of everyday experience and not on the basis of a legal formula. Also, reasonableness is not tested according to what an ordinary citizen would consider to be probable cause. The test is whether an *experienced officer* would consider probable cause existed. This allows people involved in law enforcement to weigh the circumstances in the light of their training and expertise. The rule is helpful since it ties the legal standards to the police officer's informed judgment.

The last key word, which must always be considered by officers engaged in searches and seizures, is *particularly*. Unlike the problems involved in testing and evaluating reasonableness and probable cause, which arise in cases with or without lawful search warrants, problems relating to particularity as to the person seized or the premises searched generally arise under a search warrant. The warrant must be specific,

```
                        MUNICIPAL COURT OF CALIFORNIA
                      SANTA CLARA COUNTY JUDICIAL DISTRICT
                       _____FACILITY


 1                           SEARCH WARRANT

 2    THE PEOPLE OF THE STATE OF CALIFORNIA
      To any Sheriff, Constable, Marshal, Policeman or Peace Officer in
 3    the County of Santa Clara:

 4           Proof, by affidavit, having been made before me this day by

 5    _____ that there is probable cause

 6    for believing that

 7

 8

 9

10

11           You are therefore commanded, in the daytime or _____

12    _____, to make search
      (Magistrate's initials)
13

14

15

16

17

18    located at _____, County

19    of Santa Clara, State of California, for the following property:

20

21

22

23

24

25

26

                                   -1-
```

FIGURE 3.3 Search warrant for narcotics.

not only as to who or what is to be searched but also as to the items that are to be seized—for example, narcotics (Figure 3.3). *People* v. *Rainey* supports the rule of specifics, or particularity:

CASE

People v. *Rainey*, 197 N.E. 2d 527 (N.Y., 1964). The defendant was convicted of forgery and receiving stolen goods. On appeal, the defendant contended that the trial court erred in denying his pretrial motion to vacate a search warrant and to suppress evidence, and in receiving as evidence, over his objection, material seized pursuant to a defective search warrant. The Court of Appeals of New York *reversed* the conviction and dismissed the indictment. Since the search warrant described an entire building, one part of which (for which probable cause was shown) was occupied by defendant and another part (for which probable cause was not shown) by an innocent third party, the warrant was obviously constitutionally deficient for not *"particularly describing the place to be searched."* The Court noted that the innocent third party's failure to complain about the search of her apartment was immaterial, since the pertinent issue was whether or not the warrant was constitutional when issued.

The requirement of particularity not only restricts the items or places that may be searched but also limits the type of search that may be conducted. A search of "Warehouse A, 1000 Jones Street, for illegal liquor stills" restricts officers to that location and that purpose. They cannot go into the warehouse and search file cabinets in the office, because the specific items in the warrant are stills, which could not be built in a file drawer. To search the file drawer would violate the rule of the particularity.

Particularity as to what people and objects are sought in obtaining a search warrant is perhaps the most technical of the three standards. It is also the standard most directly under the control of the police officer. An affidavit for a search warrant should be carefully thought out in advance to ensure correctness of the address, the person's name, the items sought, and the factual basis for seeking the warrant (Figure 3.4). If there is sufficient time to obtain a search warrant, there is sufficient time to ensure that it is validly drawn to cover the situation believed to exist.

This brief introduction to the Fourth Amendment's effect on the law of searches and seizures should be kept in mind at all times. In

```
                    MUNICIPAL COURT OF CALIFORNIA
                 SANTA CLARA COUNTY JUDICIAL DISTRICT
                 _____FACILITY


      THE PEOPLE OF THE STATE OF CALIFORNIA, )   DECLARATION IN SUPPORT
                                             )   OF ARREST AND PRE-TRIAL
 1                               Plaintiff,  )   RESTRAINT ON LIBERTY
                                             )
 2          vs.                              )
                                             )
 3    _____ Defendant.  )

 4        I hereby declare:

 5        That I am a duly acting peace officer of the _____

 6    _____ and in the performance of my

 7    duties, I have been assigned to collect and present evidence that

 8    the above-named defendant committed the offense(s) described in the

 9    complaint filed herein.

10        That I have personally reviewed and incorporated by reference

11    each of _____ pages of written reports and statements attached

12    hereto which are official records prepared by persons known to me

13    to be law enforcement officers or employees of other governmental

14    agencies as shown on said reports and statements and believe them

15    to be true and reliable.

16        That from the foregoing facts I am satisfied that there is

17    probable cause for the arrest and pre-trial restraint on liberty

18    of the above-named defendant.

19        That the defendant  has been arrested  and a warrant  is not
                              is not in custody                 is
20    therefore requested for the offense(s) set forth in the complaint

21    on file in this case.

22        I state upon information and belief and under penalty of

23    perjury that this Declaration is true and correct.

24        Executed on _____ in Santa Clara County,

25    California.                      _____

26
```

FIGURE 3.4   Affidavit for a search warrant.

conducting a search, the guidelines of *reasonableness* of the search, *probable cause* to warrant the search, and *particularity* as to the items seized or persons searched must all be tested in the officer's mind to ensure that her actions are lawful and that any arrest or seizure of property will stand up in a court of law.

ASPECTS OF PROBABLE CAUSE

In order to make a valid arrest, the peace officer must make sure probable cause does exist. An arrest made without suspicion, or probable or reasonable cause, would ultimately be viewed as invalid. The validity of such an arrest could be attacked on the grounds that the suspect had been deprived of his constitutional rights—specifically his rights under the Fourth Amendment. If the arrest is ruled invalid, evidence seized during a search made incident to the arrest will be excluded.

There have been numerous definitions of *probable cause*, but perhaps the best is the one given by Chief Justice E. Harold Hallows, of the Wisconsin Supreme Court:

> An arrest without a warrant for a felony is valid if there is reasonable
> and probable grounds of suspicion or to suspect that the person
> arrested has committed a felony. Reasonable grounds to believe means
> a "reasonable ground or suspicion supported by circumstances
> sufficiently strong in themselves to warrant a cautious man in believing
> the accused guilty." The word "suspicion" does not mean mere
> suspicion. Nor does probable cause, or as sometimes stated, "reasonable
> cause to believe," depend upon the outcome of the subsequent
> prosecution resulting from the arrest. Probable and reasonable cause
> in this case depended upon the factual information given to the police
> and its sufficiency and the reliability of the informants.[6]

The Wisconsin Supreme Court held that there was probable cause to make an arrest on the basis of an undisclosed, reliable informer's statements, when the use of such information was in the best public interest.

Before every arrest, according to Gardner (who cites *Brinegar v. U.S.*), the officer must ask himself whether he has probable cause, and in most situations the answer is easy. Not only must the police officer make a value judgment as to what the amount of evidence available to him is worth,

> ... but he must also be able to articulate this because in determining
> the existence of probable cause, the law is concerned with the knowledge
> of the law enforcement officer and also his motives before he: (1)
> makes an arrest; or (2) makes a search subsequent to arrest; or (3)

petitions a court for a search warrant. Because probable cause is determined by the knowledge and motives of the police officer, hearsay evidence may be considered by the officer, in part, in determining whether he has probable cause. The officer may even testify to, and repeat, hearsay evidence in court to show that he did have probable cause when he acted "so long as there . . . [is] a substantial basis for crediting the hearsay."[7]

However, according to Gardner, hearsay evidence alone, or good motives alone, will not sustain a finding that probable cause existed.

As we shall see later, when we discuss search warrants, probable cause for an arrest is identical to the standard of probable cause for a search warrant. The only difference is that in one case (arrest) the facts and circumstances must be enough to justify a man of reasonable caution in believing that the *suspect has committed a particular crime,* whereas in the other case (search warrant) a man of reasonable caution must be justified in believing *the property to be seized will be found* in a particular place or on a particular person. Therefore, the following principles, which apply to search warrants, also apply to arrests.

1. Probable cause can be based on *hearsay information*—which usually means information received from police informants—if this information is reasonably corroborated by other facts known to the officer.
2. There is sufficient corroboration when the informant is *known from experience* to be reliable and when he gives a precise description of the appearance and location of the defendant that is verified at or before the time of arrest.
3. There is insufficient corroboration, however, if the information is from an undisclosed source of *unproven* reliability, even though the defendant's physical appearance and previous criminal record are known to the arresting officer.

CASE

State v. *Beck,* 191 N.E. 2d 825 (Ohio, 1963). Defendant was convicted of possessing clearinghouse (policy) slips, a misdemeanor. On appeal, defendant contended that illegally obtained evidence was used against him, and that the trial court erred in refusing to compel disclosure of the name of an informer upon whose information the police in part relied for probable cause to arrest the defendant. The Supreme Court of Ohio *affirmed.* Since the clearinghouse slips were seized incident to defendant's lawful arrest without a warrant, the evidence was not the product of an unlawful search and thus was properly admitted. Since it was not shown that disclosure of the informer's name would have been of any real value to the defendant, the defendant was not entitled to the informer's name. The policy against disclosure, based on the desire to protect and encourage informers and to keep open the avenues by which they pass along information important to the police, would be outweighed only by compelling considerations.

4. The police need only testify to the informer's reliability to show probable cause. If the identity of the informant is not directly material to guilt or innocence of the defendant, the police need not reveal the informer's identity in order to establish probable cause for an arrest or search. *State* v. *Beck* (above) is an excellent example of this point.

Most authorities on criminal law agree it is extremely unlikely a list could be compiled including *all* the factors that might be construed as probable cause. The following list, however, serves as an excellent example.

1. Incidents that alone and in themselves would amount to probable cause:
   a. A crime is committed in the presence of an officer.
   b. An admission or confession to the commission of a crime is made.
   c. Circumstances are such that the officer can reasonably conclude only X could have committed the crime, although the officer did not see the crime committed.
   d. It is reasonable to believe that one of a small group of persons must have committed the crime. (Mass arrests of 142 people in Detroit in April 1969 were held illegal, although it was reasonable to believe that one of the 142 killed the police officer whose death was being investigated.)
2. Knowledge that a crime was committed plus one or more of the following, would, in most cases, amount to probable cause:
   a. Fingerprints that put the suspect at the scene of the crime.
   b. Identification by the victim or a witness (by photograph, or line-up, for instance).
   c. Identification by unusual characteristics (a one-armed man with red hair, for instance).
   d. Information from a reliable informer.

    e. Flight from the crime zone or an attempt to hide.
    f. An attempt to destroy evidence.
3. *Suspicion that a crime has been committed* or is being committed, plus two or more of the following, might amount to probable cause:
    a. Flight or an attempt to hide.
    b. Evasive and inconsistent answers.
    c. A suspect's refusal to identify himself or refusal to explain the circumstances surrounding his presence in the area.
    d. Knowledge of the suspect's past record or past weaknesses (drug addiction, alcohol, or gambling, for instance).
    e. Hearsay evidence from the general public, another police officer, or informant.

STOP-AND-FRISK

Stop-and-frisk is the detaining and searching of suspects without probable cause. A much-debated issue for police is whether, and under what circumstances, a police officer is permitted to stop a person in an automobile* or walking in a public place in order to question him about his identity and activities and to frisk him for illegal weapons. This practice is supposedly justified by the strong public interest in crime prevention, but it is based on the assumption that a citizen can be temporarily restrained when there is no probable cause to arrest him.

Several states have passed "stop-and-frisk" laws, which permit a police officer to detain a person in a public place if he has a reasonable suspicion that the person being detained has committed or is *about* to commit a felony. The officer may demand that the individual identify himself as well as explain his actions. Such actions on the part of law enforcement agencies have been judicially upheld in many state and federal courts even without statutory authorization. Underlying both statutory and judicial approval of stop-and-frisk is the theory that this practice does *not* constitute an arrest under state law, so it can be justified by some standard less than that required for a lawful arrest.

In *Terry* v. *State of Ohio*, Chief Justice Warren said:

> It is frequently argued that in dealing with the rapidly unfolding and often dangerous situations on city streets, the police are in need of an

---

* The *search* of an automobile is presently being considered by the U.S. Supreme Court (*Minjares* v. *California*). The California State Supreme Court ordered a new trial (Paul Michael Minjares was convicted in 1975 of robbery) for Minjares declaring that the search of Minjares automobile was illegal because police did not obtain a warrant before opening a tote bag in which the evidence (i.e., clothing, guns, and coins) was found.

escalating set of flexible responses, graduated in relation to the amount of information they possess. For this purpose it is urged that distinctions should be made between a "stop" and an "arrest" (or a "seizure" of a person), and between a "frisk" and a "search." Thus, it is argued, the police should be allowed to "stop" a person and detain him briefly for questioning upon suspicion that he may be connected with criminal activity. Upon suspicion that the person may be armed, the police should have the power to "frisk" him for weapons. If the "stop" and the "frisk" give rise to probable cause to believe that the suspect has committed a crime, then the police should be empowered to make a formal "arrest," and a full incident "search" of the person. This scheme is justified in part upon the notion that a "stop" and a "frisk" amount to a mere "minor inconvenience and petty indignity," which can properly be imposed upon the citizen in the interest of effective law enforcement on the basis of a police officer's suspicion.

On the other side the argument is made that the authority of the police must be strictly circumscribed by the law of arrest and search as it has developed to date in the traditional jurisprudence of the Fourth Amendment.

The United States Supreme Court (*Terry* v. *Ohio,* 392 U.S. 1, [1968]) upheld the police officer's constitutional privilege to detain an individual and conduct a reasonable search for weapons (a frisk) if the officer has reasonable grounds for believing that the individual is armed and dangerous and that preventive action, to protect herself and others, is called for.[8] The U.S. Supreme Court has ruled that if such a search produces weapons or any other evidence of guilt, the evidence may be used in court against the person who was searched.[9] This decision, contained in two opinions written by former Chief Justice Earl Warren, emphasized the need to protect police officers in their efforts to control street crime.

An important aspect of these opinions is that they marked the first time the Court had held that police can detain and search persons without the probable cause mentioned in the Constitution's Fourth Amendment. This ruling assured the police of virtually the full range of powers law enforcement representatives had sought. It rejected appeals by civil rights and civil liberties groups to limit the stop-and-frisk power of the police.

Chief Justice Earl Warren laid down a rule of reasonableness that would permit policemen to search suspects. The chief justice indicated the police may search the suspect when "a reasonably prudent man in the circumstances would be warranted in the belief that his safety or that of others was in danger."

The major elements of the new rule were announced in the case of

John W. Terry, who was stopped and searched on a downtown street in Cleveland on October 31, 1963.

CASE

In *Terry*, Officer McFadden, the arresting officer, a veteran of 19 years with the Cleveland Police Department, first noticed Terry and a cohort about 2:30 P.M. on the afternoon of the arrest. Officer McFadden could not recall what first brought them to his attention, but he testified that the situation was inappropriate and extremely suspicious. The arresting officer observed the suspects making several trips (approximately five or six apiece) down the street, stopping at a certain store window, continuing on in the same direction for another half block, turning around and returning to the spot they had come from, again pausing to look at the same window. The suspects conversed furtively after each journey. At one point during the time they were observed, they were joined by a third man, who conferred with them and then moved on. The pair continued their "measured pacing, peering and conferring." After approximately twelve minutes, the pair left and followed the route taken by the third man. By this time Officer McFadden suspected that the two were "casing a job, a stickup." He followed them because he felt it was his duty as a peace officer to investigate the case further. In following the pair, he discovered that they had joined the third man again. Officer McFadden then decided that "the situation was in need of direct action." Therefore, Officer McFadden approached the three suspects, identified himself, and requested that the subjects identify themselves. When Terry mumbled something, Officer McFadden "spun him around so that they were facing the other two, with Terry between McFadden and the others, and patted down the outside of his clothing. In the left breast pocket of Terry's overcoat, Officer McFadden felt a pistol." Terry was relieved of his weapon, and a subsequent search of his partner revealed a similar gun. The two men were ultimately convicted of carrying concealed weapons. Terry's appeal was based on the contention that the weapon was the product of an illegal search and seizure and as such should not have been used against him. The United States Supreme Court disagreed and upheld his conviction.

Although the police in most communities have been stopping and searching for suspects for years, the question of whether the practice violated the Fourth Amendment was not very important until 1961.

In that year, the Supreme Court held that evidence obtained in violation of the Fourth Amendment could not be used in state courts. The Fourth Amendment declares in part that "the right of the people to be secure in their persons, houses, papers and effects, against unreasonable searches and seizures shall not be violated, and no warrants shall be issued, but only upon probable cause."

This has been construed by the Supreme Court to mean that the police could not make an arrest *or* search unless they had objective evidence that a crime had been committed by the suspect.

In most search situations, the police act on the basis of suspicious circumstances but do not have probable cause. Thus, the court would have ruled inadmissible the fruits (the objects for which the crime was committed) of most searches if it had insisted on the probable-cause standard.

Former Chief Justice Warren declared that the Fourth Amendment still applied but that because the amendment rules out "unreasonable" searches, the probable-cause requirement can be ignored if a search for weapons is otherwise reasonable.

However, the *Terry* case applies only to weapons uncovered and seized during such a search. The Court has yet to rule on the admissibility of other evidence obtained through such a stop-and-frisk, such as drugs, burglars' tools, and perhaps even incriminating statements overheard during the search.[10]

MANNER OF MAKING ARRESTS

An arrest is made for criminal-law violations and, in certain situations, for civil-law violations, by actual restraint of the person or by the person's submission to the custody of an officer. Any person arrested may be restrained as much as necessary for her arrest and detention. In making the arrest, the police officer must inform the person to be arrested of:

1. his intention to arrest her
2. the cause of the arrest
3. his authority for making the arrest

There are three general exceptions to this procedure. The person making the arrest is not required to comply with the foregoing procedure: (1) if he has reasonable cause to believe that the person to be arrested is actually engaged in the commission of, or is attempting to commit, an offense; (2) if the person to be arrested is pursued immediately after commission of a crime; and (3) after an escape. The person making the arrest must, on request of the person he is arresting, inform her of the offense she is being arrested for. Submission to custody is shown when the person to be arrested recognizes the presence of the authority for the arrest and is advised of the alleged offense.

Authority to arrest may occur in either of two ways: (1) when the peace officer is in uniform and (2) when the person being arrested should, by exercising ordinary care, recognize the officer's authority. Immediate pursuit is not used here in the sense of an escape from custody but rather in the sense of flight from the scene of a crime. As soon as the complete arrest and restraint are made by the officer, he must advise the arrestee of her constitutional rights, whether or not she is a citizen of the United States. Every person arrested in the United States enjoys this privilege. It is preferable that there be a witness to the advisement of rights. After the advisement of rights, the arrestee must be asked if she understands her rights. If she answers yes, then and only then may the peace officers begin interrogation of the suspect.

Exemptions from Arrest

Two classes of people are exempt, within certain limits, from criminal arrest. The first group is ambassadors and other diplomatic officials of foreign nations, together with their families and members of their official households, except when and where it is necessary to prevent these persons from committing acts of violence. Consular officials lack this immunity unless it is given them by treaty. The second group is witnesses who are brought into, or are traveling through, a state in obedience to a subpoena or who have been ordered to testify at a criminal or grand jury proceeding in connection with circumstances that occurred before the witnesses entered the state.

On occasion, peace officers have arrested persons who are immune to arrest. These arrests, when they occur, are voidable but not illegal. The arrestee, in this situation, must submit to the authority of the arresting officer and later establish her immunity in a judicial proceeding. People belonging to the classes listed above are also exempt from civil arrest. In addition to these two classes, the following categories are exempt from civil arrest: (1) *witnesses* under court order or subpoena going to or returning from court; (2) *voters* at, going to, or coming from polls on election day; (3) state and federal *legislators;* (4) *state militia* members at, going to, or returning from their place of military duty.

Arrests by Peace Officers without a Warrant

A peace officer may make an arrest in obedience to a warrant, or she may arrest a person without a warrant whenever she has *reasonable and probable cause* to believe that the person to be arrested has committed a public offense in her presence. In addition, an officer may arrest a person who has committed a felony, although not in her presence.

She may arrest a person whenever she has *reasonable cause* to believe the person has committed a felony, whether or not a felony has, in fact, been committed.

Most arrests are made without warrants, and they are frequently made in situations where calm, direct, and deliberate action is impossible. As a result, peace officers are obliged to have a thorough and exact understanding of their powers, obligations, and limitations to make arrests without a warrant. Why is this understanding necessary? There are four basic reasons: (1) an unlawful arrest may subject an officer to a suit for false arrest; (2) the arrestee, under limited circumstances, may have a right to resist the arrest; (3) any subsequent search is considered unlawful and evidence seized may be suppressed or excluded; and (4) a later confession is considered to be obtained through duress and coercion and is not admissible. The following case is an excellent example of the problem.

CASE

United States Ex Rel. Everett v. Murphy, 329 F. 2d 68 (CA-2 1964). The petitioner was sentenced to life imprisonment upon conviction for felony murder by a New York State court. After having exhausted his state remedies, the petitioner applied for a writ of habeas corpus to the United States District Court for the Northern District of New York. On appeal from the district court's summary denial of the writ, the petitioner contended that his state conviction was obtained through an involuntary confession and thus violated his Fourteenth Amendment right to due process of law. The Court of Appeals for the Second Circuit ordered New York to release the petitioner unless he be retried within a reasonable time. The petitioner's confession was made after he was *illegally arrested*, held incommunicado for about seven hours, questioned without benefit of counsel and without being informed of his right to counsel and to remain silent, and falsely told that the robbery victim was not seriously hurt and that a detective would "help" the petitioner if he confessed—therefore the confession was not voluntary. Since the confession was used as evidence against the petitioner, his state conviction was obtained in violation of due process.

In this chapter, several references have been made to reasonable cause. Further discussion of this concept, when discussing arrest procedure, is relevant. The peace officer may make an arrest for a felony or a misdemeanor without a warrant if she has reasonable cause to believe the person to be arrested has committed a crime in her presence. The term *reasonable cause* is not defined by statute. However, an officer must understand its meaning in order to make arrests properly, effectively, and justly. To illustrate its meaning fully would require an extensive discussion of judicial decisions. This would go beyond the scope and purpose of this chapter, which is designed to acquaint students and new law enforcement officers with the subject of arrest procedure and technique. However, *reasonable cause* has been defined as a state of facts that would lead a person of ordinary care and prudence to believe, and conscientiously to entertain an honest and strong suspicion, that the person is guilty of a crime.

The term *probable cause* is used interchangeably with *reasonable cause* by courts throughout the country. However, *probable cause* has been defined as an opinion supported by evidence that inclines the mind to believe but leaves room for doubt. It does not apply to evidence that would be admissible at a trial to prove guilt.

No method exists for determining what is reasonable cause. It depends on all the facts and circumstances of each case.* The circumstances that should be considered have already been discussed in the section dealing with probable cause. However, it is worth reemphasizing that it is vitally important that there be reasonable cause before a search or an arrest is made. If reasonable cause is lacking, evidence uncovered by the search will be held inadmissible by the courts.

Arrests by Peace Officers with a Warrant

A warrant of arrest, based upon a declaration (Figure 3.5) is a written order of a magistrate, directed to a peace officer, commanding him to arrest a particular individual and bring him before the magistrate (Figure 3.6). When obeying such a command, an officer has no liability and cannot be sued for carrying it out. An officer with a warrant that is regular upon its face acts without malice if he reasonably believes the person arrested is the person referred to in the warrant.

The phrase *regular upon its face* is important to officers. They must know the procedure for securing a warrant, and the warrant's form and content. The Supreme Court of the United States (*Vallandras* v. *Massachusetts*) has said regularity is not to be determined on the basis of what a trained legal mind would know. It is sufficient that the warrant, upon its face, has every appearance of validity in the judgment of an ordinary intelligent, informed layman.

When an officer serves a warrant, he must act in good faith, take

---

* It is usually construed as a question of law (to be decided by the judge rather than the jury)—*Beck* v. *Ohio*, 379 U.S. 89.

```
                    MUNICIPAL COURT OF CALIFORNIA
                 SANTA CLARA COUNTY JUDICIAL DISTRICT
                 _____FACILITY


 1  STATE OF CALIFORNIA    )
                           ) ss.          AFFIDAVIT IN SUPPORT
 2  COUNTY OF SANTA CLARA  )
                                          OF SEARCH WARRANT
 3

 4       Personally appeared before me this _____ day of _____

 5  19_____, _____

 6  who, on oath, makes complaint, and deposes and says that there is

 7  just, probable and reasonable cause to believe, and that he does

 8  believe, that there is now in the possession of _____

 9  _____, on the premises

10  located at _____

11  _____, which premises consist of: _____

12  _____

13

14

15  personal property described as follows:

16

17

18

19

20

21

22

23

24

25

26
                                -1-
```

FIGURE 3.5   Declaration for an arrest warrant.

W A R R A N T

MUNICIPAL COURT OF CALIFORNIA, COUNTY OF SANTA CLARA

_____ JUDICIAL DISTRICT

* * * * * * *

The People of the State of California to any peace officer of said State:

Complaint upon oath having been this day laid before me, a Judge of the _____ Court, by _____ _____ that the offense(s) of California _____ _____ _____ a felony(ies) has been committed, and accusing _____ _____ thereof.

You are therefore commanded forthwith to arrest the above-named defendant and bring him/her before me, forthwith, at the Municipal Court, located at _____ _____, County of Santa Clara, State of California, or in case of my absence or inability to act, before the nearest or most accessible magistrate in this County.

This warrant may be served at night, and defendant admitted to bail in the sum of

CASH OR BOND $_____
Assessment $_____
TOTAL to be
deposited $_____

Witness my hand and seal, at _____, California, on this _____ day of _____, A.D., 198___.

_____
JUDGE OF THE MUNICIPAL COURT

WARRANT (Felony)

FIGURE 3.6   Arrest warrant.

precautions to determine that the person about to be arrested is the party against whom the warrant is issued, and be alerted to consider information given to him that might reveal that an error has been made. If the officer arrests the wrong person as a result of his own carelessness or malice, he may be sued.

Through a series of cases, rather strict requirements have been laid down for the issuance of an arrest warrant. In seeking a warrant, an officer need not always act on the basis of personal observation. He may, and policemen often do, rely upon information obtained from others. But his informants must be known to be reliable, either from the officer's own observation and experience or from the experience of other officers.[11] Such reliable information will suffice even if it would be excluded at a criminal trial as hearsay. In addition, the officer must set forth the information that gives him probable cause in sufficient detail and particularity to enable the magistrate, judge, or other official to make an independent appraisal before issuing the warrant. A warrant is usually initiated by the filing of a written complaint with a county prosecutor (Figure 3.7). A *complaint*, like an *indictment* or *information*, is an accusatory pleading. It constitutes the formal charge to which the defendant must respond at his arraignment before the magistrate who issued the warrant.

The complaint must contain the same allegations that are required for indictment and information. Criminal complaints are frequently made on the information and belief of the peace officer. This means a criminal complaint may be issued in situations in which no one is available who possesses absolute knowledge or information about all the facts of the alleged offense. The peace officer's oath "on information and belief" generally says the complainant believes that the facts alleged are true and founded upon information and knowedge she has actually received.

A warrant may be issued by any magistrate. The term *magistrate* includes justices of the supreme and appellate courts and judges of the superior, municipal, and justice courts. It is the duty of these justices and judges to issue a warrant of arrest for a person if they, in fact, are satisfied that the complainant has based her request for a warrant on reasonable information and knowledge that the person to be named in the warrant committed the crime for which the warrant is requested.

Whenever a judge of the justice or municipal court acts as a magistrate, she has countywide jurisdiction and is not limited by the territorial jurisdiction of her particular court. It has been a convenient practice for many years for officers to file their felony complaints in the municipal court of the city or in the justice court of the district in which the alleged crime was committed. A justice of the supreme court, which has only appellate jurisdiction, may act as a committing magistrate.

MUNICIPAL COURT OF CALIFORNIA
SANTA CLARA COUNTY JUDICIAL DISTRICT
_____FACILITY

THE PEOPLE OF THE STATE OF CALIFORNIA,)   COMPLAINT _____
                          Plaintiff,)
)
     vs.   )
)
)
)
                     Defendant(s).)
_____)

    I, the undersigned, hereby certify, or, on information and belief declare:

    That in the County of Santa Clara, State of California, on or about the _____ day of _____, 19____, a FELONY/MISDEMEANOR/ INFRACTION, to wit: a violation of CALIFORNIA _____
_____
was committed by the above-named defendant(s), as follows, to wit: The said defendant(s)

    Complainant therefore prays that the said defendant(s) may be dealt with according to law.
    I certify under penalty of perjury that the foregoing is true and correct. Executed on _____ at _____, California.

Warrant received for service by: _____
_____
on _____
Cash or Bond $ _____

_____
JUDGE OF THE MUNICIPAL COURT

FIGURE 3.7 Complaint.

The warrant must describe the offense charged and contain the name of the accused, or if his name is unknown, some description by which he can be identified with reasonable certainty. A "John Doe" or "Jane Doe," or blank, warrant, without some more particular description of the accused, may be held void and no basis for a valid arrest. The warrant is directed to, and may be executed by, *any peace officer* in the jurisdiction. The arresting officer does not have to have the warrant in his possession at the time of the arrest as long as he shows it to the accused, if he is requested to, after the arrest. A warrant issued in one county or judicial district may be served by peace officers of any other county or district of the same state where the accused may be found.

Some states, by statute, give local peace officers statewide powers of arrest. This allows police officers in the county or district where the warrant was issued to make the arrest anywhere in the state. However, a warrant has no authority beyond the territorial limits of the state in which it is issued. An arrest in state A *cannot* be based on a warrant issued in state B. Many states have eliminated this problem by adopting a uniform act authorizing a peace officer from one state who enters another in "fresh pursuit" of a person to arrest him for a felony committed in the first state. But the process of extradition from the second state must still be followed.

There are four special forms of warrant: (1) coroner's warrant; (2) warrant on writ of habeas corpus; (3) bench warrant; and (4) warrant for bail jumper. The *coroner*, throughout most of the United States, is thought of as a medical doctor whose task is to determine the cause of death through examination of human remains. Although this is an accurate description for many areas, the coroner may assume three specific roles—physician, hearing officer, or peace officer. His role as a physician has been mentioned. As a hearing officer, the coroner presides over inquests into the cause of deaths. If the coroner's jury, composed of citizens in the area, finds that the death of a person was caused by some person under circumstances not excusable or justifiable by law, or that the death was the result of a criminal act, and if the subject who committed the act is known and is not in official custody, the coroner is required to issue a warrant for the person's arrest and detention. The coroner may act as a peace officer in serving the warrant he himself has issued.

A warrant is issued instead of a writ of habeas corpus when it appears to a judge or a justice, authorized to issue a writ of habeas corpus, that a person is illegally jailed or under detention and that if he is removed from the jurisdiction of the court, he may suffer irreparable injury.[12] The warrant of arrest recites the facts and requires the sheriff, coroner, or constable of the county to bring the person before the court at once. The same warrant may command the apprehension and arrest of the individual responsible for the illegal jailing or detention. Warrants of this type are generally issued by the court clerk and signed by the judge or justice. Without exception, they must bear the seal of the court. An example of a writ of habeas corpus and related court problems is shown *In re Fitts:*

CASE

In re Fitts, 197 A. 2d 808 (Vt. 1964). After the petitioner's conviction for petty larceny, the trial court suspended sentence and placed her on probation. About 10 months later, the trial court found that the petitioner violated the terms of her probation and ordered the petitioner to serve the original sentence of four to six months. Petitioner's father instituted a petition for writ of habeas corpus for petitioner's release, which was granted by the county on the grounds that legal cause had not been shown for petitioner's imprisonment. On appeal by the state from the county court's order, petitioner contended her discharge on writ of habeas corpus was not subject to appeal by the state. The Supreme Court of Vermont dismissed the state's appeal, holding that no Vermont statute expressly authorized appeal by the state from a habeas corpus proceeding. Vermont statutes indicate that habeas corpus proceedings were intended by the legislature to be a quick, summary, and final procedure for release from illegal imprisonment. Appeal by the state from an adverse habeas corpus proceeding was not provided for by the general appellate statutes. Consequently, the appeal was unauthorized.

To compel the appearance of witnesses or the presence of defendants before the court, a *bench warrant* is issued either by the clerk of the court as directed by the magistrate commanding the appearance, or by the magistrate at the request of the prosecuting attorney. If there is no court clerk, then the magistrate issues the warrant directly. These warrants are executed in the same manner and fashion as a warrant of arrest.

A *warrant for a bail jumper* is issued for the protection of the bonds-person, or individual who gives bail, for a bail jumper from one state who is found in another state. A warrant for the arrest of such a fugitive can be obtained.

Arrest by a Private Person (Citizen's Arrest)

Various statutes throughout the United States cover arrests made by private persons.[13] The statutes generally provide that a private person may arrest another (1) for a public offense committed or attempted in her presence; (2) when the person has committed a felony although not in her presence; (3) when a felony has in fact been committed and she has reasonable cause for believing that the person arrested did, in fact, commit the felony. It is not necessary that a citizen's arrest be accompanied by a warrant of arrest.

An offense is committed in the presence of a person when the person can testify to sufficient facts, known personally, to show that the offense in question has been committed.* If a crime is committed in the presence of the person making the arrest, the powers of arrest possessed by a peace officer and a private citizen are equal. The principal difference is that the peace officer may make an arrest for a felony that, in fact, has not been committed (if he has reasonable cause for believing it has been committed). The private person may make an arrest only if the felony has been committed.[14] The general view is that a peace officer or private citizen has the power to arrest without a warrant for a misdemeanor only if it has *in fact* been committed or attempted in her presence and the person arrested is actually guilty. Courts are inclined to be liberal in determining what constitutes the "presence" of the arresting officer. It is sufficient if he becomes aware through any of his senses (sight, hearing, smell) that a crime is being committed. In some states, a police officer is empowered to arrest for a misdemeanor if he reasonably believes that an offense is being committed in his presence and that the person arrested is guilty.

An arrest for a misdemeanor must be made within a reasonable time. If the arrest is made after the occasion has passed, even though the crime was committed in the presence of the person making the arrest, the arrest is not justified. A continuous effort to make the arrest must be made. If instead of making the arrest when the violation is committed in her presence, the citizen goes about other matters, she loses her right to make the arrest without a warrant. To make a valid arrest, a warrant of arrest must be sought.

When a private person makes an arrest, she must conform to the same rules peace officers follow. A private person's arrest is made if she merely announces in a clear and audible voice that she is making a citizen's arrest, even though she does not touch the arrestee or direct a peace officer to detain the arrestee.

Can one arrested private person arrest another? There is nothing to indicate that the private person loses his privilege to arrest because he himself is under arrest. In a California case (*Lorenz* v. *Hunt*, 89 Cal. App. 6), the court said a private person who is under arrest may arrest

---

* Private persons are bound by common law to arrest in such instances (*Kennedy* v. *State* 107 F.2d 144).

another and also that a private person may arrest a peace officer. Opinions of the appellate courts are scarce in this area. Until a statute or court opinion says otherwise, it should be presumed that a private person who is under arrest may arrest another.

A peace officer has a duty to advise a private person of her power to arrest. The officer is also bound by law to take custody of a person arrested by a private person if the officer believes the arrest is lawful. The officer should assist the private person with the arrest only when the person being arrested resists. If the officer believes the arrest is unlawful, he should advise the private person, and if the private person continues, the officer's duty is to aid the person being unlawfully arrested. One private person has the right to resist an unlawful arrest by another private person.

A private person who assists a peace officer in making an arrest is not liable for false imprisonment. The courts have said it is manifestly unfair to impose civil liability upon private persons for doing something the statutes require them to do.

A private person making an arrest is justified in killing a fleeing felon who cannot otherwise be taken if she can prove the person is actually guilty of the felony. Deadly force (serious injury or killing) may not be used in making a misdemeanor arrest.

For the purpose of protecting her property, the owner, in most jurisdictions, may restrain for a reasonable time and for the purpose of investigation anyone she has reasonable and probable cause to believe has interfered with or stolen her property. In most jurisdictions, physically resisting lawful arrest by a private person is considered an assault upon the arrestor.

Resisting arrest by a private person and by a peace officer differ. A person who resists a peace officer may be guilty of resisting arrest per se. This may be either a felony or a misdemeanor. Most statutes provide that a person may not resist an arrest, lawful or unlawful, made by a peace officer. It is the duty of the citizen to submit (he has no privilege to use any force) regardless of the validity of the arrest.[15] A person being unlawfully arrested by a private person, however, may use force to resist. Even deadly force may be used if it is reasonably required. Any person making an arrest may take from the person arrested any weapons that he may have about his person in order to protect herself and those about her. Such weapons must be delivered to the magistrate before whom the arrested person is taken.

A peace officer is not required to accept custody of an arrested person from a private citizen if he does not believe the arrest is lawful. One deciding factor in determining the legality of an arrest is the competence of the arresting party. Competence may be seriously questioned with regard to three groups:

1. *Children.* Age alone does not determine the competence of a child. It appears there is no age limit for the arresting person.
2. *Insane or mentally ill persons.* A peace officer, in most cases, should not take into custody a person who has been arrested by an insane or mentally ill person. The unstable person is incapable of making a sound decision serving as a competent witness.
3. *Intoxicated persons.* An officer may reasonably assume the arrest to be unlawful if the person making the arrest is under the influence of alcohol or drugs.

When any person makes an arrest she may summon as many persons as she deems necessary to aid her. Refusal to respond is morally wrong as well as a violation of law.

Special Statutes Authorizing Arrest Without a Warrant

Eight special statutes in the United States provide for arrest without a warrant. In some states, all eight have been enacted. In others, only a few will be found. Because of the varying ways the states apply these laws, they will be discussed here only briefly.

1. A *magistrate* is authorized to order any peace officer or private person to arrest anyone committing, or attempting to commit, an offense in his presence.
2. The *Uniform Fresh Pursuit Act* authorizes peace officers of one or more states entering another state in fresh pursuit of a person wanted for a felony in the first state to arrest without a warrant.[16] Their authority is the same as that of peace officers in the state in which the arrest is made. People they arrest must be taken before a magistrate, who is required to determine the legality of the arrest. The magistrate may commit the arrestee for a reasonable time to await extradition.
3. A *felony fugitive*—an escapee— can be arrested at any time or place, and county jail "walk-aways" can be retaken without a warrant.
4. A *bail bondsman* or other person who has posted bail with a court for the release of a defendant can arrest the defendant without a warrant for the sole purpose of returning her to custody. A person of suitable age and discretion can be empowered by the bondsperson or another person to act in his place. However, when the fugitive is from another state, a warrant of arrest is required.
5. *Unlawful-assembly* statutes require that peace officers, city officials, and certain others order persons unlawfully or riotously assembled to disperse. Failure to do so is a criminal violation.
6. A *probationer* reasonably believed to have violated the terms of his probation may be arrested by a probation or peace officer, returned to custody, and brought before the court that granted probation.

7. A *parolee* who leaves the state where he is paroled, or violates the conditions of his parole or whose parole is suspended or revoked, is considered an escaped prisoner. He can be arrested at any time and at any place without a warrant.
8. Finally, a *defendant* released by a magistrate on her own recognizance can be ordered arrested and returned to custody if she fails to give security or bail when required by the magistrate, or if she fails to appear in answer to a grand jury indictment or to an information filed by the prosecuting attorney charging a felony.

SUMMARY

By arresting a law violator, the arresting officer initiates the system of judicial due process. Therefore, the arresting officer ought to be familiar with the legal framework and restraints that govern her actions. The arrest procedure and the procedures immediately following the arrest must comply with edicts that have been handed down by appellate court decisions in the form of *case law* (i.e., precedents). In order for the district attorney to prosecute a case successfully, the arresting officer must follow legal procedures and techniques when taking a suspect into custody.

In this chapter, the authors have attempted to cover areas that are important enough to be considered a necessary part of a police officer's fundamental knowledge. An overview, therefore, is presented in laws of arrest—including probable cause—and arrest procedures; distinction between the rules of arrest and the rules of search and seizure; manner of making arrests; exemptions from arrests; the much-debated stop-and-frisk issue and the major elements of the new rule announced in the *Terry* case, in which the United States Supreme Court ruled that the probable-cause requirement can be ignored if a search for weapons is otherwise reasonable; arrests by peace officers with or without warrants and the basic reasons why police officers must have a thorough and exact understanding of their powers, obligations, and limitations when making arrests without the aid of a warrant, as well as the four special forms of warrant (i.e., coroner's warrant, warrant on writ of habeas corpus, bench warrant, and warrant for bail jumper); arrest by private persons (citizen's arrest); special statutes authorizing arrest without a warrant (such as an order by a magistrate, the Uniform Fresh Pursuit Act, a felony fugitive, a bail bondsperson, unlawful assembly statutes, and a probationer or parolee who violates conditions of probation or release); and search and seizure.

In the area of search and seizure, methods such as observation, surveillance, actual searches and seizure of evidence, and interrogations of the suspect and victim are a significant part of police work. The legal framework within which these techniques should be carried out is discussed, with some actual decisions of appellate courts serving as illustrations.

The United States' *constitutional protections and their significance to the law enforcement officer is discussed.* The Constitution is important to law enforcement officers not only because it sets out general standards and protects personal liberties, but also because a misunderstanding of its separate parts will hinder the law enforcement officer's proper performance of his duty.

NOTES

1. New York State Criminal Procedure Law, 1978–79, Sec. 1.20(33).
2. For additional information on arrest procedures, refer to E. Eldefonso, A. Coffey, and R. C. Grace, *Principles of Law Enforcement*, 2d ed. (New York: Wiley, 1974), pp. 251–260, 263–270.
3. L. Ed. 2d 1737.
4. ALI Code of Crim. Proc. 18.
5. Information here relating to the Fourth and Fifth Amendments was taken from *Handbook on the Law of Search and Seizure* (Washington, D.C.: U.S. Government Printing Office, 1967), pp. 11–20. For a more detailed treatment, refer to this source.
6. *State* v. *Cos*, 262 Wis. (1952).
7. *Brinegar* v. *United States*, 338 U.S. 160.
8. *Gilbert* v. *United States*, 366 F. 2d 923; cert. denied, 388 U.S. 922.
9. *Terry* v. *Ohio*, 392 U.S. 1 (1968).
10. See *Wonglun* v. *United States* infra for exclusion of seized conversation.
11. *Draper* v. *United States*, 358 U.S. 307.
12. *Barton* v. *Saunders*, 16 Ore. 51.
13. *Graham* v. *State*, 143 Ga. 440.
14. *Kurtz* v. *Moffitt*, 115 U.S. 487.
15. California Penal Code, Section 834(a).
16. *District of Columbia* v. *Perry*, 215 A. 2d 845.

PRACTICAL EXERCISES

1. How does probable cause relate to arrest?
2. What are the advantages and disadvantages of making an arrest with or without a warrant?
3. How does arrest by a private person differ from arrest by a peace officer?
4. List the four forms of warrant.
5. List and briefly discuss the special statutes authorizing arrest without a warrant.

ANNOTATED REFERENCES

Bonsignore, John J.; Katsh, E.; d'Erico, P.; Pipkin, R. M.; and Arons, S. *Before the Law*. 2d ed. Boston: Houghton Mifflin, 1977. A book of timely cases and readings on the legal process, designed to enhance a general understanding of the law. It draws upon contemporary and classic courses to give the reader an enlightened view of how law really works.

Bristow, A. P., and Williams, J. B. *Criminal Procedure and the Administration of Justice*. 3d rev. ed. Encino, Calif.: Glencoe Press, 1976 An excellent overview of the law, judicial, and postjudicial system in the United States. The authors are well known for their excellent work in this area.

Gardner, T. J. "Aspects of Probable Cause." *Police Work: Concerning Criminal Evidence*, December 1969. *Probable cause* or *reasonable grounds to believe*—terms that are used interchangeably—must exist before an arrest can be made. This requirement is thoroughly analyzed in Gardner's article. An extremely good and complete resource in an important area.

Eldefonso, E.; Coffey, A. R.; and Grace, R. C. *Principles of Law Enforcement*. 2d ed. New York: Wiley, 1974. Chapter 12, on arrest procedures, is of tremendous value to the student not familiar with the law of arrest. This chapter introduces the reader, in simple language, to the requirements of physical arrest. See also by E. Eldefonso and A. R. Coffey, *Process and Impact of the Justice System*. Encino, Calif.: Glencoe Press, 1976.

LaFave, W. R. *Arrest: Decision to Take a Suspect into Custody*. Boston: Little, Brown, 1976. The student enrolled in a police science program must have this book in his private library. LaFave discusses arrest and the various problems involved in initiating such an action. An outstanding dissertation on the subject of arrest.

Chapter 4

RULES
OF EVIDENCE

LEARNING OBJECTIVES

The learning objectives of this chapter are:
1. To explore constitutional limitations on rules of evidence, interrogations, and confessions.
2. To become cognizant of the *"chain" of evidence, rules of exclusion, prohibition* from obtaining evidence through illegal searches or arrests, and *degree* of evidence.
3. To understand that evidence obtained through illegal searches or arrests is inadmissible in both federal and state courts.
4. To be able to distinguish between evidence obtained through *primary* and *independent* means and to determine how the two types of evidence will be accepted or excluded at the trial.
5. To analyze the *Escobedo* and *Miranda* U.S. Supreme Court decisions and to comprehend the distinction between them, in a continuation of the material on interrogations and confessions introduced in Chapter 3.

In 1967 THE PRESIDENT'S COMMISSION on Law Enforcement and Administration of Justice issued a report entitled *The Challenge of Crime in a Free Society*. Under the section "Court Proceedings," the following comment was made:

> The cases decided by trial are only a small fraction of the total of cases, but they are most impoitant to the process because they set standards for the conduct of all cases. The trial decides the hard legal issues, and reviews the rules of claims of official abuse. Trial procedures have evolved over centuries and in general have proven that they can resolve disputed cases effectively. Unlike the administrative proceedings in the pretrial stage, court proceedings are continually being studied by lawyers and are now receiving intensive scrutiny from other groups.

In societies that presume the innocence of an accused person until there is *proof* of guilt, the theoretical task of the criminal court is simply to determine the adequacy of evidence—the hard legal issues. In practice, of course, the hard legal issues involve considering proof of innocence as well. As the statement by the President's Commission implies, determining the adequacy of proof is anything but simple. Even eyewitnesses, as will be discussed in this chapter, make mistakes.

PRESERVATION OF EVIDENCE

When police officers make an arrest, thus invoking the initial phases of the criminal-justice process, their first responsibility—aside from ensuring that the arrestee retains his rights of due process—is the preservation of evidence.

Preservation of evidence is an extremely important aspect of police work. The evidence must, at all times, remain sterile, or untainted— that is, divorced of any suspicion that it was tampered with. There are many rules designed to preserve evidence until the time of trial. The technical term *preservation* means retention of the evidence's "persuasive quality."

Since judges and juries do not witness the crimes being tried, a defendant's guilt is largely a matter of proof—proof established by enough evidence to remove all reasonable doubt. Whether there is reasonable doubt might depend on how well the evidence has been preserved. By "preserving" such evidence, the "chain" (record of evidentry progression, i.e., a log is maintained on "movement" or examination of evidence). The following example, though exaggerated for purposes of illustration, reflects, in part, some of the problems of protecting and preserving evidence.

EXAMPLE

Officer A arrests a suspected narcotics peddler in the early morning, and, before going off duty, places on the desk of a narcotics detective an envelope containing what officer A believes is heroin. This evidence has a note instructing the narcotics detail to have the envelope contents analyzed.

Officer B makes a similar arrest on another patrol beat and follows the same procedure, using the same narcotics detective's desk.

On arriving at work, the narcotics detective finds the janitor picking the two envelopes up off the floor, where they had allegedly been pushed by the cleaning woman's dusting cloth.

Nothing more is thought of the situation until the crime lab declares the contents of one envelope to be baking soda and the other envelope to be heroin.

An investigator for the prosecutor's office then determines that the janitor is the brother of officer A's suspect, and the cleaning woman is the wife of suspect B. It is further discovered that the cleaning woman is divorcing suspect B.

A jury might now wonder is the janitor changed the contents of one of the envelopes to "protect" his brother. Perhaps the cleaning woman switched the envelopes after learning what the janitor had done because of guilt feelings about divorcing suspect B—or perhaps she inserted heroin in the soda-filled envelope to ensure suspect B's conviction before the divorce. A jury might also wonder if the janitor misjudged the cleaning woman's motives and made an inappropriate switch himself. For that matter, someone else might have tampered with the evidence left completely unprotected on the detective's desk.

Of course, a little common sense would have prevented all these problems from developing in the first place. Nevertheless, they represent the very real kinds of difficulty encountered in protecting and preserving evidence. When we consider the importance of knowing the many rules for preserving evidence, one fact emerges: the quality of the evidence is no greater than how well it is preserved. Since the function of evidence is to *persuade,* evidence of marginal quality is virtually valueless.

ADMISSIBILITY OF EVIDENCE

Exclusionary Rule

In order to prohibit police from continuing unlawful practices by obtaining *evidence through illegal searches or arrests,* the U.S. Supreme Court has held such evidence inadmissible in federal courts.[1] This prohibition, however, was to remain on the federal court level alone for the next 35 years. In 1949 in another case, the U.S. Supreme Court reaffirmed the rule—known as the "exclusionary rule." The court declined to impose the rules on the states, but suggested that the states impose it on themselves. Finally, in 1961, (*Mapp* v. *Ohio,* 367 US 643), the U.S. Supreme Court made the exclusionary rule the law of the land. And back in 1914, after acknowledging there were valid arguments for both positions regarding the exclusion of illegal evidence, Justice Oliver Wendell Holmes wrote: "We have to choose, and for my part I think it is a less evil that some criminals should escape than that the government should play an ignoble part. . . ."

In *federal* cases, the landmark rulings on exclusionary rule of search and seizure are: *Weeks* v. *United States* (1914)—U.S. Supreme Court ruled that evidence seized as a result of an unreasonable search and seizure is inadmissible in a federal court; *Burdeau* v. *McDowell* (1921) —U.S. Supreme Court held that the exclusionary rule does not apply to evidence obtained by private citizens in a civil procedure; *Wolf* v. *Colorado* (1949)—U.S. Supreme Court ruled that evidence obtained in an unreasonable search and seizure is admissible in a state court prosecution; *Mapp* v. *Ohio* (1961)—U.S. Supreme Court overruled earlier decision in *Wolf* v. *Colorado,* and instead decided that evidence gathered in an unreasonable search and seizure is *not* admissible in state court.

The Fourth Amendment's guarantee against unreasonable searches and seizures is an essential part of the Fourteen Amendment, which restrains the actions of the states and their officers. Evidence seized in an unreasonable search must be excluded, since there is no other effective way to enforce the guarantees of the Fourth Amendment—and the Fourteenth Amendment—against unreasonable searches and seizures. The exclusion of evidence seized in an unnecessary search is called the *exclusionary rule.*

From these amendments, the Court has evolved several basic principles. *First,* searches must only be made for certain classes of materials, specifically (1) the tools of crime, (2) the fruits of crime, (3) contraband goods (things forbidden by law to be kept or possessed), and (4) goods on which an excise duty is due. *Second,* searches may be carried out only (1) with the consent of the person to be searched, or the proprietor of the premises to be searched; (2) with a search warrant that conforms to the requirements of the Fourth Amendment (and a few other requirements that have been added by rules of criminal procedure); and (3) incident to a valid arrest. The Constitution clearly forbids the use of "general warrants" or dragnet searches, which were so odious to the American colonies before the Revolution.

The wisdom of the exclusionary rule has not gone unquestioned. Michigan, which has long followed the rule, twice amended its constitution to provide that illegally seized evidence of certain violations (concealed weapons and narcotics) may nevertheless be used in court. The change in Michigan was in response to serious crime problems. In California, it has been suggested that the exclusionary rule followed in the state courts be relaxed to permit the use of evidence seized illegally in narcotics cases. The fact remains, however, that the exclusionary rule is now the law in both federal and state courts. That the exclusionary rule plays a vital part in the gathering of evidence for successful prosecution is a fact established by practitioners in the field:

> The police play a vital part in the process of prosecution in that they are in the best position to assure the evidence needed by the prosecutor is not excluded by the court because it was obtained by improper methods. In the area such as seizure, recent decisions have greatly increased the necessity of obtaining a search warrant. The decisions in *Chimel (Chimel v. California* [1969]) and *Morales (Morales v. California)* complement each other in requiring and then providing a workable warrant system. In terms of police workload, this imposes an additional burden on the officer. . . . In the context of prosecution, however, the warrant requirements encouraged the police officer to fulfill his role in providing dependable admissible evidence.[2]

Derivative Rule

Law enforcement agencies could easily escape the sanctions of the exclusionary rule if the rule applied only to primary evidence (evidence precipitating arrest). In the early 1920s the Supreme Court held not only that illegal evidence was inadmissible at trials but that any evidence *derived from* the illegal primary evidence should also be inadmissible. (The Supreme Court did *not* say that any evidence obtained that could be later traced to the primary evidence was automatically excluded. If the evidence was obtained through independent means, it could be introduced at trial.)

The *derivative rule* is extremely important in field arrests. For example, when an officer stops an automobile to issue a traffic citation and, in the course of issuing the citation, she discovers incriminating evidence, the court will consider such evidence inadmissible.

The Supreme Court has excluded confessions even though the requirements of the *Miranda* doctrine were met. In *Wong Sun* v. *United States* (*Wong Sun* v. *United States*, 371, U.S. 471), federal narcotics agents broke into an apartment without a warrant. Information obtained from the occupant led to the arrest of the defendant. The court held that the first party's statements were the product of an unlawful search and seizure. Any information obtained as a result was inadmissible. In other words, the police officers could not use the information, or the fruits of the information, obtained through the first party's confession. The court further held that any statements made by the first party after arraignment, with full knowledge of his Constitutional rights, could be used in a subsequent criminal prosecution because the voluntary statement made by the first party were "so extenuated as to dissipate the taint."

As we have mentioned, independent sources of evidence are acceptable. The prosecution may also prove that the illegally obtained information was not the basis upon which the jury returned its verdict. If the prosecution can show that the evidence came within what is called the *harmless error concept*, the illegally obtained evidence will not contaminate the lower-court verdict.

Evidence Obtained by Private Citizens

In addition to this vortex of rules surrounding illegally obtained evidence, there are still others that apply to evidence obtained by private citizens. The reasoning behind this distinction is as follows: Criminal prosecutions are brought against the defendant by the state. If law enforcement personnel were able to introduce evidence that was obtained illegally, the criminal trial would be unjust in itself. This constitutional protection, however, does *not* apply to the activities of a private citizen. The rationale for this rule is found in the due process clause of the Fourteenth Amendment. The Fourteenth Amendment provides: "No state shall . . ." This phrase has been interpreted to mean that only state action is prohibited. As a result, evidence obtained by private citizens that would be inadmissible if obtained by a law enforcement officer *is* admissible evidence. This rule does not permit law enforcement agencies to authorize or indirectly employ private persons to obtain this type of evidence.

Cases

The following cases are the foundation of the Supreme Court's prohibition of private activities that would otherwise be outside the scope of the Fourteenth Amendment's due process protection.

CASE

In *Screws* v. *United States* (*Screws* v. *United States,* 325 U.S. 91 [1945]), the defendants, three state police officers, arrested Robert Hall at his home for the theft of an automobile tire. While transporting him to the courthouse, they beat him into unconsciousness. He died within one hour of his beating. The defendants were tried for violation of Section 20 of the Criminal Code, 18 U.S.C. 52. This statute provides that it is a federal crime to deprive any party of any rights, privileges, or immunities secured or protected by the Constitution and laws of the United States. The jury returned a guilty verdict. A writ of certiorari was granted by the Supreme Court.

The question before the Supreme Court was: Is it unconstitutional to pass laws making acts that violate the due process clause of the Fourteenth Amendment *criminal?* The Supreme Court held that no construction of the federal statute, as it was then written, could save it from the claim of unconstitutionality. The Supreme Court remanded the case back to the lower court to allow the jury to pass on the issue of *specific* intent, because specific intent is a necessary ingredient of the statute (Sec. 20 of the Criminal Code, 18, USC 52).

The Supreme Court did find that the defendants were acting under the "color of law." The color-of-law concept means that the activities of the defendants were classified as state action (officers acting as state's agent) and would have been otherwise prohibited by the Fourteenth Amendment due process clause if the statute was not unconstitutionally vague. The *only issue* before the Court, then, was whether the State of Georgia alone had the power and duty to punish, or whether there *was* a violation of the Fourteenth Amendment and open for federal prosecution. The Court concluded that the statute does not come into play merely because some federal or state law or administrative ruling is violated. It is applicable only when someone is deprived of a federal right by that action. The mere fact that a state law has been violated does not necessarily preclude federal prosecution for the same act.

CASE

In *Williams* v. *United States* (*Williams* v. *United States*, 341 U.S. 97 [1951]), the defendant, a private detective who had been issued a special police officer's badge, was employed by a private firm to investigate theft. After showing his badge, and accompanied by a regular police officer, he took four suspects into a small shack on his employer's property and beat them until they confessed. He was indicted and tried by a jury, which found him guilty of violating 18 U.S.C. 242.

The Court found that the defendant acted willfully and purposely with the semblance of police power and that his actions indicated his assertion of the authority granted to him. He was not acting as a private person. Because he was acting under color of law, the due process clause of the Fourteenth Amendment was applicable.

CASE

In 1951, in the case of *Collins* v. *Hardyman* (*Collins* v. *Hardyman*, 341, U.S. 65 [1951]), a federal statute provided for civil damages when two or more people conspire for the purpose of depriving any person of equal protection of the laws or of equal privileges and immunities under the law (42 U.S.C. Sec. 1985-3). The defendant allegedly conspired to deprive plaintiffs of their rights as citizens of the United States to assemble for the purpose of discussing national issues. The defendant broke up the plaintiff's meeting and was sued for this action.

The Court made it clear that an individual or group of individuals not in public office cannot deprive citizens of their constitutional rights. However, the statute named above is directed toward people who deprive anyone of equal protection of the law or equal privileges and immunities under the law. The Court concluded that breaking up a meeting was not the type of injury the law was designed to prohibit. It was no more a deprivation of equal protection of equal privileges and immunities than it would be for one person to assault and batter one of his neighbors rather than everyone living on his block. This private discrimination was not inequality under the law. There is no question that the plaintiffs' rights were disregarded and violated. However, the equality of their rights was not intended to be denied or impaired. California courts were available to the plaintiffs. California law provides for redress in such cases.

Congress does have the right to create a federal cause of action for anyone injured by a private individual if that individual abridges some federally created constitutional right. Therefore, the courts began to open the door for Congress to legislate against such private action, based on the application of the due process clause of the Fourteenth Amendment.

Case

In *United States* v. *Price* (*United States* v. *Price*, 393 U.W. 787 [1966]), three law enforcement officers and fifteen private parties were alleged to have killed three civil rights workers in Mississippi.

The conspiracy charge stemmed from allegations that the law enforcement officers released the victims from jail and subsequently recaptured them and killed them all in order to punish the victims without trial. By doing so, they deprived the victims of their Fourteenth Amendment right not to be punished without due process of law by any person acting under color of law. The Supreme Court held that private persons, when jointly engaged with state officials in a prohibited action, act under color of law for purposes of the statute. Therefore, state action does not mean only acts of officers of the state or their agents. It is now enough that a private party is a willful participant in such prohibited activity.

The Court further held that Section 241 must be read to include conspiracies "to injure . . . any citizen in the free exercise or enjoyment of any right or privilege secured to him by the constitution or laws of the United States." The statute includes any rights or privileges protected by the Fourteenth Amendment. Therefore, all parties were properly indicted under Section 241. The Court thus held this type of activity to be of federal concern. This is an area in which federal jurisdiction has been growing for the past hundred years and has been most actively manifested through the civil rights cases.

CASE

In *United States* v. *Guest* (*United States* v. *Guest*, 383, U.S. 745 [1966]), six defendants were indicted for criminal conspiracy in violation of 18 U.S.C. 241. The complaint alleged a conspiracy by the defendants to prevent black citizens from freely exercising and enjoying specific rights secured by the Constitution and laws of the United States.

The second paragraph of the indictment alleged that the defendants conspired to injure, oppress, threaten, and intimidate black citizens in order to deny them their right to "the equal utilization, without discrimination upon the basis of race, of public facilities in the vicinity of Athens, Georgia, owned, operated or managed by or on behalf of the state of Georgia or a subdivision thereof."

Whereas the *Price* case involved rights under the due process clause, this case involved rights under the equal protection clause of the Fourteenth Amendment. The Court held that if one type of right must be guaranteed, so must the other.

The main defense argument in this case was that the equal protection clause did not apply to wholly private action. However, the Court held that the language of Section 241 incorporates the equal protection clause itself. The Court made it clear that state action is not necessary to create rights under the equal protection clause. This does not mean that every criminal conspiracy that interferes with an individual's right to interstate travel falls under 18 U.S.C. 241. However, if the purpose of the conspiracy is, in fact, to impede or prevent the exercise of the right to interstate travel, then whether or not it is motivated by racial prejudice the conspiracy is a proper target *for federal sanctions.*

A concurring opinion of Justice Brennan emphasizes the complete power of Congress to legislate in all areas necessary to guarantee rights under the Constitution and laws of the United States. Justice Brennan could find no principle of federalism or word of the Constitution that would deny Congress the power to determine that in order to protect the right of equal utilization of state facilities, the United States must punish individuals, other than state officers, who engage in conduct aimed at frustrating equal protection.

In order to help build a more perfect society, the Supreme Court of the United States is searching for some other basis on which it may prevent private discrimination or injustices that go unpunished because of the failure of state laws to provide for punishment or because of the refusal of state prosecutors to bring action against certain citizens.

DEGREE OF EVIDENCE

Inasmuch as proof requires evidence but not all evidence actually proves, the law enforcement officer's responsibility to gain enough evidence for proof is crucial. Consideration of the *degree* of evidence required is, therefore, necessary. Table 4.1 reviews the levels of evidence supporting prosecution by the district attorney's office.

In general terms, the amount of evidence needed to prove will depend on the type of court. Various civil courts use the "preponderance of evidence" standard, in which an attorney producing as little as 51 percent of the evidence theoretically "wins" over the attorney presenting only 49 percent of the "persuasion."

By contrast, the standard in criminal court is "beyond a reasonable doubt" (Table 4.1). This standard places on the prosecution, and therefore on law officers, the responsibility for presenting evidence of guilt to "persuade" a jury that there is no reasonable doubt of guilt. The various aspects of criminal evidence will be discussed in this chapter in the context of this responsibility—a responsibility of awesome dimensions in a free society of ever-increasing individual rights.

Evidence to persuade the court that there is proof of guilt beyond a reasonable doubt may come from one of three categories: *circumstantial evidence*, including testimony; *witness evidence* other than circumstantial evidence; and any *confessions* or *admissions*.

In most instances, confessions eliminate any need for other varieties of evidence in persuading the court of proof of guilt—except, perhaps, where the confession may be *inadmissible*, which will be discussed later in this chapter.

Circumstantial Evidence

A great deal of what is referred to as evidence in criminal court is called "circumstantial." Many complicated rules govern circumstantial (preponderance of relevant or related evidence) evidence. The key rule (in circumstantial evidence), however, is that evidence must be related, or *relevant*, to the issue before the court. The "relevancy" of evidence can best be determined through contrast with the concept known in law as *materiality* of evidence. The *American Law Review* (see 63 ALR 595) states:

> The *materiality* of evidence depends on what specific issue is to be proven in the court. If the evidence presented tends to prove anything

TABLE 4.1   Levels of Evidence Supporting Legal Action

DEGREE OF EVIDENCE	AUTHORIZED LEGAL ACTION
Beyond All Doubt (absolute certainty)	Required by law for police or court action
Beyond Reasonable Doubt	Adjudication of delinquency and verdict-conviction in criminal cases
Probable or Reasonable Cause	Arrest without warrant OR Filing of legally sufficient (1) information; (2) simplified information; (3) misdemeanor and felony complaint Issuance of dropping warrants, search warrants, and revoking parole
Preparation of Evidence	Burden on defense to establish "affirmative defense" and revoking probation
Reasonable Suspicion	Stop-and-frisk
Suspicion (evidence without legal significance)	No authorization action—further investigation necessary to develop evidence that will either (1) increase competency of evidence or (2) reveal no basis for suspicion

other than the specific issue, it is considered "immaterial"—therefore, unacceptable to the court.

Relevancy, on the other hand, deals with the relationship between evidence and "facts" in general. In this sense, evidence that is immaterial could be considered relevant.

An example might be evidence showing a defendant was seen in a bar with a lady who is not his wife, introduced to show that he and his wife are separated. Now, if the defendant is accused of burglary, evidence that he has been seen in a bar with another woman is not *material* to this trial, but may, indeed, be relevant to the issue of whether or not he is separated from his wife.

When it is material and relevant, circumstantial evidence can be thought of in terms of the inferences that might be drawn from the circumstances presented. The "circumstances" of a defendant's fingerprints being on a murder weapon may indeed support the proposition that the defendant is guilty. Ownership of the weapon might either reinforce this proposition, or it might lead to the alternate proposition that the defendant is innocent—depending on the circumstances. If, in addition to the fingerprints, there is admissible evidence that the defendant was on the scene, there begins to emerge the basis for the logical conclusion that the defendent is guilty.

Consider the famous trial that took place in 1935.

CASE

Colonel Charles A. Lindbergh, the first person to fly solo across the Atlantic, in 1927, became a great national hero. When his infant child was kidnapped from his home one evening in March 1932, public excitement reached fever pitch. A ransom of $50,000 was paid, but the child was not returned. Instead, its dead body was found a short time later near the Lindbergh home in a shallow, hastily dug grave.

Two years later, some of the ransom money began circulating, and it led to the arrest in September 1934 of Bruno Hauptmann.

Hauptmann took the stand after the prosecution's evidence, mostly circumstantial, had been completed. That evidence, if believed, was sufficient to convict him, for he had been identified as the man who wrote the notes demanding ransom, [who] received the money, [who] spent part [of] it and still had some left when he was arrested, [who] was enjoying sudden and unexplained prosperity, whose tools and lumber had been used to make the ladder employed in the kidnapping, and who was seen in the vicinity of Hopewell, New Jersey, where the Lindberghs lived, near the time when the crime was committed.[3] [Hauptmann was found guilty on the preponderance of circumstantial evidence which his attorney could not contradict.]

But most circumstances have alternative explanations, and in these cases more evidence is needed to prove guilt—at least in a court system requiring proof beyond a reasonable doubt.

The actual evidence depicting circumstances takes many forms and has endless variety. Generally, however, it is presented either as the testimony of witnesses or by "exhibits" before the court.

Witnesses and circumstantial evidence. When circumstances are presented by testimony, the criminal court usually requires the witness to have observed everything to which his testimony refers. So-called "hearsay testimony," often referred to in motion pictures depicting the court process, *is acceptable*, but only under very special conditions —conditions usually relating to the expertise of the witness involved.

An example of admissible hearsay evidence might be a physician offering an opinion as to the time of death or a physician giving "expert testimony" on the defendant's knowledge of "right and wrong" at the time of an alleged offense. (For information on psychological defenses, refer to "Criminal Defenses" in Chapter 5.) Under such other special circumstances, police officers are acknowledged "experts" in certain areas and therefore able to testify to matters not directly observed.[4] An example might be the officer's testimony regarding a vehicle's speed at impact in an accident. Even though the officer did not observe the collision, his expertise in measuring skid marks on arrival at accident scenes constitutes a reasonable degree of expertise. Another occasional example is a policeman's expert testimony on a defendant's sobriety, even though the officer did not witness alcohol being consumed.*

Exhibits and circumstantial evidence. When exhibits are used to persuade that circumstances exist, the court process assumes an even greater variety than it does with testimony. Hardly a year passes without extremely significant discoveries from the sciences of criminalistics —a major source of circumstantial evidence. Fingerprints, ballistics, chemical analysis, photography, and graphology are but a few of the sources of exhibits.[5]

The purpose of criminalistics is to furnish recognition, identification, and evaluation of physical evidence by application of the natural sciences. Insofar as the criminal court is concerned, criminalistics serves to persuade. By contrast, law enforcement officers customarily conceive of criminalistics in terms of apprehending suspected law violators.

The crime laboratory, when staffed with well-trained technicians and adequate equipment, has proved efficient for both functions. The crime laboratory has provided the criminal court with persuasive exhibits— including spectographic, serological, toxicological, metallurgical, and radiological analysis—and has provided officers with many of the clues leading to the arrest of suspects ultimately involved in a court process.

Scientific experiment and circumstantial evidence. Scientific experiments are another method of persuading the court of the guilt or innocence of the accused person. Traditionally, the courts expect experiments used as evidence to be acceptable among scientists in general. On special occasions, however, courts have ruled on "scientific experimental evidence" solely on the basis of the "relevant conclusions" produced. In other words, if the evidence is relevant by the standards discussed earlier in this chapter, courts have held that this evidence is

* Hearsay evidence is admissible—if no objection is raised.

admissible whether or not it would be acceptable among scientists in general.

Scientific experiments may be designed for purposes as diverse as determining the "average" travel time between points or researching the time required under water to make a firearm inoperable. The officer's interest in such experiments is frequently connected to evidence he gathered originally that the prosecution wishes to elaborate upon.

Eyewitnesses

The testimony of witnesses who have allegedly observed the actual commission of crimes is subject to many of the same complicated rules that govern circumstantial evidence. In terms of materiality and relevance, however, the rules on eyewitness testimony can be greatly simplified.

Exhibits and testimony about circumstances frequently evoke lengthy legal discussions regarding the materiality or relevance of such evidence. Eyewitness testimony relating to an observed crime is rarely challenged on the grounds of either materiality or relevance. When the testimony of an eyewitness is challenged, it is usually in terms of how competent or how valid the testimony may be.

> Men are prone to see what they want to see. . . .
>
> "It must be admitted that at the present day the testimony of even a truthful witness is much over-rated. . . ."
>
> "No doubt the eyes of some witnesses are livelier than those of others, and the sense of sight may be quickened or diminished by the interest or bias of he who possesses it. . . ."
>
> "Even where witnesses are upright or honest, their belief is apt to be more or less warped by the partiality or prejudice for or against the parties. It is easy to reason ourselves into a belief in the existence of that which we desire to be true, whereas the facts testified to, and from which the witness deduces his conclusions, might produce a very different impression on the minds of others. . . ."
>
> "It frequently happens that a person, by long dwelling on a subject, thinks that a thing may have happened, and he, at last, comes to believe that it actually did occur. . . ."[6]

The challenge—or the questions, when raised—deals with the "credibility" of an eyewitness, or any witness for that matter. Efforts to challenge the credibility of a witness are known as *impeachment*. Impeachment is based on the assumption that for one reason or another the witness cannot be believed.

Impeachment does not necessarily imply that the witness is lying;

in many instances it simply means that the witness's perception, or memory, is not reliable. Attempts to impeach any witness, but particularly eyewitnesses, are actually efforts to undermine the persuasion of the evidence being offered. Such attempts are, or should be, based on the *examples of unreliability*. An example of unreliability would be a nearsighted witness testifying to observations allegedly made at some distance without his glasses. Observations supposedly made in poor lighting (in identifications of suspects, for example) are also frequently challenged.

Impeachment might also be based on the relationship between the defendant and the witness, especially when circumstances might motivate particular styles of testimony. Financial matters, accumulated anger, and other "motivational factors" are often brought out in court in an effort to impeach a witness. Any evidence that demonstrates a probable influence on the motives of the witness, whether or not brought out on cross-examination, is likely to become a major part of efforts to impeach a new witness—particularly an eyewitness.

Because law enforcement officers customarily identify and screen eye witnesses for the prosecution, these considerations are extremely important to them.

In addition to the varied and complex rule systems that have been discussed so far in this chapter, other controls have been imposed by the United States Supreme Court in its continuing interpretation of the United States Constitution.[7] Many of the questions relating to these rules and controls are dealt with elsewhere in this text (Chapter 3). However, there are additional areas of concern in terms of what evidence can be admitted in criminal court and under what circumstances. Therefore, police interrogation, voluntary confession, and demonstrative evidence must be considered here.

POLICE INTERROGATION

There is no doubt that the two most important decisions dealing with police interrogations and voluntary confessions are the Supreme Court decisions relating to the *Gideon*,* *Escobedo*, and *Miranda* cases.

It has been said that American courts function as social controls of values and attitudes toward law, while at the same time reconciling grievances—grievances between either the state and the individual, or

---

* The Sixth Amendment guarantees defense counsel in federal court and the Fourteenth Amendment guarantees defense counsel in state court.

between individuals.[8] And while the press has carried prominent articles about the need for strong judicial measures on behalf of the state in every decade for the past 50 years,[9] only recently has general concern focused directly on court reconciliation of grievances between the state and individuals.

A traditional role of law enforcement in constitutional forms of government is *apprehending* law violators, leaving *punishment* to the judicial process. Philosophically, at least, such a role permits crime prevention to be a mutual, although secondary, responsibility of both police and courts. But in recent times, police and courts are increasingly faced with "crimes" stemming from growing demands for social reform rather than merely from the violation of criminal statutes. One apparent reaction by the courts, particularly the Supreme Court, has been a number of decisions tending to have great impact on police procedures in general, and on the relationship of police to social change in particular. In effect, the Supreme Court has handed down rulings that judge not only the lower courts' functions but the police function as well.

Much of the basis of the increasing Supreme Court assessment of police practice is the Fourth Amendment, and to some degree the Ninth Amendment. The implications of the Fourth Amendment to the police function have received more than adequate concern in the literature.[10] Nonetheless, a brief review of the highlights of the more significant court decisions may serve to clarify these implications.

CASE

In 1914 the United States Supreme Court ruled in *Weeks* v. *United States* that a federal court could not accept evidence that was obtained in violation of search-and-seizure protection, which is guaranteed by the Fourth Amendment.

CASE

In 1963 the Supreme Court ruled on the appeal case of *Gideon* v. *Wainwright*. The effect of this ruling was that a new trial could be demanded by anyone convicted of crime who had not had legal counsel.

CASE

Moving closer to the function of the police, in 1964 a decision was handed down in the case of *Escobedo* v. *Illinois*. This decision, based on a five-to-four majority, held it the constitutional right of an indigent to be provided with legal counsel at the time of the police interrogation. A graphic representation of the rulings affecting all interrogations is given in Figure 4.1.

CASE

In June 1966, again by a five-to-four majority, the Court ruled on the case of *Miranda* v. *Arizona*. The *Miranda* decision had the effect of providing legal counsel during police questioning for persons *suspected* of crimes (see also the *Miranda* distinctions discussed later).

Because this and previous rulings were made on the basis of "constitutional rights," law enforcement found itself compelled to regard many traditional investigative methods as unconstitutional. So if constitutional rights have been violated by certain previously practiced police methods, the question became one of alternative approaches. And determination of such approaches is at best difficult when the overall function of the courts is undergoing change, resulting from Supreme Court interpretations of the United States Constitution.

Fortunately, the pattern of Supreme Court decisions in recent years has been to reduce the *direct* impact upon law enforcement—at least when compared with the Supreme Court decisions of the 1950s and 1960s. Indeed, if a pattern is discernible at all, it appears to show faint signs of recognizing the implications of the following:

America decries her rising crime rate, people board themselves into their homes at night, they walk the darkened streets with dread. More and newer laws are enacted. While all along the police officer knows the solution; rehabilitate in an all-out effort those criminals who are salvable; those who have proven themselves unrehabilitable should be permanently incarcerated for the protection of society.

Failure to cope realistically with crime and the criminal has caused widespread suspicion of government among the police. The policeman distrusts his government and its facilities for justice, while at the same

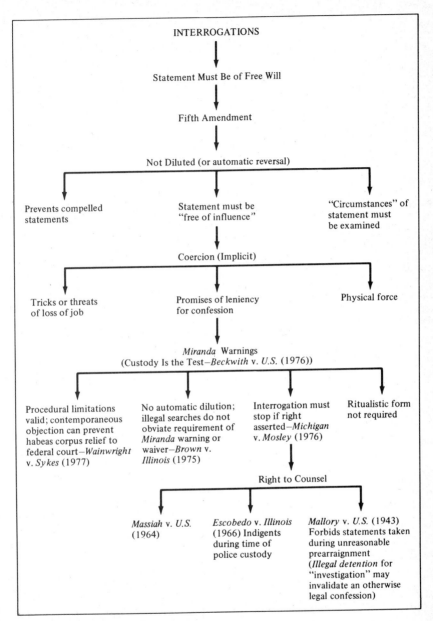

INTERROGATIONS

Statement Must Be of Free Will

Fifth Amendment

Not Diluted (or automatic reversal)

Prevents compelled
statements

Statement must be
"free of influence"

"Circumstances" of
statement must
be examined

Coercion (Implicit)

Tricks or threats
of loss of job

Promises of leniency
for confession

Physical force

Miranda Warnings
(Custody Is the Test—Beckwith v. U.S. (1976))

Procedural limitations
valid; contemporaneous
objection can prevent
habeas corpus relief to
federal court—Wainwright
v. Sykes (1977)

No automatic dilution;
illegal searches do not
obviate requirement of
Miranda warning or
waiver—Brown v.
Illinois (1975)

Interrogation must
stop if right
asserted—Michigan
v. Mosley (1976)

Ritualistic form
not required

Right to Counsel

Massiah v. U.S.
(1964)

Escobedo v. Illinois
(1966) Indigents
during time of
police custody

Mallory v. U.S. (1943)
Forbids statements taken
during unreasonable
prearraignment
(Illegal detention for
"investigation" may
invalidate an otherwise
legal confession)

FIGURE 4.1   Interrogations.

time he fears the elements of turmoil and crime operating almost
without restriction. This places the policeman in the unenviable
position of truly being the middle man. Intellectuals, reformists, and
government-sponsored groups attack the police from one side; criminals,

revolutionists and anarchists attack from the other side, and the police find themselves even more alienated, defending a precarious middle ground they are not sure anyone values.[11]

Beyond doubts of law enforcement personnel regarding the value of the middle ground being defended, the Supreme Court looms large in the area of defining the "interests" of the community as opposed to "interests" of the *individual*—critically significant contrasts for police in attempting to integrate these conflicting interests.

Police cope with the conflicting interests of groups representing themselves as the community, but in any given situation the Supreme Court exerts its influence on police practice through the individual. A clear definition of such interest is called for.

Regardless of the importance of defining interests, such a task cannot be easy in an era of articulate yet divergent explanations of interests. The difficulty is increased still more by Supreme Court decisions that influence not only the definition of what *due process* is but also the definition of the interests served through due process. Nevertheless, defining interests remains crucial to law enforcement.

Miranda and *Escobedo*: Distinction

Ther are four basic differences between the *Escobedo* guidelines and the *Miranda* requirements.

First, the *Miranda* case was based on the question of "custodial interrogation" as defined in the Supreme Court opinion below:

> The prosecution may not use statements, whether exculpatory or inculpatory, stemming from custodial interrogation of the defendant, unless it demonstrates the use of procedural safeguards effective to secure the privilege against self-incrimination. By custodial interrogation, we [United States Supreme Court] mean questioning initiated by law enforcement officers after a person has been taken into custody or otherwise deprived of his freedom of action in any significant way. As for the procedural safeguards to be employed, unless other fully effective means are devised to inform accused persons of their right to silence and to ensure a continuous opportunity to exercise it, the following measures are required. Prior to any questioning, the person must be warned that he has the right to remain silent, that any statement he does make, may be used as evidence against him, and that he has the right to the presence of an attorney, either retained or appointed. The defendant may waive effectuation of these rights, provided the waiver is made voluntarily, knowingly, and intelligently.

Escobedo, on the other hand, involved the focus of investigation on a particular subject coupled with his being in police custody.

Second, *Miranda* was concerned with the right of the subject to the presence of his own or appointed counsel, while *Escobedo* only recognized the right to consult with the suspect's own attorney.

Third, *Miranda* did not prohibit the states from adopting any experimental legislation that would protect a suspect's Fifth Amendment guarantees.

Fourth, *Miranda* is predicated on the Fifth Amendment privilege against self-incrimination; Escobedo was based on the Sixth Amendment right to counsel. The court's emphasis has switched from right to counsel, which materializes some time before trial, to the focus of inquiry on a particular suspect. This focus usually occurs immediately before arrest.

The *Miranda* holding also provides that if a suspect indicates he wishes the assistance of counsel, his own or court-appointed, law enforcement agencies *cannot* ignore his request even if they do not continue questioning him. More specifically, once a suspect indicates at any time and in any manner that he wishes the assistance of counsel, all questioning must cease until counsel is present. If an individual suspect cannot obtain counsel and wishes to remain silent, law enforcement agencies must respect his decision.

What is custodial interrogation? Although the *Miranda* decision seems clear, a frequently encountered dilemma of law enforcement agencies is to decide what constitutes in-custody interrogation.

The United States Supreme Court did not have, in either case, an opportunity to illustrate in detail what is meant by custodial questioning. The facts of *Escobedo* and *Miranda* were not presented in such a manner that the Court would have been justified in taking this collateral issue and expanding upon it.

The *Miranda* guidelines are not limited to police station interrogation. Evidence that *Miranda* should not be limited to police station interrogation is shown by *Mathias* v. *United States* (88 S. Ct. 1503 [1968]). In that case, an Internal Revenue agent failed to give the taxpayer the *Miranda* warnings before questioning him about income tax returns while the taxpayer was serving a jail sentence in a state facility. However, three justices dissented in the *Mathias* case and held that the reasoning behind the *Miranda* decision was not applicable to *Mathias* because a police station and court atmosphere were absent. Therefore, in the absence of the inherently coercive surroundings, the warnings were not necessary. This dissenting opinion was expanded and made a law by Congress through the Omnibus Crime Control Act.

Suspects: focal point of investigation. *Escobedo* applied only to prime suspects or to suspects upon which the focal point of the investigation centered. A different challenge faces the court when it is asked whether the *Miranda* warnings should apply to a suspect who was neither deprived of his freedom of movement nor in custody but yet was a prime suspect for the crime charged.

The custody test breaks down into a number of circumstances, the most important of which are: (1) officers do not have to record on a scale or timepiece the exact incident that made the defendants become a focus of criminal investigation; (2) nor do the officers have to establish focus when minor offenses occur. Therefore, the *Miranda* custody test is much easier to apply and relates to a broad spectrum of criminal violations whether they are petty or serious.

Escobedo places a great deal of weight on the efficiency or quantum of evidence that constitutes a basis for a law enforcement officer to focus his interrogation on the particular subject. However, *Miranda* looks to the totality of the circumstances surrounding interrogation, including the defendant's state of mind as a result of being placed in a position where he must answer questions that come from an inherently coercive source. The inherent-pressures-or-coercion rule implies that the *Miranda* doctrine will apply whether the subject is a witness or a prime suspect, or whether the interrogation has focused on him.

The United States Supreme Court's rationale was simple. A law-abiding citizen should give whatever information he may have to law enforcement agencies to ensure the administration of enforcement of justice. Difficult problems arise when, as a result of such general questions, the potential suspect gives law enforcement officers answers that focus attention on himself. When does a police officer cease general questioning and have to give the *Miranda* warnings? The Supreme Court has not dealt with every conceivable factual situation to which the *Miranda* warnings may apply. With continuing interpretation of such rulings, law enforcement agencies will find it is increasingly clear what their procedures should be in procuring information.

VOLUNTARY CONFESSION

A *confession* is a voluntary statement made by a person charged with the commission of a crime, communicated to another person, wherein he acknowledges himself to be guilty of the offense charged and discloses the circumstances of the act or the share and participation that he had in it. A confession is one species of admission—namely, an admission consisting of a direct assertion by the accused in a criminal case of the main fact charged against him or of some fact essential to the charge.

Confessions, like admissions, may be either judicial or extra-judicial. It is a judicial confession when it is made by the defendant on the stand or in a plea of guilty or *nolo contendere*. All other confessions are extra-judicial.

It is presumed that a confession is true, because it is against the interest of the person making it, but it must be secured in a manner free from threats, coercion, fear, or hope of benefit or reward, which might induce the prisoner to make a false confession. If the defendant is persuaded to confess by threats, or by promise of leniency, or by any inducement of reward other than the easing of his conscience, the confession will not be admitted against him.

The taking of statements or confessions, either written or oral, is of paramount importance to police officers. A thorough and timely investigation may become worthless and a case lost in court due to taking a statement or confession improperly or without regard to due process of law as guaranteed by United States Constitution, and interpreted and upheld by the United States Supreme Court.

Police officers must realize that in the entire United States, the law is enforced as the United States Supreme Court interprets it. The Court's recent opinions of statements or confessions and the right to counsel are what we must abide by. These opinions are obligatory on State as well as federal authorities.[12]

Most difficulties arise when a party gives a voluntary confession to a law enforcement officer. The United States Supreme Court has held:

There is no requirement that police stop a person who enters a police station and states that he wishes to confess to a crime, or a person who calls the police to offer a confession or any other statement he desires to make. Volunteered statements of any kind are not barred by the Fifth Amendment and their admissibility is not effected by *Miranda* v. *Arizona*, 384 *U.S. 436.* . . .

If a voluntary confession is made to police officers, the whole is admissible in evidence, even though it may contain the admissions of other offenses or be related to the one for the commission of which the defendant is on trial.

The United States Supreme Court added that a confession obtained under the influence of placing the prisoner under oath to tell the truth may not be admitted. It is proper, however, to have the prisoner sign and swear to a confession that has been reduced to writing after it has been made. Each page of a written confession should be signed and witnessed in order that no page be substituted. Carrying this one step further: Where a prisoner charged with homicide was taken before a committing magistrate, and there sworn to tell the truth and told "if you do not tell the truth I will commit you," a confession thus exacted is not admissible as evidence against the prisoner on trial. When a previous confession is unduly obtained, any subsequent confession given on this basis is not admissible.

In 1968, Congress adopted Title II of the Omnibus Crime Control and Safe Streets Act of 1968. The legislation attempted to overrule the *Miranda* warning requirements. The congressional legislation provided that in federal prosecutions, the question of admissibility of confessions should be determined *solely* by voluntariness and not by whether the *Miranda* guidelines have been complied with. The new congressional legislation has not been challenged yet, but Congress cannot, by itself, overturn *Miranda*. Even if it attempted to do so, the United States Supreme Court could interpret the legislation as something that Congress did not mean or did not intend, or simply hold that Congress had no right to make such legislation. The United States Supreme Court has centered its recent criminal-procedure decisions regarding confessions on the Fifth Amendment safeguards against self-incrimination. But the recent upheaval stems from the basic right to counsel at time of trial.

RIGHT TO COUNSEL

The Sixth Amendment of the United States Constitution provides, in part: "The accused shall enjoy the right to . . . have the assistance of counsel for his defense." This amendment guarantees the criminal defendant's right to counsel in federal courts. The state courts were bound by the same provisions through the due process clause of the Fourteenth Amendment, discussed in Chapter 3.

Althought his right to counsel may be waived, the burden is on the prosecution to prove that the defendant knowingly, intelligently, and voluntarily waived his right to counsel "at any stage of the proceedings."

The United States Supreme Court has held that the right to counsel is limited only to criminal prosecutions. There is no right to counsel before investigative or administrative tribunals such as grand jury or fire marshal proceedings. The United States Supreme Court also held recently that the right to counsel exists "at every stage of criminal proceedings where substantial rights of the criminally accused may be affected." The guidelines established by the Supreme Court in the *Mempha* (probation revocation hearing) case border on the equivocal definition of the *Escobedo* decision, which called for Sixth Amendment rights at any "critical stage" of the proceedings.

Although the Supreme Court has given a definition of sorts in the

Mempha case, the question arises as to how this definition may be applied to specific proceedings. The United States Supreme Court has held that critical stages include the following:

Custodial interrogation by law enforcement agencies
Preliminary examination
The entering of a guilty plea at any time
Sentencing of the defendant
Probation revocation hearing
Juvenile proceedings that may lead to confinement of the defendant in
   an institution
Line-up for identification purposes

The right of the accused to be represented by counsel is common in all jurisdictions. Until recently this safeguard was completely effective only for the defendant whose financial circumstances permitted him to employ an attorney, whereas those defendants who were indigent frequently found their right to representation more theoretical than real. In 1972 the United States Supreme Court ruled (*Argersinger* v. *Hamlin* 407 U.S. 25) that the indigent defendant is entitled to counsel at public expense not only for *serious* crimes but also for *petty* offenses (those punishable by *fines* or *short* periods of imprisonment). This step by the Supreme Court clearly strengthens the value of the *Gideon* decision (see Chapter 5).

DEMONSTRATIVE EVIDENCE

Demonstrative evidence is any nontestimonial evidence taken from the person of the defendant. The police have the right to secure demonstrative evidence from the defendant, in addition to interrogating or receiving voluntary confessions.

The main type of evidence that may be extracted was clarified and defined in *Rochin* v. *California* and *Schmerber* v. *California*.

CASE

In the *Rochin* case (342 U.S. 165, 72 S. Ct. 205) police officers who had "some information" that the suspect was selling narcotics forced open a bedroom door of the suspect's house. They attempted to extract two capsules that the suspect had placed in his mouth, but they failed. They then took Rochin to a hospital and had his stomach pumped. This procedure yielded two morphine capsules. The court held: "We are compelled to conclude that the proceedings by which this conviction was obtained do more than offend some fastidious squeamishness or private sentimentalism about combating crime too energetically. This is conduct that *shocks the conscience*. . . . They are methods too close to the rack and screw to permit of constitutional differentiation."

Case

In the Schmerber case (*Schmerber* v. *California* 384 U.S. 757, 86 S. Ct. 205), the defendant, upon advice of counsel, objected to the arresting agency's taking a sample of his blood to determine the alcohol content. Analysis of the defendant's blood was nevertheless admitted as evidence. The Court answered the four basic questions raised by Schmerber's appeal in the following manner:

Right to Counsel: "Since petitioner was not entitled to assert privilege, he has no greater right because counsel erroneously advised him that he could assert it."

Self-Incrimination: The *Miranda* doctrine did not apply to this particular defendant. The court held that the protection of the privilege against self-incrimination "reaches an accused's *communications*, whatever form they may take." In this case, there was no testimonial compulsion of communication forced from the lips of the defendant.

Due Process: The *Rochin* doctrine described above did not apply to the effects of this particular case either. The court held that since the blood was extracted in a medically acceptable manner within the antiseptic environment of a hospital, there was no basis to conclude that this activity "shocked the conscience of the court."

Search and Seizure: The court concluded that the Fifth Amendment's privilege against self-incrimination *did not* apply. However, the Fourth Amendment's right to protection against unreasonable search and seizure *did* apply.

Although the protection of the Fourth Amendment applied in this case, the Court concluded that these protections were not violated by the activity of the arresting agency. Because there was possible cause for the officer to arrest the defendant, and because the possible presence of alcohol created an emergency that required immediate analysis, and because a test was performed in a reasonable manner, activity of the arresting agency was not illegal.

As a result of the Rochin and Schmerber cases, arresting agencies have now apparently been given a green light to extract *nontestimonial* evidence from the defendant after his arrest as long as it is done in a reasonable manner. Extending this proposition to its logical conclusion, the courts apparently allow almost any type of nontestimonial evidence to be extracted from a defendant, including clippings of hair from his head or beard, dirt from his fingernails, or dry blood from his skin—*reasonableness* is the key.

ENTRAPMENT AND EVIDENCE

In *Black's Law Dictionary, entrapment* is defined as "the act of police in inducing a person to commit a crime not contemplated by him, for the purpose of prosecuting him." Entrapment is generally recognized as a defense to criminal charge in both state and federal courts.

CASE

[A person] who has committed a criminal act is not entitled to be shielded from the consequence merely because he was induced to do so by another. Again, in considering the question of public policy, the clear distinction, founded on principle as well as authority, is to be observed between measures used to entrap a person into crime in order, by making him a criminal, to aid the investigator in the accomplishment of some corrupt private purpose of his own, and artifice used to detect persons suspected of being engaged in criminal practices, particularly, if such criminal practice vitally affects the public welfare rather than the individual's (*Com v. Wasson*, 42 Pa. Super 38; *Com v. Kutler*, 173 Pa. Super 153 [1953]).

CASE

A police officer approached a woman who was known to be a prostitute on a street and, after greeting her, stated, "You're not still in business, are you?" Following her reply that she was still sometimes in business but not at that spot, he asked her into a car and drove to a place where the crime was to be committed, at which point the officers identified themselves and arrested the prostitute.

The court held that these actions did constitute entrapment, inasmuch as the suggestion to commit the crime for which defendant was arrested originated in the mind of the arresting officer (*Com v. Hess*, 53 D & C 339 Allegheny [1948]).

Case

The mere furnishing of opportunity to another who is ready and willing to commit the offense is not as such entrapment, but where the owner of the property upon which the arrest was made, either by his own or his agent's act, promotes and instigates his staff, for the purpose of trapping the thief, and does trap him, the accused may defend on the ground that the instigation on the owner's part amounted to his consent that property should be taken and, therefore, prevented the accused's act from being larceny.

Case

Where the criminal intent originates in the mind of the accused, the fact that means were used by others to furnish him opportunity or aid for the commission of the crime, in order that they may prosecute him therefor, constitutes no defense (*Price v. United States*, 56 F., 2d, 134).

Case

Artifice and stratagem may lawfully be employed against those engaged in the commission of a crime, but it is a different matter when the criminal design originates with the officer of the law, and she incites an innocent person, or anyone not contemplating an offense at the time, to commit a crime in order that she may prosecute (*Sorrels v. United States*, 287, U.S. 435).

The rule prohibiting entrapment does not prohibit procurement of evidence by deception, or the setting of a trap to catch a criminal (*People v. Mattei*, 381, Ill., 21).

Since the main purpose of the law is to prevent crime and not encourage it, the defense of entrapment may be used when an officer is the *procuring* cause of the crime and puts the unlawful design of intent in the mind of the accused. If the intent to commit a crime *originates* in the mind of the defendant, the mere offering of an opportunity to commit it will not constitute a defense. In short, an officer may afford opportunities for the commission of a crime and may lay traps to detect the offender.

Entrapment is a defense to criminal act when, for the purpose of prosecuting him, a person is incited, induced, inveigled, or lured into the commission of a crime he did not contemplate by a law enforcement officer or agent. "It is recognized as a defense only in federal courts and a few states. In other states, the instigation of the crime is immaterial; the competency of evidence showing criminal conduct depends only upon its inherent probative value rather than other circumstances."[13]

There is very little difference between dictionary definitions for entrapment of a criminal and catching one. The terms have been used synonymously. It is the duty of the police to catch criminals, and if the term *entrapment* is used in this ordinary dictionary sense, this "catching" of a criminal means the same thing as entrapping a criminal. This is not so, however, under the court decisions, and since officers of the law must abide by statutes and court decisions, it is suggested that they ignore dictionary definitions and be aware of the judicial decisions that apply to peace work.

The prevalent judicial test for entrapment is the "innocence" test. The supposed legislative intent of the innocence test is to avoid tempting innocent persons into violations. Under this test, courts ask whether a crime was a result of *creative activity* by the police or the result of the police merely affording an opportunity for the suspect to commit a crime.

CASE

An excellent illustration of the difference between catching and creating criminals is the case of *People* v. *Hanselmen* (76 Cal 460), in which a constable in a small town was concerned with the number of thefts involving drunk-rollers. In order to detect the defendant, the constable disguised himself, feigned drunkenness, and lay in an alley with marked money on his person. When the subject approached him, the constable made no effort to prevent the theft but remained passive until the suspect had removed the marked money from him. At that point, the constable jumped to his feet and placed the suspect under arrest.

The court said there was no entrapment when an officer disguises himself, feigns drunkenness, and makes no objection when money is taken from his person. The court then quoted the famous "plans to entrap," in which the authorities on the subject hold:

> If a person suspects an offense is to be committed, and, instead of taking precautions against it, sets a watch and detects and arrests defendants, he does not thereby consent to the conduct, or furnish them an excuse. And, in general terms, exposing property or neglecting to watch it, of furnishing any other facilities or temptations to such or any other wrongdoer, is not a consent in law.

It would seem that officers may set traps for suspects, and such traps do not constitute entrapment. Of course, officers are not required to take steps to prevent the commission of the crime except when the general obligation of an officer to protect life and property would compel him to act. For example, an officer would try to stop a time bomb from going off if she knew of its existence before the potential explosion. In California, there is a law that requires officers to prevent duels if they have prior information about them (California Penal Code, Section 230). Generally speaking, if the officers learn beforehand that a crime will be committed at a certain time at a particular place, they may stake it out and wait until some criminal act has been committed before making an arrest.

There are two extremely important questions in the area of entrapment. First, did the police actually engage in an *impermissible degree of inducement*—"setting a trap for the unwary innocent"? Second, was the defendant *predisposed to commit the crime anyway?* Generally, the defendant must plead and prove that the police induced him to act. If he does so, the government has the burden of proving predisposition, which will negate any entrapment.

The issue of entrapment can only be decided by a jury. The jury's decision will be reversed only if entrapment is proved as a matter of law. This will be established only if proper inducement appears in the government's own witnesses and there is insufficient evidence of predisposition. The government is generally permitted to introduce a great deal of evidence as to the suspect's prior conduct and reputation, including past criminal convictions and hearsay evidence, to prove his predisposition to commit a crime. Some courts, however, have excluded unreliable hearsay of a highly prejudicial nature.

The problem here is to interpret what is meant by *overzealous and superinducement, or overpersuasion.* Generally, "if the accused entertained a criminal intent before he was afforded the opportunity to violate the law, he is not improperly entrapped because he is not led into the commission of the crime by the officer."[14] In other words, the defense of entrapment involves the issue of whether intent to commit the crime originated with the officer or the defendant. It is a question of fact whether criminal intent was first conceived by the law enforcement officer or whether he simply encouraged the defendant. There must be factual evidence introduced to show that the defendant was inveigled into commission of the crime or that the officers were the procuring cause or instigators of the criminal intent.

In conclusion, it can be said that many courts have taken the bold step of establishing a judicially inspired defense of entrapment, since it is a violation of entrapment laws to woo or lure an apparently innocent person into the commission of a crime he or she did not contemplate for the purpose of prosecuting. At the same time, courts have recognized perfectly legitimate and proper devises, decoys, and traps for the purpose of detecting crime and securing evidence. In short, officers are paid to catch criminals, not to create them.

SUMMARY

In this chapter, we discussed evidence used in criminal court in terms of *guilt beyond reasonable doubt*. Failure to provide sufficient evidence to persuade the court of the accused's guilt is evidence of innocence, inasmuch as all are presumed innocent until proved guilty.

The persuasive value of evidence was reviewed and a distinction made between *evidence* and *proof*. Proof requires enough logical evidence to persuade. When insufficient logical evidence is provided to persuade, proof had not been established. Put another way, all proof is evidence but not all evidence is proof. Degree of evidence, particular proof, admissibility, and circumstantial evidence were also discussed.

The problem of protecting and preserving evidence until the time of the trial was presented in terms of its relationship to law enforcement responsibility and to the fact that the quality of evidence is no greater than how well it has been preserved.

Eyewitnesses, credibility, impeachment, and other related matters were reviewed.

The subject of *admissibility* of evidence was presented both in the context of rules of evidence and in the context of individual rights. The guarantee of individual rights by the United States Constitution was presented as implying an increasingly significant role for the police with respect to the admissibility of confessions and other types of evidence.

Nontestimonial evidence was discussed, along with court decisions relating to the *Miranda* and *Escobedo* cases. In light of the aforementioned decisions, the problem of police interrogation was put into proper perspective. Finally, certain criminal defenses to which law enforcement agencies are frequently exposed were briefly reviewed, the last of which was entrapment.

NOTES

1. Information here relating to the Fourth and Fifth Amendments was taken from *Handbook on the Law of Search and Seizure* (Washington, D.C.: U.S. Government Printing Office, 1967), pp. 11–20. For a more detailed treatment, refer to this source.
2. D. Warren, "Search and Seizure," *Police Work: Concerning Criminal Evidence*, December 1969, pp. 9–12.
3. Karlen Delman, *The Citizen in Court: Litigant Witness Jury Judge* (New York: Holt, Rinehart and Winston, 1964), pp. 119–135.
4. E. Eldefonso, A. Coffey, and R. C. Grace, *Principles of Law Enforcement*, 2d ed. (New York: Wiley, 1974), chap. 4.
5. *Ibid.*, chap. 11.
6. John J. Bonsignore, E. Katsh, P. d'Erico, R. Pipkin, and S. Arons, *Before the Law: An Introduction to the Legal Process* (Boston: Houghton Mifflin, 1977), p. 74.
7. E. L. Barrett, "Personal Rights, Property Rights and the Fourth Amendment," 1960 *Supreme Court Review* (Chicago: University of Chicago Press, 1961), p. 65. See also C. R. Sowle, ed., *Police Power and Individual Freedom* (Springfield, Ill.: Thomas, 1972); W. H. Parker, "Birds Without Wings," *The Police Yearbook* (Washington, D.C.: International Association of Chiefs of Police, 1965).
8. W. Freeman, *Society on Trial: Parent Court Decisions and Social Change* (Springfield, Ill.: Thomas, 1965), preface.
9. W. Amos and C. Walford, *Delinquency Prevention*, 2d ed. (Englewood Cliffs, N.J.: Prentice-Hall, 1976), p. 208.
10. Barrett, "Personal Rights, Property Rights and the Fourth Amendment," p. 65. See also C. R. Sowle, ed., *Police Power and Individual Freedom*, and Parker, "Birds Without Wings."
11. Charles W. Sasser, "Cops Are Conventional People but . . . ," *Law and Order* 19 (August 1971), p. 50.
12. Pennsylvania State Police Association, *Pennsylvania Criminal Law and Criminal Procedure* (Harrisburg, Pa.: Telegraph Press, 1978), p. 147.
13. E. M. Dangel, *Criminal Law* (Boston: Edan Publications, 1971), pp. 174–175.
14. *Ibid.*, pp. 20–22.

PRACTICAL EXERCISES

1. Outline the police role with respect to evidence.
2. How does evidence differ from proof?
3. How does the United States Constitution impact on the admissibility of evidence?

4. What is meant by the "preservation" of evidence?
5. What is entrapment?
6. What is impeachment?
7. What is the difference between *relevance* and *materiality*?
8. What is *color of law*?

ANNOTATED REFERENCES

Alexander, Clarence. *The Law of Arrest in Criminal and Other Proceedings.* Buffalo, N.Y.: Dennis and Company, 1969. This book provides an illustrative insight into the basic concepts of arrest and interrogation prior to the "Warren Court."

Cataldo, B. F.; Gillam, C. W.; Kempin, F. D.; Stockton, J. M.; and Weber, C. M. *Introductory Cases on Law and the Legal Process.* New York: Wiley, 1978. The sections pertaining to due process and fair trial are particularly relevant to a discussion of criminal defenses.

Coffey, A., and Eldefonso, E. *Process and Impact of Justice.* Encino, Calif.: Glencoe Press, 1976. An analysis of the fundamental rights of the criminally accused and the manner in which the criminal defendant views the justice process.

Goddard, K. W. *Crime Scene Investigation.* Englewood Cliffs, N.J.: Prentice-Hall, 1977. The relationship between the Fifth and Sixth amendments is discussed indirectly.

LaFave, W. R. *Arrest: Decision to Take a Suspect into Custody.* Boston: Little, Brown, 1976. Explores the illogical problems of the policeman on the beat who is confronted with the decision of whether to arrest or warn an alleged criminal.

President's Commission on Law Enforcement and Administration of Justice, The. *The Challenge of Crime in a Free Society.* Washington, D.C.: U.S. Government Printing Office, 1967. A report of the President's Commission on Law Enforcement and the Administration of Justice.

————. *Task Force Report: Crime and Its Impact—An Assessment.* Washington, D.C.: U.S. Government Printing Office, 1967. Statistical analysis and psychological insight into the reasons and occasions of criminal activity.

Weston, Paul B., and Wells, Kenneth M. *The Administration of Justice.* Englewood Cliffs, N.J.: Prentice-Hall, 1977. A lawyer's approach to the understanding of criminal law and specifically the types of pleas that may be entered by the accused.

Chapter 5

COURT PROCEDURE

LEARNING OBJECTIVES

The learning objectives of this chapter are:
1. To understand the procedure *after* arrest and the impact of criminal law on the justice process, achieving an understanding of the various steps in the process and how the process "flows."
2. To become familiar with the defendant's constitutional and statutory rights when charged with a crime.
3. To bring into focus the entire range of defense strategies against criminal charges.

Chapters 3 and 4 focused on precourt procedure and practices (mostly covered by state and federal constitutions as well as court decisions). This chapter focuses on the violator and on the system that tries and judges the accused—the judiciary process.

PROSECUTION DISCRETION

As was stated in Chapter 3, not all offenders are arrested; police do have discretion in invoking the criminal-justice process. The same can be said for the prosecutor. The prosecuting district attorney not only possesses a great deal of responsibility in enforcing the criminal law but also exercises an enormous degree of discretion in the manner in which efficient and fair law enforcement is achieved. The decisions that he must make are numerous, and often determining the adequacy of proof is anything but simple. As we have pointed out before, judges and juries do not witness the crimes on trial, and even eyewitnesses, as discussed in this chapter, make mistakes. If the evidence has not been preserved, or is inadmissible for any reason (see Chapter 4), it would be useless and a waste of valuable resources to proceed any further.

In practice, a great deal of discussion has already occurred by the time the police officer or agent from another law enforcement body presents a report to a district attorney for approval. The liaison officer already has a good understanding of whether a case is likely to result in criminal prosecution because of her frequent contact with the district attorney. Cases that clearly do not merit further proceedings are disposed of at the police level and never reviewed by the district attorney's office. The same principle applies to cases that originate in governmental agencies other than police departments.

A substantial portion of the cases that are presented to deputy district atorneys are indeed cases that merit prosecution, and a complaint is, in fact, issued. It is not unusual, however, for the police department to present a case to the district attorney's office with the express purpose of obtaining an objective and disinterested discretionary review of the matter by that office. This happens mainly in cases of significant public interest and in cases involving very serious crimes.

It is important to note that the police officer's discretion in making arrests (discussed in Chapter 3) comes into play again in court, when she takes the stand under oath. She must be able to say at what point she believed she had probable cause to make the arrest, and which facts and circumstances led to her decision.

CRIMINAL PROCESS AND PROCEDURE

The first step in the institution of criminal proceedings, as we know, is, commenced by: (1) complaint, (2) information, or (3) the grand jury's returning of an approved bill of indictment before the arrest of the defendant, in which case the court issues a bench warrant for the arrest. (The use of the grand jury indictment in some states, notably in Michigan and California, has been curtailed. These supreme courts have ruled that defendants indicted by the grand jury are entitled to a postindictment hearing with attorneys to confront accusing witnesses and to present evidence to refute prosecution.) Other less frequently used methods of instituting proceedings involve a coroner's inquest finding and a presentment of the grand jury (see Glossary).

Upon effecting an arrest, certain requirements and rules must be observed: the right to make telephone calls, stationhouse discretion, bail, release on own recognizance, the privilege against self-incrimination, arraignment, and preliminary examination. These rules must be observed within a set period of time. Figure 5.1 gives an overview of the steps in a criminal proceeding.

Right to Make Telephone Calls

Most states provide that the suspect has the right to make at least one telephone call. Other states allow two telephone calls to be made, one to an attorney or relative and the other to a bail bondsman. Section 851.5 of the California Penal Code provides: "(a) any person arrested has, immediately after he is booked, the right, at his own expense, in the presence of a public officer or employee, at least one telephone call from the police station or other place at which he is booked, *completed to the person called*, who may be his attorney, employer, or relative."

Stationhouse Discretion

Booking is only a clerical process. Not all persons arrested and brought to a police station are detained with subsequent prosecution. When an arrest is made without a warrant, either by an arresting agency or a

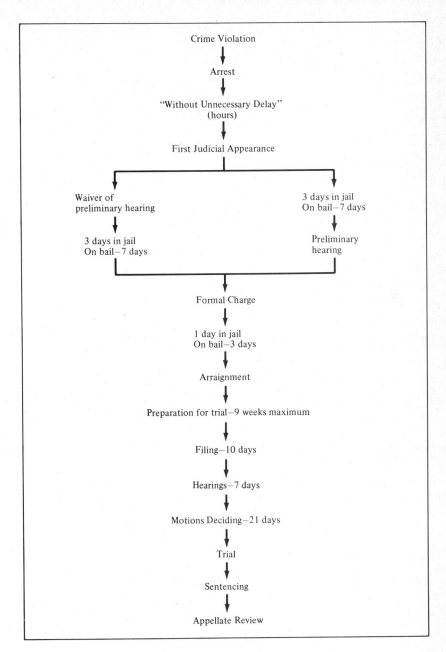

FIGURE 5.1   Steps in a criminal proceeding.

private party, a peace officer may release the person arrested instead of detaining him for preliminary arraignment when he concludes that there is no basis for filing a complaint.

Frequently, the officer in charge may decide that the arresting officer does not have sufficient evidence to detain the defendant for the offense charged and therefore he may dispose of the matter at that point. This procedure is especially pertinent in relation to domestic difficulties. Arrests for intoxication and disturbing the peace, made in and about a family home, are the types of cases that are disposed of immediately. The commanding officer may also release parties brought to the jail if those parties sign an agreement to appear in court or before a magistrate at a particular place and time.

It should be pointed out at this time that even if a person is detained, it does not mean he will be prosecuted. The district attorney may reduce the plea or dismiss the case on his own motion because of insufficient evidence. About 5 percent of misdemeanor cases are dismissed by the prosecutor on his own motion. Of all persons charged with misdemeanors, 35 percent plead guilty. Of the defendants who ultimately go to trial, 15 to 25 percent are fined and released subject to some probationary term.[1]

Bail

There are many different definitions of the word *bail*. The most popular definition is "security given for the due appearance of the prisoner in order to obtain his release from imprisonment."[2]

Bail bond is a corporate surety bond posted to secure the release of a defendant from jail. These bonds may be obtained from bail bondsmen, whose offices are usually located in the vicinity of the local courthouse or jail. The cash premium is usually 10 percent of the amount of bail. In addition to the premium, the bail bondsmen must require the defendant, before his release, to post other collateral in the form of deeds, trusts, or other securities to further ensure his appearance at the subsequent court hearing.

The amount of bail is usually fixed by the magistrate at the preliminary arraignment. In some instances, bail may be set before the preliminary arraignment. This may occur when the arrest is made under a warrant and the amount of bail is endorsed on the warrant. In other procedure for bailable offenses, any magistrate or commissioner with jurisdiction over the offense may fix the amount of bail under the following circumstances: when the defendant is arrested without warrant or has not yet been taken before a magistrate, or when no warrant fixing the bail has been established.

To avoid the pitfalls and inequities of a bail system, most state systems, and the federal system, provide that a defendant must be

4. The date when the offense is alleged to have been committed; provided, however,
   a. if the specific date is unknown, or if the offense is a continuing
      one, it shall be sufficient to state that it was committed on or
      about any date within the period of limitations; and
   b. if the day of the week is an essential element of the offense
      charged, such date or day must be specifically set forth;
5. The place where the offense is alleged to have been committed;
6. A summary of the facts sufficient to advise the defendant of the
   nature of the offense charged, but neither the evidence nor the
   statute allegedly violated need be cited in the complaint, nor shall
   a citation of the statute allegedly violated by itself be of sufficient
   compliance with the subsection;
7. A statement that the acts of the defendant were against the peace
   and dignity of that particular state;
8. A request for the issuance of a warrant of arrest of a summons;
9. A statement attested by the issuing authority, that the affiant swore
   to or affirmed the complainant before him and signed it in his
   presence; and
10. The signature of the affiant and the date of execution of the com-
    plaint (refer to complaint form in Chapter 3).

A complaint is normally made by a citizen, but the district attorney's
office issues the complaint against the defendant. The victim of the
crime *is not* the party who alleges commission of the crime by the
defendant. The *People of the State* is the proper plaintiff in a criminal
prosecution. The victim of the crime can only be a complaining witness.

A misdemeanor complaint justifies the arrest of the defendant so
he can be arraigned and required to enter his plea. When the misdemeanant is arraigned, he may either plead to the complaint or demur.
A *demurrer* is a legal attack on the face of the complaint arguing that
the complaint does not state facts sufficient to constitute a cause of
action against the defendant. In misdemeanor cases, there is no preliminary examination. If the defendant's plea raises an issue of which
reasonable men may disagree, a trial is conducted in a municipal court
or other inferior court. The defendant is then either acquitted or found
guilty and sentenced by that same court.

Information

The prosecution may also begin by filing information. Information
is like a complaint in that it is made under oath and is the first step in
the initiation of a criminal prosecution. It is the foundation upon which
all subsequent legal proceedings are based, and it is essentially the
statement of the validity of all such proceedings. It differs in that it

applies to misdemeanors that do not require the return of an indictment.

The information is normally signed by the district attorney and sworn to by him or by any member of his staff. An information, from a strictly legal point of view, is an accusation against an individual made by the prosecution attorney direct to the court without the case having been passed upon by the grand jury.

The terms *complaint* and *information*, through usage, have developed the same meaning, and yet there is considerable technical differences between these two legal expressions. The definition and basic purpose of a complaint has been detailed above; let us briefly discuss the D.A.'s information.

The key purpose of an information is to acquaint the defendant with the charge against him, and it is sufficient if it sets forth the charge in substantially the language of the act. Information must comply with the same requirements as the indictment. Information, however, need not be as specific and as technically accurate as required in an indictment if essential elements of the offense are set forth in terms of common parlance, it is sufficient.

Under the common law an information was used in a misdemeanor case. (All felony prosecutions were commenced by indictments.) However, under statutory law, an information is not necessary in misdemeanor cases. In fact, in 22 states, felonies may be prosecuted by either indictment or information at the option of the prosecutor. In most of these states, criminal proceedings are commenced exclusively by information. A few states and the federal system require indictments to commence filing any prosecutions. The majority of those states that utilize the information alternative require that prosecution by information be commenced only after preliminary examination.

Felonies that are tried in superior court must be prosecuted by indictment or information. If a district attorney elects to proceed by information, formal criminal procedures are commenced for filing the complaint in the inferior court in the county where the offense was committed. In a great majority of the cases, the police also give a copy of the police report and the arrest report to the deputy district attorney, who prepares written felony complaints. If the facts that are stated would support a felony prosecution, the complaint is prepared and filed with the magistrate. Technically, the complaint is not a plea. It becomes a plea only if dispositional facts submitted by an informant are sufficient to constitute the basis for a felony prosecution. After the complaint is filed with the magistrate or judge in an inferior court, the magistrate or court judge may issue an arrest warrant if he concludes that a crime has been committed and that there is reasonable cause to believe the defendant committed it. In other words, a prosecutor need not have personal knowledge of the facts necessary to convict the defendant but can institute proceedings on information and belief that the offense had indeed been commited.

Where a law enforcement officer or an individual signs an information based not on his personal knowledge or facts but on information that he receives from others, he must also swear that he believes the information he received. If his information is based only on rumor or some sources concerning reliability of which he is not familiar, he cannot honestly swear that he "believes" the information he received, and if he would so swear, he would be guilty of perjury. The facts disclosed to him should be of such character and from a source of such credibility that he can conscientiously swear he believes them to be true.

It is the duty of an officer to log the information at the earliest moment after the arrest so that the defendant is advised of his jeopardy and the basis of the record is established.

Grand Jury

A *grand jury* is an investigative body that is part of the judicial system. Its primary function is to initiate prosecution by indictment when the district attorney exercises his right to proceed by that method of prosecution, which may happen when he does not wish to proceed with a felony prosecution on the basis of the information. An *indictment* is an accusation in writing, returned by a grand jury to superior court, charging a person with a criminal offense. Theoretically, an indictment is a formal charge brought by the state acting through the grand jury.

The grand jury *does not* determine the guilt or innocence of a defendant. The only question it must answer is whether the defendant should be brought to trial. The grand jury hears all the evidence placed before it, and it must return an indictment when, in its collective judgment, a conviction by trial jury would result. This does not mean the jury trial must return a guilty verdict. The grand jury must determine *only* that the defendant should stand trial because there is reason to believe that he has committed a felony. If an indictment is returned before the defendant has been taken into custody, a bench warrant is issued for his arrest. If the defendant is already in custody, no secrecy surrounds the grand jury proceedings. If substantial cause exists, the state may decide to arrest the defendant before the indictment. If this is so, it must follow the complaint procedure described previously. A bench warrant is issued by the court, and the court determines bail. However, the grand jury must make a recommendation as to the amount of bail that should be set for a particular offense. The court then uses its own discretion in following the recommendation.

The grand jury must act conscientiously and without fear that the state or the court will interfere with its duties and obligations. The grand jury does not have to wait for the prosecuting attorney to commence the proceedings. It may bring to trial anyone against whom the state has neglected to commence proceedings. Grand juries also have the power to grant general or specific immunity to witnesses who refuse to testify. If they still refuse to testify after the grand jury grants immunity, they are held in civil contempt. This means the witnesses are jailed until they decide to comply with the order and answer the questions put to them. Criminal contempt is an affront to the court itself and commands an independent sentence regardless of compliance after sentencing.

It is not unusual for law enforcement officers to be called before the grand jury to testify. Under the federal court system, an indictment may be based entirely on hearsay. But the majority of state courts follow the rule that the evidence presented must be legally competent (admissible in a criminal trial). Witnesses, including police officers and in some instances defendants, do not have a right to counsel. The grand jury is an investigative body, not an adjudicative body; nevertheless, the privilege against self-incrimination is available to any witness, including the accused.

> The difference between an *indictment* and *information* is in their origins rather than their contents. Both are formal written accusations of crime against specific persons, containing statements as to the time and place the alleged offense was committed, and listing the material facts charged against the accused. The former [indictment] issues from a Grand Jury, which has voted it a *true bill*, and it is signed by the Grand-Jury foreman. The latter [information] issues merely from the prosecuting attorney's office and is signed by the chief prosecutor. . . .
>
> Grand juries are rather docile tools of the county district attorney, tending to return indictments he wishes and squashing those he prefers not to prosecute. This is quite natural, because it is the district attorney who is presenting all the evidence to them and, in most cases, the juries are correct in accepting the D.A.'s guidance, because he is leading them in the direction of justice. They always have the power to reject his guidance if they become suspicious of it, and begin demanding evidence other than that presented by the D.A.[4]

Arraignment: Lower Court

An arraignment usually follows the decision that the defendant will be prosecuted. The purpose of an arraignment is to accord the accused an opportunity to know the nature of the charge against her and to answer whether she is guilty or not and to set a date for the trial. Following an arrest, the defendant must be taken before the court for arraignment within "a reasonable length of time," generally 48 hours. The court proceeds to read the complaint, identifies the defendant by asking her name, and informs the defendant of her right to counsel and sets the bail, if such has not been done.

If the offense is a misdemeanor, at the arraignment the defendant may plead guilty to the charge and be sentenced at this time. The defendant may also request continuance before entering her plea to obtain counsel, or a continuance for a valid reason. If the defendant pleads not guilty, a date may then be set by the court for trial. This may be by jury or by judge. The defendant has the right to have the trial in 30 days; if not then, the charge is dismissed. The defendant may waive this 30-day requirement.

If the offense is a felony, at the arraignment of the lower court the defendant may plead guilty to the felony charge. The lower court has no jurisdiction to hear or to sentence the defendant and must, in less than two or no more than five days, order the defendant to appear in a superior court for sentence. The lower court cannot sentence on a felonious offense. When the defendant appears in superior court, she can then be sentenced.

If the defendant pleads not guilty at her arraignment, however, a date will be set for her preliminary hearing.

Preliminary Hearing

The preliminary hearing is often referred to as a judiciary inquiry directed toward the determination of the existence, validity, and sufficiency of probable cause.[5]

Depending on the procedure, either a judge or a prosecutor will preside over the proceedings, and an inquiry will be made of the defendant in order to determine the probability of her having committed a crime. This is the stage at which all material facts are gathered and tested and subsequently reported by the judge who prepares the case for trial. The court then determines the credibility and truthfulness of the matters discovered. It must be determined if the state's evidence against the accused is strong enough to warrant holding her for further proceedings.

Although both the grand jury* and preliminary hearing may precede a trial, there is a *definite* difference between the two (see Table 5.1). The purpose of the hearing is essentially to advise the person of his right to remain silent and his right to assistance of counsel at trial. It also serves the following purposes: (1) to determine the existence of

---

* In 1979 the California State Supreme Court ruled that an indictment by a grand jury does *not* eliminate the necessity of a preliminary hearing. A preliminary hearing *must* be held if one is requested by the indictee.

TABLE 5.1   Grand Jury and Preliminary Hearing (Contrast)

GRAND JURY	PRELIMINARY HEARING
• Decision made by layman	• Decision made by judge
• Prosecutor is present	• Prosecution and defense attorney present
• Defendant is not present	• Defendant is present
• Defendant is not present	• Defendant can cross-examine witness
• Defendant is not present	• Defendant can challenge reality of evidence
• Defendant is not present	• Defendant can challenge legality of testimony
• Defendant is not present	• Defendant can present exculpatory evidence

probable cause for which a warrant was issued for arrest; (2) to inquire into the reasonability of the arrest and search, and the compliance of the executing officer with the command of the warrant; (3) to afford the magistrate who issued the warrant the opportunity to hear the accused and determine whether probable cause still exists after the hearing of witnesses or examining evidence presented by the accused; and (4) to release the accused on bail.

At an arraignment in a lower court, the defendant may answer a plea of not guilty. The magistrate must then have the preliminary examination within five days. Postponements may be allowed at the defendant's request. The preliminary hearing is not a trial, and the district attorney does not give his case away by presenting all his evidence. Usually, the district attorney will present just enough evidence to "tie the defendant" with the felony. The preliminary hearing is a "screening" of cases so that the superior court will not waste its time hearing cases where it is obvious that the prosecution does not have a case, or where, in fact, the offense is not a felony. Further, the lower court may dismiss the case against the defendant if there is not sufficient evidence to indicate that a felony has been committed. At the preliminary hearing, it may be discovered that the offense is really only a misdemeanor. Then the defendant may be ordered to stand trial on this. If, at the preliminary hearing, the judge finds a felony has, indeed, been committed, and there is reason to believe the defendant may have been the culprit, the defendant is "held to answer," which merely means that the defendant will go to the superior court for trial. The defendant cannot be deprived of this preliminary examination. In some jurisdictions, the custody of the defendant is transferred from the city jail to the county jail. The reason is that lower courts (municipal courts) are in densely populated areas with city courts under city police, whereas the superior court is a state court and the county sheriff has jurisdiction over the prisoner. At this point, the law provides that persons awaiting trial (not convicted of anything at this point) are not to be placed in custody with persons serving sentences for the conviction of crimes.

PLEA BARGAINING

Complaints of many law violations reach the prosecutor's office in substantial volume from inhabitants of his jurisdiction and by reference from other law enforcement agencies, social welfare organizations, and attorneys. It is common, particularly in urban areas, to find legal administrative procedures that provide for inquiry into disposal of most such complaints without initiating criminal proceedings. In 1967 the President's Commission on Law Enforcement and Administration of Justice advocated the use of alternatives to divert formal prosecution for certain offenders. In discussing initial stages of a criminal case, the commission stated:

> The criminal process disposes of most of its cases without trial.
> Policemen often use their discretion not to arrest certain offenders.
> Prosecutors exercise discretion in a similar fashion. They do not charge
> arrested suspects, they frequently have wide choices of what offense
> they will charge, and they often move to dismiss charges they have
> already made. Beyond this, the overwhelming majority of cases are
> disposed of by pleas of guilty. Often these pleas are the result of
> negotiations between prosecutors and defendants or their attorneys.
> Guilty pleas may be obtained in exchange for reduction of charges or
> for agreed-upon sentence recommendations. In many instances, it is
> the prosecutor who, in effect, determines or heavily influences the
> sentence the defendant receives.[6]

About half the persons arrested on felony charges are formally charged with commission of a felony. The other half are released on the prosecutor's own motion. Seventy to 80 percent of the formally charged defendants plead guilty. The plea is normally entered after compromise and some negotiation between the prosecuting attorney and the defendant's attorney. This method of plea bargaining has not been constitutionally tested. The courts are split over the question of this voluntariness, but a majority of courts approve of this method of disposing of criminal cases. The rationale behind these dispositions is that an admission of guilt is the first step toward rehabilitation. With an opportunity for the defense counsel to present a social critique of the defendant's police record and/or background, the court usually remands the case, depending on its gravity, to the probation department for an independent investigation and recommendation. Plea bargaining usually covers three areas: (1) sentence recommendation, (2) reduction of the charge, and (3) dismissal of other counts relating to the same incident.

Plea bargaining takes place because of the high incidence of crime and the low number of prosecutors available to prosecute these cases. As a practical manner, the economics of judicial administration are very much a part of the adversary system. District attorneys realize that plea bargaining is one way to dispose of large numbers of cases in a summary manner.

Cost, however, is not the only factor in plea bargaining. Without it, citizens might have to be called on for more jury trials. These jurors might find themselves routinely pressed into service for the most obvious cases, which would tend to create apathetic juries.

This is not to say that it is not frustrating—frustrating for the police officers who make the arrests, sometimes exposing their lives to grave danger, and then having the district attorney decide to accept a plea of guilty to a lesser offense. Police officers, unfortunately, begin to question whether the risk involved justified the ultimate disposition of the case. This is not to say that a valid arrest necessarily constitutes evidence sufficient to ensure a guilty plea. But police officers see the circumstances from their viewpoint and, at times, justifiably criticize the plea bargaining system.

DEFENDANT'S CONSTITUTIONAL AND STATUTORY RIGHTS WHEN CHARGED WITH A CRIME

The person charged with a crime has certain protections set up by the Constitution and by code provisions. The United States Constitution protects the people from the federal government, and generally the first 10 Amendments (known as Bill of Rights) do not protect from the actions of a state. The "due process" clause of the United States Constitution has by inclusion and exclusion covered some of these rights of the people against the state.

Thus, it is necessary to look to the state constitution, which is a document that gives the people rights against their own state legislative acts, to determine what these protections are. Various code sections and common law rules of evidence also give the defendant every guarantee of a fair trial.

Officers of the law should have a general knowledge of these rules so that they are not placed in a position whereby a misunderstanding occurs. The following are some of these major rules.

Right to Jury Trial

Every defendant may have a common-law jury of 12 to decide the disputed facts of his case. The defendant may waive the jury trial if he fully understands the nature of the waiver. He may also waive the number and be tried by less than 12 in misdemeanor cases. To sustain a conviction, all jurors must agree. If less than all agree, then it is a "hung jury" and the defendant may be tried again. There is no limit to the number of times the defendant may be put on trial.

In lieu of the jury trial, the defendant can have the judge hear the case without jury.

Double Jeopardy

Double jeopardy simply means no one can be tried for the same crime more than once. A "hung jury" is not an acquittal, and in this instance a retrial for the same offense is not double jeopardy. Also, the same act may be an offense under two jurisdictions, and thus the defendant may be tried for both. A good example is an auto theft in San Francisco, and the car is driven to Nevada. There are, then, two crimes: a state law violation and a federal law violation (Dwyer Act). The defendant may be charged and convicted of both—one in the state court and the other in the United States court; this is not double jeopardy. In other words, unless the acts are merged, the defendant may be tried on both.

Right to Bail

Prior to conviction, the defendant always has the right to bail. In capital offenses, the right to bail is discretionary with the judge and not an absolute right. Any offense punishable by death is a capital offense. After conviction, and pending appeal, bail is discretionary with a judge and not a right. If the defendant does not have funds to put up for bail, and he does not qualify for bail on his own recognizance, he may be retained in custody but cannot be interned with those convicted of a crime.

Right to a Speedy Trial

The defendant does have a right to a speedy trial. After his arrest, he has a right to demand to be brought before a magistrate within a reasonable time—usually 48 hours. The defendant is also entitled to have his case adjudicated in an expedient manner. He may, of course, waive this right to open court. But unless he does so, in the superior court, the defendant must be brought to trial within 60 days after the indictment by a grand jury or filing of information by the district attorney. If he is not brought to trial, the case must be dismissed and further prosecution on that particular charge disallowed.

Right to Counsel

As indicated previously, the defendant has the right to counsel of his own choice at every stage of the proceedings. Most states guarantee that "if the defendant desires counsel and cannot pay the fee, the court must appoint counsel for the defendant. The court should so inform the defendant of his right."

Of course, the defendant may always waive his right to counsel. The court cannot force counsel on the defendant, because he always has the right to act as his own attorney. But the waiver and request to act as his own attorney must be an intelligent decision, and the judge must agree.

Right Not to Testify Against Oneself

The Fifth Amendment provides in part: "No person . . . shall be compelled in any criminal case to be a witness against himself." In a federal court, a witness at a civil or criminal trial cannot be compelled to give testimony evidence that might subject him to criminal prosecution. This privilege applies to all witnesses whether or not they are parties to the action. The Fourteenth Amendment's due process clause incorporates the Fifth Amendment privilege against self-incrimination. In other words, the *states* are also prohibited from forcing communicative testimony which may be incriminating (Fifth Amendment), from a witness in civil or criminal trials (the court has a duty to warn the accused of his right not to testify).

This privilege has a twofold purpose. A defendant in a criminal proceeding has the privilege to refuse to testify or to take the stand. If the defendant refuses to testify, the prosecution cannot comment on his silence (the prosecution *can* comment on his refusal to submit to *non*testimonial procedures). Although the jury may be psychologically influenced by the defendant's refusal to take the stand to defend himself, it would be a prejudicial error if a prosecutor were to comment on a defendant's exercise of his privilege not to testify.

The restriction against comment extends not only to the time of trial but also to the time of his arrest and any time before or after when he specifically claims the privilege against self-incrimination (*Miranda* v. *Arizona*, 384 U.S. 436, [1966]).

The Supreme Court has shifted from the position of protecting the accused on the basis of his right to counsel derived from the guarantees of the Sixth Amendment to protection based on the privilege against self-incrimination guaranteed by the Fifth Amendment. Even as the pendulum has swung from the Sixth to the Fifth Amendment for protection of the accused, Congress, through the Omnibus Crime Control Act of 1968, has attempted to reverse *Miranda*-type decisions by providing for the admissibility of confessions only on the basis of whether they are voluntary (see also Chapter 4). The doubtful question of the voluntariness of a confession is left to determination by the court.

Even though the prosecutor can make no adverse comments with regard to a defendant's failure to testify, improper comment does not necessarily mean automatic reversal of conviction (*Griffin* v. *California* 380 U.S. 609, [1965] and *Chapman* v. *California* 386 U.S. 18 [1967]). The conviction will not be reversed if the appellate court finds that the prosecution's comments about the accused's failure to testify were only "harmless error." The prosecution always has the burden of proving beyond a reasonable doubt that the court or jury was not influenced by such comments. However, a prosecutor's comment on a criminal defendant's failure to testify is still, apparently, permitted when the criminal defendant takes the stand and gives limited testimony. The prosecutor can then point out to the jury that the criminal defendant failed to testify about information that the prosecution is sure the defendant has.

The question of waiver must be analyzed with a two-pronged approach:

Waiver of privilege not to testify. As a general rule, whenever a criminal defendant takes the stand and testifies on his own behalf, he waives his right not to take the stand. Not only can a criminal defendant then be asked questions about the substantive nature of the alleged crime committed, but he must also answer questions that might impeach testimony. There is still a question as to whether the defendant must answer questions concerning other crimes previously committed. Some states hold that he must answer all questions because he has completely waived his right not to take the stand. Other states allow impeachment of the defendant's testimony by showing collateral crimes. If a witness takes a stand in a prior proceeding, whether it be grand jury indictment or a preliminary hearing, he does not waive his rights to refuse to testify at a trial. However, testimony given in prior proceedings may be used against him in the form of a confession or admission.

The privilege against self-incrimination. This privilege can be waived by any party, defendant or witness, when an incriminating question is asked and the party fails to assert his privilege. Difficulties lie in two areas: (1) Does partial disclosure completely waive the party's privilege against self-incrimination? Most states have held that if a party makes a partial disclosure, he may be questioned about all the facts concerning the alleged crime. (2) The second, and more difficult, question is: What is meant by an incriminating question? Most courts hold that a question can be construed as incriminating if the answer would bind a testifying party, either directly or indirectly, to the commission of a crime or provide any leads from which such criminal prosecution could result. Most courts hold that a question is incriminating only if it could result in *criminal prosecution*. If a crime is not directly or indirectly involved, the party cannot claim the privilege. For example, if a party might lose his job or disgrace his family or be subject to civil liability, he cannot claim the privilege. The court has held, in *Gardener* v. *Broderic* (392 U.S. 273 [1968]), that any public employee who refuses to answer questions directly relating to his official duties can be discharged from his job. However, even though a public employee may be fired from his job, the incriminating answers cannot be used against him at a subsequent criminal prosecution if he is compelled to testify by his superior officers. In *Garity* v. *New Jersey* (385 U.S. 493 [1967]), a police officer made a confession to a superior officer under threat of losing his job. The court held that his confession was involuntary and inadmissible at a subsequent criminal prosecution. The threat of removal from office has been held by the court to be "coercive" and inconsistent with the voluntary waiver of the privilege against self-incrimination. The court followed the same rationale and this type of enforcement complies as it did in the *Miranda* case.

Right to Be Confronted by One's Accuser

A defendant always has the right to have a witness against him testify in his presence. The defendant, or his counsel, has the right to cross-examine the witness against him, to seek the truth, and to impeach the witness to show he may be lying, mistaken, hostile, prejudiced, or whatever. The jury must weigh the credibility of the witness.

The Sixth Amendment to the Constitution provides that "in all criminal prosecutions, the accused shall enjoy the right . . . to be confronted with witnesses against him." This provision means, as previously stated, that any defendant has the constitutional right to cross-examine witnesses. The right of confrontation exists not only in federal courts but also in state courts, because the due process clause of Fourteenth Amendment includes the Sixth Amendment privilege. The right to confrontation exists in "all criminal prosecutions." The right was extended in 1967 to juvenile proceedings (*In re Gault*, 387 U.S. 1 [1967]). Criminal prosecution does not include investigative proceedings such as legislative inquiries, coroner's inquiries, or grand jury proceedings (or any proceeding that could not result in prosecution).

Informers. Regarding informers, the United States Supreme Court, in 1968, held that a police informer who testifies against a criminal defendant must reveal her name and address (*Smith* v. *Illinois*, 390 U.S.

129, [1968]). This disclosure may enable the defense counsel to impeach the informer. They can attack the informer's credibility as a witness. The court has held that the identity of police informers is not constitutionally required to be revealed in order to obtain a search warrant or an arrest warrant, but it is necessary for prosecution.

In *McCray* v. *Illinois* (386 U.S. 300 [1967]), the Supreme Court held that the police did not necessarily have to reveal the informer's identity in order to establish probable cause for arrest and search. But it is necessary that the police testify to the informer's reliability to establish probable cause.

If the identity of the police informant is not directly material to the guilt or inocence of the defendant, his identity need not be revealed. The court emphasized some pertinent guidelines, which, it determined, were sufficient to avoid violation of the Sixth Amendment's right of confrontation. The police officer, in open court, must describe in detail what the defendant told him. The lower court judge, in exercising her discretion, must be satisfied that the police officers are telling the truth. She can then allow such testimony to be admitted as evidence.

Statute of Limitations

Statute of limitations simply means that within the prescribed period of the statute, an indictment, a complaint, or information must be filed. (Even within a state, there are differences in time periods for the commencement of prosecution [New York State Criminal Procedure Law 1978–79, Section 30.10].) The time requirement does not run when the defendant is out of the state, since the purpose is to allow the defendant to get his defense together. Although it would be unjust not to set some limitation on the time that a person could be charged with the crime, many times the statute of limitations has proved to be an asset to a clever criminal.

In regard to felonies, crimes so specified have a three-year statute of limitations from the time the *information* is filed (*not* from filing of the complaint). In regard to *misdemeanors,* there is a one-year statute of limitations from the time the complaint is filed. When these time limits have expired, the defendant cannot be tried for the committed offense. This is jurisdictional, and a conviction after the statute has run out is void, even if the defendant does not plead statute of limitations as a defense. For misdemeanors the time starts to run from the date of the commission of the crime. An acceptance of a bribe by a public official has a six-year statute of limitations. There are no time limits for *murder, embezzlement of public money,* or *falsification* of public records. Furthermore, there can be *no crime committed* unless such is so designated by statute and the penalty is prescribed. The statute must be clear and not vague as to what is prohibited. The statute must also be in plain English (no Latin medical terms). There must be a clear understanding as to what the statute means.

COURT AND TRIAL

When a person is formally charged and prosecution is begun—by indictment, information, or complaint—the accused is called into court before trial, informed of the charges, and given the opportunity to make a plea. Arraignment is not a trial, and the court does not examine any matters pertaining to the accused's guilt or innocence.

Upon representation by counsel, the accused is asked to enter a plea. The plea entered can be guilty, not guilty, not guilty by reason of insanity, or *nolo contendre* (see Glossary). If no plea is offered, the court will offer a plea of not guilty for the accused. A plea of guilty will not be accepted by the court at arraignment until the nature and consequences of such a plea and the maximum penalty that may be imposed by law for such an offense have been fully explained to the defendant.

A criminal trial in the United States is always conducted by a judge. In contrast to the police officer, the judge before whom a suspect is first brought usually exercises less discretion than the law allows her. The judge is entitled to inquire into the facts of the case and ask whether there are grounds for holding the accused; in practice, however, she seldom does this. The more promptly an arrested suspect is brought into the courts, the less likelihood there is that much information about the arrest other than the arresting officer's statement will be available to the judge. Many judges, especially in urban areas, have such congested calendars that it is almost impossible for them to give any case except the most extraordinary ones prolonged scrutiny.

In practice, the most important things the judge does are to set the amount of the defendant's bail and, in some jurisdictions, to appoint counsel. Too seldom does either action get the careful attention it deserves. In many cases, the magistrate accepts the waiver of counsel without ensuring that the suspect is aware of the significance of legal representation.

Criminal-court proceedings as practiced in the United States afford the defendant an opportunity to defend himself against the charges in a court of law. In other words, if the alleged offender pleads not guilty, a significant part of the due process is a *trial*. What is a trial? Is it a drama like those portrayed on the Perry Mason show? Although, no one can deny that a trial actually is a drama which has a significant impact not only on the defendant but also on his relatives and friends, it is a drama based on specific rules and a philosophy that varies to reflect the conditions of the time.

A trial has been defined as a

> . . . procedure or proceedings, held in open court, whereby judge or a jury, after hearing evidence for or against an accused, renders a verdict of guilty or not guilty. The distinction between a court trial, i.e. trial by a judge, and trial by jury, is merely in the number of persons necessary to render a verdict. In a court trial, the judge renders the verdict. In a jury trial, the verdict is rendered by the unanimous vote of all twelve* jurors.[7]

In contrast to criminal-justice systems in other countries, the American system sets up elaborate safeguards to protect those who have been charged with a law violation. The Sixth Amendment to the United States Constitution reads:

> In all criminal prosecutions the accused shall enjoy the right to a speedy trial and a public trial by an impartial jury by the State and the district wherein the crime shall have been committed . . . and to be informed of the nature and cause of the accusation; to be confronted with the witnesses against him; to have compulsory processes for obtaining witnesses in his favor; and to have the assistance of counsel for defense.

Most of these safeguards depend on the care and thoroughness with which prescribed procedures are observed during the courtroom trial. "Perfect justice," therefore, is not always attained. This is vividly pointed out by H. E. Allen and C. E. Simonsen:

> Judges are elected or appointed to office. In either case, they can be put in a position where they owe their political depth to their backers. Because of the corrupt practices of a very few judges, it is often felt that judges, in general, are responsible only to pressure groups and will dismiss cases if told to do so by those in power. Actually, the discretion of a judge in a criminal court is quite limited.
>
> Dean Wigmore [John Henry Wigmore, 1863–1943, probably the world's foremost authority on the law of evidence] is credited with originating the "sporting theory" of justice as a description of a court trial. A trial can boil down to a legal contest between two highly skilled lawyers, with the judge playing the role of a referee. Our adversary system of justice pits two lawyers against each other in an attempt to prove the *technical* guilt or innocence of the suspect. The judge, who may be considerably less skilled at law than either the

---

* The United States Supreme Court recently handed down a decision permitting states to use fewer than 12 jurors in a criminal trial.

prosecutor or defense attorney, simply determines the outcome of various procedural disputes. If he makes one wrong decision, the offender will question it on appeal, and that alone can suffice to overturn his conviction. It is a basic concept of the American system of justice that many offenders should be permitted to go free, rather than risk a conviction of one innocent person because the procedures that protect his rights were not observed to the letter.[8]

Although many more cases are handled by plea bargaining than by the formal trial procedure, a trial is and will remain a vital aspect of the administration of criminal law. All the preliminary steps are shaped by the necessity attending those cases that do go to trial. Investigation and fact-gathering are directed to the need for proof at trial, even though they also contribute to dispositions without trial.

The manner in which an individual law enforcement officer conducts investigation and fact-finding determines the effectiveness of the court process as an instrument of justice. Misconduct or inadequate performance by the investigating or arresting officer gravely undermines the functioning of the court process in a manner generally beyond repair by the trial judge. Law enforcement's role in the court process has been vividly spelled out by the American Bar Association:

American law enforcement is literally a part of the American court system. No other profession outside the structure of the system itself is so desperately dependent upon it for day to day guidance and support. The more than professional police officer must recognize the court as an essential vehicle in administration of justice. The courts are the only public agencies ultimately responsible for both safeguarding our constitutional rights as citizens and providing restraints to ensure the reasonable safety and welfare of our country and its people.
Individually and collectively, citizens and policemen alike depend more upon the judgements of the various courts than either likely realizes.[9]

Of all the institutions and agencies through which the system of criminal justice is administered, the *court* stands first in importance and historical origin. Other institutions, from public police systems to probation and parole agencies, come much later; for many centuries the criminal law was administered without them. It is difficult, if not impossible, to conceive of a system of criminal justice without a tribunal of some kind for its administration, particularly in light of the American concepts of government and individual liberties.[10]

The Jury

The jury is usually composed of 12 men and women (juries may have varying numbers according to a recent Supreme Court decision) and is drawn to represent a cross-section of the community within the jurisdiction of the court. The method and standards of selection are established by law in each state but must satisfy the minimal standards of due process, which calls for fair and impartial procedures. No state can set standards that discriminate against its citizens by reason of race, religion, or national origin.

In all states, and in the federal system, the accused is entitled to "a speedy trial." The right to an early trial is guaranteed by the various constitutions, and the constitutional provisions are generally supplemented by legislative enactments particularizing and specifically limiting the pre-trial detention period. In Illinois, for instance, once a person is jailed upon a criminal charge, he must be tried within 120 days, unless the delay has been requested by him or an additional length of time up to 60 days has been allowed by the court to the prosecution for the purpose of obtaining further evidence. If the accused is out on bail, he can demand a trial within 160 days, although in this instance too the court can allow the prosecution an additional 60 days. Unless an accused person is prosecuted within a specific period of time, he may be released and is, thereafter, immune from prosecution for the offense.

An accused person is also entitled to trial by jury, as a matter of constitutional right. However, he may waive his right to a jury trial and be tried by judge alone. If the case is tried without a jury, the judge hears the evidence and decides for himself whether the defendant is guilty or not guilty. Where the trial is by jury, the jury determines the facts and the judge serves more or less as an umpire or referee; it is his function to determine what testimony or evidence is legally "admissible," that is, to decide what should be heard or considered by the jury. But the ultimate decision as to whether the defendant is guilty is one made by the jury alone.[11]

The jury theoretically represents a community,

. . . as does a trial judge trying the merits in a criminal case when sitting without a jury. Since the victim does not himself institute criminal proceedings (except that such a person complains to, or files a complaint with, duly constituted authorities), the legal community (state) moves against the offender. But the defendant is accorded certain measures of protection in a modern society, primarily as a safeguard against convicting innocent persons. At least, such is the avowed aim of the various procedural safeguards, though they are sometimes flaunted . . . during practical application of them. One such ingredient of criminal procedures, of significance at this juncture, is the requirement that the prosecution shall bear the burden of proof at the threshhold of a criminal trial. The sequence of proof prescribed at the trial level in criminal prosecutions enables the defendant to remain personally inactive up to the time when the prosecution rests its case. Contemporary society is required to present the accusation without invading the rights of the accused, forcing him to aid in his own prosecution.[12]

The Adversary System

Unfortunately, there is an inconsistency between the intent of justice and the impact of justice, and the adversary system is clearly a part of that problem. Ideally, the system presents two advocates in search of truth, with either one willing to accept truth once it has been found. But in reality, each lawyer will usually fight to come out on top regardless of where "truth" happens to lie. Of course, the judge and jury are theoretically objective enough to discern the truth regardless of how the attorneys approach the trial—a strong argument in favor of the adversary system. But the accused is not likely to emerge from the courtroom with an idealistic view of justice after his exposure to the conduct and demeanor of many—probably most—defense attorneys and prosecutors. Most probably, the accused finds his attention locked onto *winning* as the most significant goal of the trial, not only for himself but for the advocates as well.

Prosecutor

In a criminal proceeding, the prosecution always has the right and duty of opening the case and offering evidence in support of the case irrespective of the nature of the defense. The purpose of the opening statement is to explain to the jury the issue or issues to be tried. The prosecuting attorney has the right to state in her opening what facts the prosecution intends to prove, but she cannot cite facts for which she has no competent evidence. Following the opening statement by the prosecuting attorney, a motion to allow the defense to make his opening statement is addressed to the court. Counsel for the defendant is properly restricted from stating in his opening statement matters that would be inadmissible in evidence. He has the right, however, to state his theory of the legal principles applicable to the entire case.

Disputes on issue of fact arising in the criminal constitution are determined on the basis of evidence offered and admitted at the trial. For the most part, this will be the testimony of persons who witnessed the facts, and such testimony will be given in open court. In addition to the written or spoken word, tangible objects and tests may be admissible as evidence. Tests can be conducted by both prosecution and the counsel for defense in order to prove their case of guilt or innocence.

Defense Counsel

The presentation of the defendant's defense argument to the jury, by himself or by his counsel, is a constitutional right that may not be denied, however clear the evidence against him may seem. As pointed out by the American Bar Association, the general posture of defense counsel is that he undertakes his function with built-in handicaps arising out of the reality that by the time he undertakes his main task, a series of events has placed his client under a cloud of suspicion that is very real, notwithstanding the presumption of his innocence.

> The defense attorney often finds himself in conflict with the police and not infrequently with the judge. The conflict with the police has to do with what many defense attorneys call "police brutality," which in their view includes many forms of police action. The police, understandably, object to this characterization of their behavior, and wonder out loud as to how much attorneys really know about offenders and their unhappy tendency to repeat the offenses. The police officer also objects to the defense attorney who "tries his case in the newspapers," though police chiefs frequently do the same thing. This tendency on both sides to attempt to use the news media as an aid to prosecute or defend, particularly in cases that arouse varied public interest, has resulted in the adoption by the American Bar Association of strict new rules about pretrial publicity. The ABA's effort is directed toward preserving the defendant's right to an impartial trial, the right which, according to the news media, often conflicts with the right of free speech and the public's "right to know" about what is going on in its criminal process. Issues in this controversy involve basic constitutional rights and will not be easily resolved.
>
> Defense attorneys, particularly in the so-called "political trials," take umbrage not only with the police but with the prosecutor and the judge. The attack on Judge Hoffman in the "Chicago Seven" trial is without precedent in modern criminal factors, with many issues about the conduct of the trial to be resolved by the United States Supreme Court.
>
> Not only defense attorneys, but many lawyers concerned with preserving the rights of the accused, deplore the practices that develop in the court and stationhouse after mass arrests during riots and other forms of civil disobedience. [Usually, there is a] breakdown under the impact of larger number of persons taken into custody within a short period of time. Charging, presentment, bail procedures, and even trials become perfunctory and arbitrary.[13]

The primary role of counsel is to act as champion for his client. In this capacity, he is the equalizer, the one who raises the litigant as nearly as possible on an equal footing before the substantive and procedural law under which he is tried. Of course, as a practical matter, counsel does this not by formally educating the clent on every legal aspect of the case but by taking those procedural steps and recommending those courses of action that a client, were he an experienced advocate himself, might fairly and properly take. A lawyer cannot be timorous in his representation. Courage and zeal in the defense of his client's interests are qualities that are necessary in order to perform as an advocate. As an advocate, defense counsel has various criminal defenses he is legally entitled to present.

Criminal Defenses

A discussion of specific criminal defenses should note that western civilization had been faced with the problem of crime long before the "causes" of crime were studied. This, of necessity, has resulted in the criminal law and its specific defenses evolving primarily in terms of *self-deterministic* theories of crime. Reduced or diminished individual responsibility for criminal behavior was slow in developing. Indeed reduced individual responsibilty for crime currently relates to defense in terms of intent, instead of relieving the offender of the responsibility. That is, the ability to form intent to violate the law may, in some instances, be considered relevant even though environmental stress and psychological tension is in no way an excuse for violating the law. For this reason, the defense that will be discussed in this section—"justification"—will be discussed "technically" rather than in the context of behavioral theories.

Lack of capacity. When a criminal defense hinges on the question of "capacity," one of the following issues is customarily cited as the specific basis:

INSANITY. Most jurisdictions distinguish insanity at the time of trial from the insanity at the time of the alleged crime. Confusion sometimes arises, since a person judged insane at the time of trial cannot be held criminally responsible until he is sufficiently "sane" to "appreciate" the punishment for the crime—even if the evidence clearly indicates he was "sane" at the time of the criminal act.

In determining sanity at the time of a criminal act, virtually all courts use a legal test known as the M'Naughton Rule (California's State Supreme Court voted four to three in September 1979 to throw out the 116-year-old M'Naughton Rule, which focuses on the defendant's knowledge of right and wrong).* In effect, under this 1843 precedent, the court must attempt to ascertain whether the accused,

---

* In its place, the court substituted a broader definition of insanity, developed by the American Law Association, and now used in 15 states and most of the federal judiciary. The California Justices said that a defendant no longer must show he didn't know right from wrong—often a difficult task—and also could prove insanity by showing he had a mental defect that made him unable to stop himself from committing the crime. The rule implemented by the court states that a person is not

at the time of the act, was "laboring under such a defect of reasoning or from disease of the mind as not to know the nature and quality of the act which he was doing, or if he did know, that he did not know what he was doing was wrong."

Many of the widely publicized legal entanglements in criminal trials in which the defense of sanity is raised hinge on the definitions of "nature and quality" along with the interpretation of the words "right and wrong."

In some criminal-court jurisdictions, there are additional insanity defense pleas more directly related to behavioral science explanations of crime causes. A few of the better-known variations are the "irresistible-impulse" defense and the "delusion" defense. When such defenses are invoked, the psychiatric and sociological considerations inevitably become a great deal more involved than simple ability to ascertain "right and wrong" (M'Naughton Rule).

IDIOCY. When posing a question of capacity as a defense in a criminal trial, most jurisdictions distinguish between *idiocy* and *insanity*. Idiots are deemed to be all those persons who have never had "mental capacity" in the first place. An insane person is supposed to have "lost" his capacity through mental disease. The impact of behavioral science on this particular criminal defense is usually involved in establishing the degree of feeblemindedness necessary to establish idiocy. Such categories as morons and imbeciles are often distinguished in these psychological classifications.

INTOXICATION AND NARCOSIS. In most criminal-court jurisdictions, the voluntary use of alcohol and narcotics is not permitted as a defense regardless of how much one's "capacity" is inhibited by intoxication or narcosis. In some instances, however, the specific issue of intent to commit a criminal act can be somewhat mitigated by intoxication (California has taken this approach to first-degree murder). As an example of such mitigation, a completely inebriated person is presumably incapable of the premeditation and deliberation required to commit first-degree murder—even though he might be "convictable" of involuntary manslaughter, since no attempt is required for its commission.

Mistake of fact. Most jurisdictions recognize the defense in which the accused person's intent was motivated by "variations in facts." (Mistake of fact is not a defense for a strict-liability offense.) An exam-

---

responsible for a crime "if at the time of such conduct as the result of mental disease or defect, he lacks substantial capacity either to appreciate the criminality of his conduct or to conform his conduct to the requirements of the law" (*Drew* v. *California* [1979]).

ple of a mistake of fact might be the following: A man and a woman walking down the street are attacked by a vicious dog. The man, woman, and dog are entangled in a struggle on the ground. A well-meaning passerby thinks that a girl and her dog are being attacked by a rapist. The girl's "benefactor" slays the supposed rapist only to find himself accused of murder. The important point in mistakes of fact is that they involve only intent.

Consent. In jurisdictions that define *crime* as an act performed "without consent of the victim," proof of the "victim's consent" is customarily recognized as a defense. Examples of situations like this are such crimes as rape and certain forms of theft. Of course, such a criminal defense is invalid when further evidence indicates that "consent" was induced through some form of intimidation.

This criminal defense, like those to follow, is clearly less related to the "causal factors" of behavioral science than the criminal defenses already mentioned.

Entrapment. When a person accused of crime is able to prove that he was, in some way, induced to commit an illegal act and had no independent intention of doing so, the law customarily recognizes a criminal defense known as entrapment discussed fully in Chapter 4. This is not to say that every person responding to an offer to commit a crime is entitled to plead entrapment. An undercover police officer successfully purchasing narcotics from a suspected seller has not entrapped the defendant. The actual test is whether or not the crime originated in the mind of the defendant, and the proof lies in certain aspects of the defendant's previous conduct.

Coercion and duress. In much the same way that entrapment reduces the accused person's responsibility for a criminal act, evidence of coercion or duress is also an acceptable criminal defense in most jurisdictions. Customarily, such evidence must demonstrate that the accused acted under fear of immediate or imminent physical harm or a threat of future injury to himself or his property.

Coercion and duress as a defense become complicated when the issue of severity—the degree of intimidation involved—is raised.

Justification. The term *justification*, when used in the "legal context" acquires a technically different meaning than the "psychological and environmental justifications" discussed in behavioral science textbooks.[14] Although the criminal defense known as justification is frequently related to the term *justifiable homicide*, there are, generally, three technical categories of justification: (a) defense of property; (b) defense of one or more other persons; and (c) defense of oneself.

Law enforcement agencies generally become involved in the various forms of *defense of property* through "defense of habitation" (the owner or occupant defending his dwelling). Another instance frequently involving the law enforcement officer is when an intended victim resists force in a robbery.

The category of *defense of others* is recognized in criminal courts under certain conditions but only insofar as the defendant exerted a degree of force that he might have exerted in defense of himself. The similarity between this category of defense and the previously discussed "mistake of fact" defense is noteworthy.

The most common form of justification to which law enforcement agencies might be exposed is the category *self-defense*. This particular defense is based on the legal maxim that "one is privileged to use whatever force is reasonably necessary to prevent a physical invasion of his person by another where he knows or has reason to believe that such invasion is imminent." The degree of force legally available when defending oneself is restricted by the degree of force that is "imminent." One cannot kill in self-defense unless it is reasonable to assume one is about to be killed. The law customarily imposes a "duty to retreat," which, in effect, requires one to make every effort to avoid the assault before acting in self-defense.

SUMMARY

Chapter 5 concerns itself with the judiciary process as it unfolds in court.

In discussing the judiciary process, the authors have analyzed the three methods by which a case is injected into court: *information, complaint,* and *grand jury.* After the arrest and booking, the defendant must appear at his arraignment. If the arraignment stems from violation of a misdemeanor statute, the court reads the complaint and informs the defendant of his rights. The same procedure is followed in felony violations. After a felony arraignment, a preliminary hearing is scheduled within a specific period of time.

At the arraignment, the magistrate may set bail *if* bail has not been established by bail schedules at the time of booking or by the warrant.

At the preliminary hearing, if it is required, the prosecution must prove that a crime exists. In other words, the prosecution must prove that a crime has been committed and that it was the result of some person's criminal activity. The preliminary hearing is *not a trial.* If a complaint is not filed, the defendant can be charged either by indictment or information.

Regardless of the procedure to which the defendant is held to answer for the crime he is alleged to have committed, the prosecuting attorney has the discretion to bargain with the defense counsel.

The right to counsel is also discussed. The authors point out that the right to counsel not only extends to the trial itself but to all critical stages in a criminal proceeding, including lineups. The right to confront witnesses is often misinterpreted by the defendant. His right to cross-examine witnesses begins at the preliminary hearing for felony cases and at trial for misdemeanor cases.

Due process is discussed. Perhaps the most significant constitutional right of the defendant today is the privilege against self-incrimination. There are two types of privileges. Unfortunately, the quest for the truth must, on occasion, take a back seat to the shelter of self-incrimination. A never-ending argument as to whether the protections against self-incrimination should be restricted will remain unanswered.

Finally, certain criminal defenses to which law enforcement agencies are frequently exposed were briefly reviewed. Among those discussed were the specific pleas of lack of capacity; mistake of fact; entrapment; coercion or duress; justification (legal definition); and double jeopardy.

In terms of causal theories of criminal law, a limited distinction was made between "purely legal defenses" and the "capacity defenses," which employ the "M'Naughton right-from-wrong rule."

NOTES

1. P. Hall et al., eds., *Cases, Comments and Questions in Modern Criminal Procedures*. American Casebook Series. (St. Paul, Minn.: West, 1969), p. 10.
2. Webster's *New International Dictionary*, 2d ed., s.v. "bail."
3. Duane Nedurd, *The Supreme Court and the Law of Criminal Investigation* (Chicago: L. E. Publishers, 1969), p. 255.
4. Richard Deming, *Man in Society: Criminal Law at Work* (New York: Dell, 1977), pp. 88, 139.
5. M. C. Bassiouni, *Criminal Law and Its Processes* (Springfield, Ill.: Thomas, 1969), p. 437.
6. The President's Commission on Law Enforcement and Administration of Justice, *The Court* (Washington, D.C.: U.S. Government Printing Office, 1967), p. 19.
7. R. G. Wright and J. A. Marlow, *The Police Officer and Criminal Justice* (New York: McGraw-Hill, 1970), p. 83.
8. H. E. Allen and C. E. Simonsen, *Corrections in America: An Introductory Text: An Introduction*, 2d ed. (Encino, Calif.: Glencoe Press, 1978), p. 85.
9. Wright and Marlow, *Police Officer and Criminal Justice*, p. 1.
10. *Administration of Criminal Justice in the United States: Plan for Survey* (Chicago: American Bar Foundation, 1955), p. 94.

11. F. E. Inbau and J. R. Thompson, *Criminal Law and Its Administration* (Mineola, N.Y.: Foundation Press, 1970), pp. 5–6.
12. W. L. Clark and W. Marshall, *A Treatise on the Law of Crimes*, 7th ed. (Mundelein, Ill.: Callaghan, 1967), p. 15.
13. H. V. Kerper, *Introduction to the Criminal Justice System* (St. Paul, Minn.: West, 1972), pp. 444–452.
14. For a thorough discussion of psychological, sociological, and physiological "justification" in the context of committing crimes, refer to: Alan R. Coffey and Edward Eldefonso, *Process and Impact of Justice* (Encino, Calif.: Glencoe Press, 1975), chap. 2; A. R. Coffey, E. Eldefonso, and W. Hartinger, *An Introduction to the Criminal Justice System and Process* (Englewood Cliffs, N.J.: Prentice-Hall, 1974), chaps. 6, 9; E. Eldefonso, *Youth Problems in Law Enforcement* (Englewood Cliffs, N.J.: Prentice-Hall, 1972), chap. 3; E. Eldefonso and A. R. Coffey, *Process of Impact of the Juvenile Justice System* (Encino, Calif.: Glencoe Press, 1976), chap. 6; E. Eldefonso, A. R. Coffey, and R. C. Grace, *Principles of Law Enforcement* (New York: Wiley, 1974), chap. 5; E. Eldefonso and W. Hartinger, *Control, Treatment and Rehabilitation of Juvenile Offenders* (Encino, Calif.: Glencoe Press, 1976), chap. 4; and W. Hartinger, E. Eldefonso, and A. R. Coffey, *Corrections: A Component of the Criminal Justice System* (Pacific Palisades, Calif.: Goodyear, 1973), chap. 8.

PRACTICAL EXERCISES

1. When does the accused have a right to counsel?
2. Explain the difference between violation of the defendant's right to counsel at a lineup and a violation of the due process clause of the Fourteenth Amendment at a lineup.
3. Contrast the criminal defenses of mistake of fact and entrapment. Contrast coercion and justification.
4. What is the difference between filing information and grand jury indictment?
5. What entails an arraignment?
6. What entails a preliminary examination?

ANNOTATED REFERENCES

Bonsignore, John J.; Katsh, Ethan; d'Errico, Peter; Pipkin, Ronald; and Arons, Stephen, *Before the Law: An Introduction to the Legal Process*. Boston: Houghton Mifflin, 1974. Contains contemporary and classic cases and readings that provide students with background and current information on a range of important areas: legal theory, penology, police science, and social problems in law.

Grilliot, Harold J. *Introduction to Law and the Legal System*. Boston: Houghton Mifflin, 1975. Through a balance of theory and case material, Grilliot covers fundamental areas of the law and the judicial system—particularly criminal law.

Hermann, Robert; Single, Eric; and Boston, John, *Counsel for the*

Poor. Lexington, Me.: Lexington Books, 1977. This book examines the extent and quality of legal defense provided to criminal defendants who are too poor to afford counsel fees.

Kratcoski, Peter C., and Walker, Donald B. *Criminal Justice in America: Process and Issues.* Glenview, Ill.: Scott, Foresman, 1978. An in-depth coverage of the American criminal justice process as well as of critical issues facing the administration of justice in our society. In addition to chapters on juvenile justice, legislation of criminal law, and future trends in criminal justice, there are chapters that cover material discussed in Chapter 5 of this book. This is one of the most complete introductions to the field of criminal justice. See also Steven Schlesinger, *Exclusionary Injustice: The Problem of Illegally Obtained Evidence* (New York: Marcel Dekker, 1977); Lloyd L. Weinreb, *Denial of Justice* (New York: Free Press, 1977); Alan R. Coffey and Edward Eldefonso, *Process and Impact of Justice* (Encino, Calif.: Glencoe Press, 1975).

Sowle, C. R., ed. *Police Power and Individual Freedom.* Springfield, Ill.: Thomas, 1972. A discussion of the title subject with emphasis on the potential impact of authority.

PART TWO

THE LAW OF CRIME

Basic in [the] theory of justice is the principle that there
can be no punishment for harmful conduct unless it was so
provided by some law in existence at the time: *nulla poena sine
lege*—no punishment without a law for it.

R. M. Perkins,
Criminal Law

Part two will serve as an introduction to a more detailed exploration of *crimes* and of what constitutes a crime. As noted elsewhere throughout this volume, the various states and other jurisdictions have literally thousands of criminal statutes, most of which define one aspect of the word *crime*. To grasp the significance of the problem of defining crime, one need only consider that an act that is "serious" or "felonious" crime in one jurisdiction may be merely "minor" or "misdemeanant" crime in another jurisdiction. Indeed, crime in some jurisdictions is not crime at all in others.

Added to this complexity is the question of whether *all* law violation is "actually" crime. Even law violation with clear *intent*, as discussed in earlier chapters, may not "be" crime. Consider, for example, that if one were to define every law violation as crime, virtually every American adult, in all probability, would be a "criminal." Inclusion of the concept of *intent* would scarcely reduce the vast majority of "criminals" in the American population.

The tens of thousands of laws, codes, and ordinances continuously passed by legislative bodies in towns, cities, counties, and states form a maze through which the uninformed cannot pass without violation. Add to this the complexity of federal law, and military law, and it becomes reasonable to assume that every adult violates some form of statute.

INTENT

In order to narrow an otherwise insurmountable complexity, discussion of *crimes* will depend heavily on the concept of *intent* as presented earlier in this volume. Because of the *mens rea* basis of crime definitions in this country, the use of the concept of intent is the *only* conceivable manner in which discussion of crime in the United States can be meaningful.

As already noted, intent can be held apart from "awareness"—the individual's intent to do something illegal remains important even if what he or she intended was not understood as "illegal." It can then be said that all crimes are law violations, but not all law violations are crimes.

Another crucial variable in examining what constitutes "crime" is the variable of *public tolerance*.

Tolerance

It could be argued that the very reason that so much variation exists in law between jurisdictions has to do with the vast differences in what can be "tolerated." Horse stealing, for example, may be totally "intolerable" in a rural western jurisdiction where horses are the basis of livelihood. Conversely, horse stealing may be more or less of a "joke" in some metropolitan urban centers of the east, where horses are rare and considered a luxury. Moreover, the probable consequences of stealing a horse in an area where horses are generally a luxury are likely to be far less severe than stealing a horse in an area where horses are a key part of the economy—the penalty also becoming a matter of tolerance.

In spite of the strength of the argument that there is variation in what can be tolerated by various jurisdictions, there are certain activities that are universally illegal and generally not tolerated. The purpose of the remaining chapters is to explore these intolerable crimes, while at the same time acknowledging that there are many other violations of laws that are "crime" only in certain areas where the activity cannot be tolerated.[1] The remaining chapters will address those violations of statutory laws that, when accompanied by intent, constitute criminal acts regardless of the jurisdiction. These "universal" crimes, rooted mostly in old common law, will be divided for discussion into two parts: crimes against the person and crimes against property.

The distinction between crimes against the person and crimes against property is a fundamental distinction. The distinction is fundamental because society, in any form, must—if the society is to survive—provide *personal* safety to members who follow the societal rules. When a society is "free"—that is, when a society permits "freedom"—individuals are usually permitted to acquire property. Society has an obligation, again on the basis of survival, to afford some protection to this property acquired as well as to the individual acquiring it—at least insofar as

[1] For a more elaborate discussion of public tolerance, see, for example, A. R. Coffey, *The Prevention of Crime and Delinquency* (Englewood Cliffs, N.J.: Prentice-Hall, 1976), chaps. 1–3.

the individual follows the societal rules. From this frame of reference, the crimes that can be perpetrated within the society can be either against the person or individual or against the property he or she has been permitted to acquire—or both, as, for instance, when a person is murdered for his or her property.

Because punishment varies so widely between jurisdictions, even for the same offense, penalties will here be considered only in terms of earlier discussions of felony and misdemeanor.[2]

2 For a technically detailed discussion of the legal ramifications of varied punishments for offenses, see, for example, M. C. Bassiouni, *Substantive Criminal Law* (Springfield, Ill.: Thomas, 1978).

Chapter 6

CRIMES AGAINST THE PERSON

LEARNING OBJECTIVES

The learning objectives of this chapter are:
1. To achieve a complete understanding of the difficulties posed by variations between various state jurisdictions in defining crime.
2. To understand the problems posed for law enforcement by these variations in crime definitions.
3. To recognize the contradiction that is inherent in law enforcement being expected to enforce some sex laws while ignoring other sex laws.
4. To understand why assault can occur without physical injury.

The main categories of crime against the person, in order of severity, are murder (most severe), assault, kidnapping, sex crimes, and slander (least severe) (see Figure 6.1).

Of the various offenses against the person, murder is by far the most universally rejected crime, the most intolerable in virtually all jurisdictions. Murder, then, will be the first crime considered. Since in order to understand the crime of murder, it is necessary to have an overview of homicide, which is the killing of one human being by another—in some cases not criminal and in some cases criminal—we will begin with a discussion of homicide (see Figure 6.2).

HOMICIDE

A *homicide* occurs whenever a human being kills another. This simple definition serves as a starting point for determining which homicides the law will punish as criminal.

As another matter of definition, for our purposes here, it can be said that all murders are homicides but not all homicides are murders, murders being *homicides with malice aforethought*.[1]

All murders are criminal; some homicides that are not murders are criminal and some are not criminal—they are innocent, or justifiable, homicides.

Consider, for example, suicide—the taking of one's own life. Since

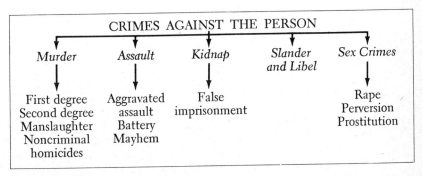

FIGURE 6.1 Crimes against the person.

DEATH OF A HUMAN BEING

I. HOMICIDE (Caused by another human being)
    Abortion
    Criminal
        Intentional
            Murder (with malice aforethought)
                First-degree (premeditated and deliberate)
                Second-degree (spontaneous)
            Voluntary manslaughter (under emotional stress, for example)
        Unintentional
            Murder, Special Case ("statutory" murder)
            Involuntary manslaughter (accident, fighting, criminal
                negligence)
    Not Criminal (Innocent, no criminal intent or guilt is involved)
        Excusable
            Defense of others
            Self-defense
        Justifiable
            Police officer killing in line of duty
            War

II. NOT HOMICIDE (Not caused by another human being)
    Accident Not Involving Another Person
    Sickness
    Suicide

FIGURE 6.2   The death of a human being.

it is not one human being taking the life of another, suicide cannot be homicide—at least by the definitions used in law. If a rabid dog should attack and kill a person, the dog does not commit homicide, since the definition is one human killing another. This definition encompasses abortion in the sense that once a fetus is sufficiently formed within the mother's womb to become a human being, the abortion is homicide—however contradictory the various explanations of an "unformed fetus" may be.

Innocent Homicide

Innocent homicide, as a matter of law, means the taking of a human life without "criminal intent."[2]

Justifiable homicide. Under certain circumstances, a police officer is obligated to use his pistol in the performance of his duties. If he kills someone in the proper scope of his responsibilities, he is not charged as a criminal, as this homicide was "justified." The officer, having no criminal intent, and discharging his lawful responsibilities, was "justified" in the homicide—therefore "innocent." Homicide is justifiable whenever it is *commanded*, or authorized by law.

Excusable homicide. Further clarification of innocent homicide emerges through consideration of "excusable homicide."[3] Excusable homicide is a concept known to most as "self-defense." Self-defense means simply that one is permitted to kill if it is necessary to defend oneself against a threat on one's life or a threat of great bodily injury. Self-defense, then, is also innocent homicide in the sense that no criminal intent or guilt can be involved.

Criminal Homicide

Criminal homicide is the taking of one human life by another human being and doing so without legal justification or excuse. *Murder* is one form of criminal homicide. To understand murder, however, it becomes necessary to recognize that murder is not the only form of criminal homicide—there is also manslaughter.

Murder can be thought of in various degrees and perhaps even types. An assassin who plans and prepares, then kills another, has committed a somewhat more severe murder than an impassioned jealous lover plotting the death of a rival. Both are presumably severe in the eyes of the law in terms of "premeditation," but they are at different levels of "cold-bloodedness." The contrast becomes clearer when the assassin is compared to an enraged jealous lover striking out in "the heat of passion" without premeditation. These are clearly different levels of criminal homicide.

The distinction between murder and other criminal homicides becomes even clearer if the two forms of criminal homicide are thought of as intentional killings and unintentional killings. Intentional killings include both murder and voluntary manslaughter, and unintentional killings are involuntary manslaughter—which could, in some technical instances, be murder. The reason for what may be a confusing overlap will become clear as unintentional killings are discussed.

Intentional killings (murder). Murder, as one of the two forms of intentional killings, can be charged as either first-degree or second-degree. First-degree murder is murder committed with premeditation and deliberation.[4] *Premeditation* refers to the state of mind of the killer—the killer entertains the idea of murder beforehand and had time to reason it out. The word *deliberation* indicates that the killer acted in a calm and reasoned manner in completing the act. When one human being premeditates and deliberately takes the life of another, and does so in a predetermined fashion, first-degree murder has occurred —an assassination is an example of this type of murder.[5]

Murder in the second degree is the kind of criminal homicide that is *intended* by the killer but without a measurable period of either premeditation or deliberation.[6] Someone having a fistfight, may for instance, decide to kill his opponent on the spur of the moment while still in full control of his faculties. The question of how "controlled" one might be of his faculties when enraged enough to kill during a fist-fight is debatable. For purposes of clarification, however, the assumption that the person was in control of his faculties at the time he decided to kill would be the basis of a charge of second-degree murder—*intent* to kill making it a murder, but absence of premeditation and deliberation distinguishing it from first-degree murder.

In some jurisdictions, there is another category of murder—called felony murder—which is similar to second-degree murder in that it is not premeditated.

Manslaughter

One of the better approaches to understanding manslaughter is to compare what the law requires as a state of mind for the killer in this case with what is required in the case of murder. When there is insufficient intent to do great bodily harm, or if there is insufficient evidence of ruthless indifference to human life, the homicide is likely to be of the manslaughter variety. Manslaughter, then, forms what the law recognizes as a category of homicide similar to second-degree murder. Manslaughter can be either "voluntary" or "involuntary."[7]

As in the case of the distinction between first- and second-degree murder, there is a difference in "severity" between voluntary manslaughter and involuntary manslaughter—voluntary manslaughter being, of course, the more severe.

Voluntary manslaughter, because of the intent to kill, or at least an intent to incur a high risk of killing, can actually be considered in the same category as second-degree murder in many respects.[8] However, as noted in the previously discussed example, when one totally loses one's temper in a fight and becomes unable to control oneself, the homicide may indeed be intentional but, because of the mitigating circumstances of the emotional stress, may not be second-degree murder —it may be voluntary manslaughter instead.

The involuntary manslaughter category encompasses homicide in which the intent to kill was not present, such as in a fist fight when a lethal blow is "accidentally" struck. The intent was to strike the victim, but not to kill him.

ASSAULT, BATTERY, AND MAYHEM

Assault

Battery is the inflicting of great bodily harm upon the individual. Before we consider battery, however, we must consider the concept of *assault*—the effort to inflict bodily harm upon another. Contrary to popular view, assault may not be a serious crime in certain instances—the assault being the *effort* to inflict injury rather than the actual inflicting of an injury.

The early common law from which much of American criminal law is drawn did not recognize that there were categories of assault. Assault was, and still is in many states, defined as an attempt—or "offer," as it is sometimes called—to inflict injury on another.[9] Rather than break these "attempts" into categories, early common-law judges tended to vary punishment in terms of the degree of seriousness of the threat—an attempted "kick in the pants" was deemed less serious than attempted blow to the head with a hammer.

The complexity of defining assaults has evolved through variations in statutes passed by various jurisdictions, as well as through the fundamental problem associated with determining what constitutes an attempt."[10]

Since assault is an "attempt" rather than the actual doing of bodily harm, defining what constitutes the attempt requires definition of what it is being attempted. As already noted, *battery*, or physical injury, is what is usually being attempted in the case of assault.

For purposes of this discussion, the assault, then, is the "attempt" to do bodily harm to another, and the *battery* is the actual doing of the harm.[11] This definition allows further clarification of the definition of "attempt."

An *attempted* crime is generally punishable as a separate offense, differing from the crime that is being attempted. As already noted earlier in this volume, the attempt itself is a crime. This, technically, is the case with assault—the attempt itself constitutes a crime. The attempt usually must be an overt act that clearly establishes the intent to commit a crime but without, for some reason, the intended crime having been committed.

Many jurisdictions have passed laws that define assault as including the *capability* to commit the battery. In other words, if there is no *ability* to batter another, the attempt to do so is no assault. An example might be useful:

EXAMPLE

Clifford confronts George with a demand that George discontinue calling on Clifford's wife. George laughs, whereupon Clifford raises his fist, threatening to strike George.

Ability—If George is sufficiently smaller than Clifford to support the contention that George was fearful of bodily harm, it could be argued that Clifford had the *ability* to commit battery, and he therefore could be *assaulting* George, *even if George ducked, causing Clifford to miss.* Clifford is guilty of assault because he had the ability to batter George.

However, if Clifford is much smaller than George, and furthermore Clifford is confined to a wheelchair, many jurisdictions would contend that Clifford did not have the *ability* to batter George, and therefore his threat to strike him was not an assault.

This somewhat oversimplified example could be misleading if emphasis is not placed on the general requirement that numerous elements are always involved in the simplest assault case—the case of assault, even when there is no actual battery, requires not only an overt act but an *intent* as well.

Recalling earlier discussions of *mens rea* (the state of mind during an act), the crime of assault is complicated further in many jurisdictions by consideration of the victim's state of mind as well. In other words, many jurisdictions require that the victim "feel threatened" and furthermore have reason to feel threatened. In the example just given, George's fear or lack of fear would be, in these jurisdictions, yet another factor in even "simple" assault.

As a practical matter, police usually find prosecutors far more successful with the crime defined as "assault and battery" than with "simple assault."

Assault and Battery

This crime, as defined, is superfluous in one sense: the battery could not be a crime without the assault, nor could the assault be a crime without the intended battery—therefore, the assault could be assumed once injury was inflicted. Nevertheless, this redundant joining of a second term to battery does point up the variations in assault statutes and further simplify the determination of whether or not a crime has been committed. In this regard, some jurisdictions have attempted to clarify assault even further with the category of "aggravated assault."

Aggravated Assault

In jurisdictions that legislate against the crime of "aggravated assault," the crime is generally a felony and defined as the most serious category of assaults—*aggravated* meaning a particularly vicious battery, or assault that is in some way related to another felony. California, for example, has two aggravated-assault laws dealing specifically with prisoners who commit aggravated assaults while under sentence in prison (Section 4500 and 4501 of the California Penal Code), and has an additional five laws defining felonious assaults in relation to other crimes:

Administering poison (CPC 216)
Assault with intent to commit murder (CPC 217)
Assault with intent to commit rape, robbery, etc. (CPC 220)
Assault with intent to commit any felony (CPC 221)
Administering stupefying drugs (CPC 222)

When taken in the extreme, the aggravated, felonious assault and battery can be so severe that it becomes yet another category of crimes against the person—mayhem.

Mayhem

Mayhem laws in most jurisdictions are along the same lines as assault and battery laws, but with the added requirement that the injury to the victim be permanent in nature. In contrast with assault, which is often a misdemeanor, most mayhem is felony.

As a practical matter, evidence that a *permanent* injury was *intended* is very difficult to prove even in cases where a malicious intent to injure is evident. Mayhem has lost some of the historical common-law significance it once had, since early common law based mayhem on an intent to deprive the victim of the physical ability to defend himself.[12]

KIDNAPPING

In many ways, the *felonious* crime of *kidnapping* is the most sensational of all the crimes against the person—in the sense that kidnapping often achieves a wider range of publicity than the other crimes against the person. This sensational facet of kidnapping is not clearly rooted in history, because whereas ancient Jewish law, for example, held that kidnapping was a capital offense, the old common law from which much of American criminal law is drawn conceived of kidnapping as nothing more than a misdemeanor—and not a particularly serious misdemeanor at that.

The common-law definition of kidnapping is "the forcible abduction of a person"—in early times for the purpose of sending the person into another country.[13] Contemporary law has dropped the concern with being forced to another country and replaced it with concern for being abducted for ransom and reward.[14]

The federal law known as the Federal Kidnapping Act[15] was amended in 1934 in a way that tends to allow motives other than ransom and reward—a broader definition of kidnapping that influences many statutes in many jurisdictions. The infamous Lindbergh-Hauptmann kidnap case, leading as it did to the high national interest in the crime of kidnapping, may have had far more influence on this crime than can be measured—both in legislative act and in national concern.[16] But in any event, it has become generally true that only the "forcible abduction" segment of early common-law kidnapping remains, other concepts totally replacing the requirement that abduction be for the relatively "minor purpose" of forcing someone into another country.

In many jurisdictions, kidnapping has evolved to a point of integration with the crime of false imprisonment.

False Imprisonment

False imprisonment is a *felonious* crime that means just what the term implies: illegally depriving someone of her freedom of movement —obviously related to kidnapping.

False imprisonment generally includes assault or assumes that it has occurred. To falsely imprison someone, she must be unwilling to be imprisoned—thus the assault. Needless to add, the victim who is actually battered in order to force the "false imprisonment" makes a clearer case than the more subtle forms of intimidation, but in any case, the loss of freedom is the basis of this serious crime against the person.[17]

If effort is made to establish some sort of common threads that link the crime of kidnapping with the crime of false imprisonment in jurisdictions where the crimes are integrated, terms such as *unlawful detention* and *abduction by force* serve the purpose very well.[18] As a practical police matter, the effort to relate false imprisonment to kidnapping is probably unnecessary in that penalties and degrees of required evidence are similar enough that the prosecutor's preference can be the total basis of the charge—as it is in many cases.

SLANDER AND LIBEL

Although law enforcement professionals have little to do with enforcement of laws on slander and libel, it is worth note that, at least in jurisdictions that define slanderous or libelous acts as crimes, these crimes are against persons.

Both slander and libel are forms of defamation—the maligning of the reputation of another. The two terms differ in that *libel* is a *written* form of such defamation, and *slander* is the *spoken* form, both presumably exposing the victim to ridicule or other painful consequences.

Although of little practical value to law enforcement, the legalistic pros and cons of slander and libel are interesting in that they relate to two variables rather than just one—the two variables being whether the accusations are true and whether the accusations actually defame. Both variables are conceptually related to the other crimes against the person.

SEXUAL CRIMES AGAINST THE PERSON

Obviously, rape with force is a crime against the person, but not all "sex crimes" are "against" the person—prostitution, adultery, and certain "crimes against nature" are sex crimes but not against the person. For the sake of simplicity, these sexual crimes that are not against the person will be included in this section.

Rape

The classic definition of rape is obtaining carnal knowledge of a female without her consent. *Consent* is defined in several ways, creating several categories of rape. *Carnal knowledge* is the attempt to have sexual intercourse with a female to the point of the slightest penetration of her vagina by the penis with or without sperm ejaculation.[19]

The various categories of rape created by the definition of *consent* have to do with the female's legal ability to consent. All other things being equal, an adult female *can* consent to sexual intercourse, which means that her refusal to do so becomes the key element in an "ordinary" rape case. Conversely, the laws of most jurisdictions specify that a female juvenile cannot legally consent to sexual intercourse, and the question of consent becomes instead a matter of age—the term *statutory rape* is the most common term for this crime. In other words, a female juvenile can personally agree to have intercourse, but the law does not recognize her ability to consent; therefore, a male having intercourse with her did so "without her consent."

Also statutory in nature is rape based upon the female being unable to give consent by virtue of some mental defect, or some form of intoxication. Technically, a man can be charged with rape if he induces intoxication in the female prior to her "consent" or, in many jurisdictions, if she is feebleminded or in other ways incapacitated mentally.

Further clarity of the variations in consent can be gained by considering the female's *resistance*. While it is not necessary for the female to resist in order to have a rape case, in cases where resistance has occurred, the rape is far easier to prove. Resistance, in and of itself, does not constitute the basis of rape: The Model Penal Code (*MPC: An Invitation to Law Reform*, 49 ABAJ 452 [1963] Swartz) expresses explicit what most jurisdictions practice—that a *wife*, even a common-law wife, has not been raped even if she violently resists the sexual intercourse forced upon her by her husband while she is resisting. Her recourse is in the civil divorce courts and not in the criminal courts. The technical point in relation to resistance here is that the husband is presumed to have already the carnal knowledge and had, therefore, not "taken it."[20] Confusion between jurisdictions on a comparative basis emerges when this same point is applied to a rapist raping a victim a second time. By and large, however, when a female resists sexual intercourse, a case of rape can be considered.

Statutory rape waives the requirement that the female resist. The absence of resistance, however, is not *consent* in "statutory" cases or, for that matter, in other cases where it can be shown that the woman was so intimidated that resistance would be unrealistic. In cases of forcible rape,[21] resistance should be present or evidence of grave intimidation substituted. In cases of statutory rape, concern with resistance is usually irrelevant.

To have a case of forcible rape, the force need not have been actually applied; even if it is merely threatened it is considered to be present. The victim need only have reasonable certainty that she is in danger of bodily harm or some other intimidating circumstances if she fails to comply with the demands for intercourse.

As a practical police matter, the bulk of courtroom defense of rape defendants directly or indirectly focuses on the female's "willingness," which, in turn, increases the need for evidence of intimidation. In other words, when physical resistance has not occurred, evidence of intimidation becomes more important.

Child Molesting

In the crime of child molesting—attempting to gain or gaining sexual gratification using small children—statutes vary widely in their definitions of both the crime and the punishment, but laws generally have in common the recognition that a child clearly cannot consent.

In cases of child molesting, most jurisdictions hold that when force has been used, rather than persuasion, it constitutes a more serious felony, even when sexual gratifications other than intercourse are involved.

Incest

Sexual intercourse with close blood relatives is both a social taboo and legislatively forbidden. The laws defining incest as crime differ radically between jurisdictions, both in definition and in penalty. The consent concept of rape is irrelevant to the crime of incest in the majority of jurisdictions—the crime can exist even with the consent of both parties.

Seduction

One of the sexual crimes against the person that does clearly incorporate the *consent* concept of rape is seduction—usually meaning the persuasion of a woman to surrender her chastity by promise of marriage or some similar inducement.[22] The vastly different statutes among jurisdictions usually have in common "chastity" as a requisite to the offense, and the fact that the female consents is offset by her belief that she could marry the offender. In other words, the statutes usually imply that her consent was not valid in that she was tricked. Obviously, seduction is not a crime under these circumstances if the chastity had been surrendered prior to the "seduction," or if the female knew, for example, the offender was married at the time the inducement was offered.

Sex Perversion Laws

The rapidly changing concepts associated with "consenting adults" have increased the variations in law between jurisdictions to the point that little can be said of universal importance on enforcement of law dealing with perversion.[23] Nevertheless, most jurisdictions retain some statutes that are usually called such things as *crimes against nature* or *perversion*—sexual acts identified as sexually perverse in the statute even though the statute is usually unenforcible.[24] The only way these laws could possibly be enforced as a practical matter would be the total elimination of personal freedom and privacy. Nevertheless, many sexual practices, considered by many people to be common, are defined as crime in most jurisdictions.

Sodomy. Sexual intercourse via the anus or intercourse with animals is defined as crime in many jurisdictions. Common law held sodomy, or "buggery," a felony whether the sex partner was a man or a woman. Jurisdictions with sodomy laws usually permit prosecution of both partners rather than declaring either of the partners to be a victim— the basis of the significance of many of the "consenting adult" statutes being considered in many jurisdictions which would remove the basis for prosecution entirely. As a practical police matter, the increased reporting of rape also includes an increase in reports of sodomy as an additional crime forced upon the victim, in some cases the anal intercourse being the primary crime. Furthermore, male homosexual rape, or forcible anal intercourse, between males, has become increasingly prevalent in penal institutions.

Oral Copulation. Most jurisdictions retain statutes that declare fellatio and cunnilingus as crimes—many times even felonies. *Fellatio* is the stimulation of the male genitalia by the mouth and *cunnilingus* is the stimulation of the female genitalia by the mouth. Many of the laws written on these two subjects are written without regard to the marital status of the defined offender, which technically makes a married person liable for prosecution for oral copulation with his or her spouse. In some jurisdictions, the more passive spouse could also be prosecuted for allowing it. As a practical police matter, this practice, like sodomy, is increasingly reported as part of a rape or as the primary act in a rape. Many jurisdictions indicate that women are increasingly including in rape reports complaints of being forced to orally copulate the rapist—in many cases, the oral copulation being the entire "rape." The legislative structure of most jurisdictions permits the prosecution to utilize a broader definition of carnal knowledge in such cases.

OTHER SEXUAL CRIMES

In a chapter addressed to the subject of crimes against the person, many of the sex crimes carried as law by most jurisdictions are difficult to integrate. Nevertheless, some of them constitute major law enforcement problems and deserve consideration in the context of sexual crime.

Solicitation and Prostitution

Not all jurisdictions hold that prostitution is a crime. Prostitution is usually defined as a female engaging in activities of sexual gratification for hire—the "hire" segment of the definition usually amounting to any form of "reward" that is explicitly in return for the sexual service provided.

From a law enforcement perspective, it is worth note that even those jurisdictions that permit prostitution as a lawful activity tend to regulate the sexual practices in terms of both location and public health.

The vast majority of jurisdictions retain statutes that ascribe at least misdemeanor status not only to the actual prostitution, or "soliciting for sexual activity," but for the pimping, or pandering, segment as well when they are involved.

Pimping is the "soliciting" of customers for a prostitute by a third party, and when it is done by the prostitute herself, and *pandering* is the procurement of a place for the prostitute to work.

As a practical police matter, it is worth note that in most jurisdictions organized crime takes over both the pimping and the pandering functions of organized prostitution.

The historical Mann Act, known to many as the "White Slave Act," elevated prostitution to federal status from its status as a local problem. It is safe to say that local police jurisdictions still bear the brunt of enforcement responsibility even though the federal statute exists.

In jurisdictions, that hold the seeking of a prostitute to be in violation of the law, successful enforcement is often achieved through policewomen arresting men for offering to pay for sexual services. Some prosecutors point out that juries are reluctant to convict the "offender" in these cases, often assuming he was "entrapped," even when the enforcement occurred totally within local legal restrictions. Veteran police and prosecutors generally agree that the chances of successful prosecution are usually greater when a prostitute either openly solicits an arresting officer or when prostitutes are arrested in a whorehouse.

Other difficult cases often include call girls and male prostitutes hired by females.

Males hired by homosexual males are usually dealt with in terms of the local jurisdiction's approach to laws on homosexuality.

Homosexuality

The nationally publicized gay liberation movement, accompanied by "consenting adult" laws, has obscured law enforcement responsibility for enforcing homosexual laws where they exist.

Where enforcement is practiced, laws dealing with "vagrancy" or similar laws are often associated with the enforcement effort. Contradictions abound in areas where homosexuals are charged as misdemeanants though all homosexual acts in a particular jurisdiction may be defined as felonies. In some jurisdictions there is a "reverse double standard": lesbian activity is totally overlooked while antihomosexual laws against males are vigorously enforced.

Many veteran vice officers contend that law enforcement will gradually evolve to the point of being responsible for nothing more than ensuring that homosexual practices do not occur in public—and perhaps ensuring that homosexuals do not molest minor children. Those holding this view point to a time in which enforcement of laws on homosexuality will be essentially no different than enforcement of laws on heterosexual behavior.

Indecent Exposure

Communities that define nude beaches as lawful often contend that the crime of indecent exposure has not been mitigated because the core of indecent exposure law is the shocking of the public's sense of decency—the public's sense of decency on a beach reserved for nudity is presumably not shocked.

This is important to police in that the "public" invariably calls the police for aid when a "flasher" exhibits his genitalia in public—the complaint itself establishing the evidence of "shock." An interesting point would occur if a flasher exhibited himself on a nude beach— conceivably the public, even if the public itself were nude, could be shocked by the exhibition.

Though a nonserious misdemeanor in the overwhelming majority of jurisdictions, indecent exposure remains a law enforcement problem for police.

Obscenity

One need merely hear a group of criminal-court judges from any jurisdiction, or any combination of jurisdictions, trying to discuss obscenity to conclude that there is no consistent basis for even defining obscenity, let alone enforcing obscenity law consistently.

As a local matter, however, there can be consistent law enforcement in this area.

As a practical police matter, *local* obscenity laws when *definitive* are continually gaining support from the general public and court trends as well, even when local law is vastly divergent from law elsewhere. From the police perspective, this tends to diminish the demand on local police to be knowledgeable on the "general body of the law" related to obscenity.

The complexity customarily emerges when obscenity is associated with the theater or some publication or other form of pornographic media. More often than not, such crime as obscene phone calls can be enforced on a different statutory basis, found in either explicit local legislation or some combination of law violations dealing with obscenity and with communication in general.

Adultery and Fornication

Even though enforcement is practically nonexistent, most jurisdictions retain laws against adultery and even fornication—adultery being the crime of sex relations of a married person with someone other than the spouse, and fornication usually the crime of an unmarried person engaging in sexual intercourse.

Cohabitation

It would be difficult to locate an enforcement program seeking to prevent the crime of cohabitation—even in jurisdictions having relatively recent laws on this subject. Why the low profile on enforcement of laws against unmarried males and females living together?

Were law enforcement as a profession ever to achieve the ideal status of having only laws that *must* be enforced, then presumably law enforcement as a profession could enforce *all* the laws. In the meantime, such laws as these remain a part of the many laws police neither have the manpower nor the priority to enforce.

In many ways, declaring adultery, fornication, and cohabitation crimes that are *not* prosecuted weakens the general police effort to enforce other laws, since many people hold consistency as the primary basis for their respect for law enforcement in general.

SUMMARY

This chapter forms the transition point in this volume from the general concepts of criminal law to the specific crimes of criminal law.

Emphasis was placed on the vast difference between jurisdictions in terms of varying definitions of crime. The "common crimes" defined by all jurisdictions were presented in terms of the taking of human life, or homicide, in a variety of contexts. Within the broad distinction between property crime and crimes against the person, homicide was considered both in terms of innocent or justifiable homicide and in terms of criminal homicide, including the various categories of murder and manslaughter.

Other crimes against persons were discussed—assault, battery, and mayhem, along with the categories of kidnapping and false imprisonment. Sexual crimes presented included rape and the variety of activities defined as sexual crime in most jurisdictions.

NOTES

1. For law implications, see American Law Reports, 22 ALR, 2d, 846.
2. For law implications, see American Law Reports, 100 ALR, 2d, 761.
3. For law implications, see American Law Reports, 89 ALR, 2d, 392.
4. For law implications, see American Law Reports, 71 ALR, 2d, 1017.
5. For law implications, see American Law Reports, 12 ALR, 2d, 854, and 46 ALR, 895.
6. For law implications, see American Law Reports, 96 ALR, 2d, 1422.
7. For law implications, see American Law Reports, 86 ALR, 2d, 892.
8. For law implications, see American Law Reports, 12 ALR, 658.
9. For law implications, see American Law Reports, 79 ALR, 2d, 1415.
10. For law implications, see American Law Reports, 79 ALR, 2d, 597.
11. For law implications, see American Law Reports, 79 ALR, 2d, 587.
12. For law implications, see American Law Reports, 16 ALR, 2d, 949.
13. For law implications, see American Law Reports, 17 ALR, 2d, 993.
14. For law implications, see American Law Reports, 95 ALR, 2d, 441.
15. Found in Sections 1201 and 1202 of Chapter 55, of Title 18, United States Code.
16. For a more elaborate discussion of the Lindbergh kidnaping, see F. Inbau and J. Thompson, *Criminal Law and Its Administration*, 2d ed. (Mineola, N.Y.: Foundation Press, 1970), pp. 207–209.

17. Three Blackstone Commentaries 127; 2 Coke, Institutes, 589; *People* v. *Wheeler*, 73 Cal. 252, 14 p. 796; *State* v. *Lunsford*, 81 UC 528.
18. See for example, W. L. Clark and W. Marshall, A *Treatise on the Law of Crimes*, 7th ed., M. Q. Barnes, revising editor, (Mundelein, Ill.: Callaghan, 1967), pp. 745–746.
19. For law implications, see American Law Reports, 70 ALR, 2d, 814.
20. For law implications, see American Law Reports, 18 ALR, 1063.
21. For law implications, see American Law Reports, 8 ALR, 2d, 996.
22. For law implications, see American Law Reports, 91 ALR, 2d, 592.
23. A vast sociological, psychological, counseling, and psychiatric literature has evolved that suggests that sex activities defined as crime are practiced on a far wider basis than legislation would indicate. For a fine example of literature to this point, written in the context of criminal law, see, for example, Inbau and Thompson, *Criminal Law and Its Administration*, pp. 269–281.
24. See, for example, S. Slovenko and P. Phillips, "Psychosexuality and the Criminal Law," 15 *Vanderbilt Law Review* 3 (1962): 799.

PRACTICAL EXERCISES

1. Sketch a "flow chart" of activities involving an offender, law enforcement, prosecution, defense, and the courts for a crime against the person. Show either victim or evidence, or both.
2. Using the state penal code, summarize sections on any three crimes against the person.

ANNOTATED REFERENCES

Bassiouni, M. C. *Substantive Criminal Law*. Springfield, Ill.: Thomas, 1978. This volume provides the technically oriented reader with a comprehensive method to utilize what was introduced in this chapter as the ALR (American Law Reports), available in law libraries.

Clark, W. L., and Marshall, W. *A Treatise on the Law of Crimes*. 7th ed., M. Q. Barnes, revising editor. (Mundelein, Ill.: Callaghan, 1967). This volume is an outstanding "original source" treatise, drawing directly upon many base sources collected in broad form by the ALR (American Law Reports).

Coffey, A. R. *The Prevention of Crime and Delinquency*. Englewood Cliffs, N.J.: Prentice-Hall, 1976. This volume elaborates in depth the concept noted in this chapter having to do with public tolerance of certain law violation.

Inbau, F. E., and Thompson, J. R. *Criminal Law and Its Administration*. Mineola, N.Y.: Foundation Press, 1970. This technically analytic work affords in-depth detail for the content of this chapter.

Chapter 7

ROBBERY

LEARNING OBJECTIVES

The learning objectives of this chapter are:
1. To achieve an understanding of the basis for considering similarities between the victim's *resistance* in rape and in robbery.
2. To recognize that robbery is a combination of crimes.
3. To become aware of the fact that violence or the threat of violence preceding the crime of larceny becomes the basis for the crime of robbery.
4. To be cognizant of the relationship between property ownership and the crime of robbery.

THE PENAL CODES IN MANY STATES identify the crime of *robbery* as a crime against the person. This is not surprising, because in more than one sense robbery can be discussed either (1) in terms of the violence or the threatened violence against the person or (2) in terms of the property that the robber is seeking to steal. From a historical perspective, robbery is a crime against property because in common law it was simply larceny in which the theft occurred by the use of violence or the fear of violence.[1]

While this chapter will discuss robbery as one of the several crimes against property (see Figure 7.1), it is worth note that robbery includes *assault* as discussed in the preceding chapter as a crime against the person: robbery includes either a threat of violence or actual violence, both against the person.

While it is not critical to either the discussion of robbery or the enforcement of robbery laws to insist that the crime be classified either as a crime against the person or a crime against property, it should be recalled that the essential core of the crime of robbery is *property*, the stealing of property. For that reason, initial attention in the discussion of robbery in this chapter will be directed toward property and property ownership. However, attention will also be directed toward the assault segment of robbery, because the crime of robbery is both larceny and assault. This can be likened to what was was discussed earlier as assault and battery. The assault in the crime identified as assault and battery is the threat of injury. Robbery, in a somewhat similar vein, includes assault as a threat to injure the person, but rather than for the sake of injury, the threat is for the purpose of stealing the victim's property, the "battery" presumably forthcoming only if the property is not delivered (the frequency of victims being battered after delivering the property notwithstanding).

Of course, many victims are "battered into" surrendering their property to robbers, and the battery emerges as the most salient feature of the crime in such cases. Nevertheless, *property* is the salient focus of robbery.

From the frame of reference of robbery as essentially a crime against property, a definition of robbery must necessarily include reference to property, as virtually all statutory robbery law does.[2] Later in this chapter, one state's robbery law will be quoted for the purpose of providing

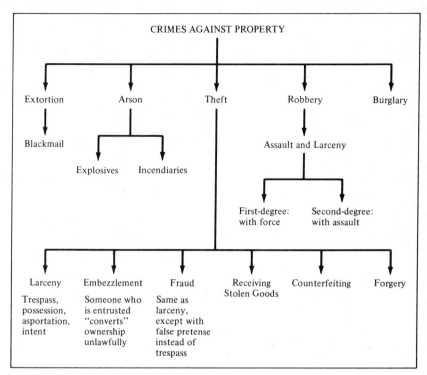

FIGURE 7.1   Crimes against property.

an example of how the language of robbery law combines the crime of assault and larceny. For purposes of the present discussion, *robbery* can be defined as *a felony made up of the act and the intent of taking the property of another by the threat of violence or the use of violence.*

Since robbery is one of those crimes that actually embodies more than one crime, understanding the crime of robbery requires consideration of both criminal segments. The crime of assault, already discussed in the preceding chapter, will be elaborated in the context of robbery later in this chapter. The crime of larceny will be discussed later in this volume in detail as a specific crime. For purposes of clarifying robbery, however, it is necessary to clarify the crime of larceny sufficiently to permit consideration of larceny in relation to assault as a basis of robbery (see Figure 7.2).

LARCENY AS IT RELATES TO ROBBERY

Larceny can be defined as the crime of taking the property of another and carrying the property away—*carrying* being a term held over from

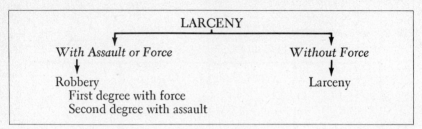

FIGURE 7.2   Larceny.

old common law. In terms of its relationship to robbery, larceny can be broken down into three legalistic parts:

1. a victim's property as the thing "taken away"
2. the actual "taking away" of the property—known legalistically as "trespass and asportation"
3. an intent to deprive the victim of the taken property—fraudulently and *permanently*

If we think of robbery as larceny, as defined above, combined with assault, it becomes apparent that these same three larceny factors are crucial to the understanding of robbery. In other words, the relevance of each one of these factors in larceny is as significant to robbery as it is to the crime of larceny, as will be discussed later in this volume. Each factor, then, is worthy of consideraiton. Let us examine each of these elements of larceny as they relate to robbery—first property, then the "taking away," and, finally, the intent, or the "fraudulent intent."

Property

In law, there is a requirement that some legal basis for ownership exist before the crime of larceny, and therefore the crime of robbery, can exist. In other words, there can be no larceny or there can be no robbery if the property taken was not owned by the victim in terms recognized by law. Court decisions tend to hold that property that has been abandoned and not reclaimed and property that has been wrecked and not immediately recovered are outside the sphere of ownership as defined for larceny and robbery.[3] In other words, ownership can exist but can be eliminated by loss or wrecking, the main point here being that a victim has to be a "legal owner" of property taken or there can be neither larceny nor robbery.

In most cases, however, the ordinary definition of ownership can be applied to property for purposes of determining if a robbery has occurred. Put another way, if the entitlement to property as understood by the "common man" applies, it is probable that this much of the crime of larceny or robbery has been satisfied. It is worth note that this "ordinary definition of ownership" can, and does, come under strain when property has more than one owner. This problem is not uncommon and is therefore worth consideration. Consider, for example, the property owned by both husband and wife.

EXAMPLE

Husband Harry purchases a fine new sports car. Wife Wilma asks for the privilege of driving it but is told by Harry to "get lost." Harry carries the ignition keys on his person at all times to enforce his rule against Wilma driving the new car.

In desperation, Wilma removes the huge Buffalo gun from the mantel, loads it, and threatens to blow Harry's head off if he fails to hand over the keys.

Now, since the keys *are* property, and the wife "takes and carries away" this property through the threat of violence, and the wife furthermore *intends* both to do bodily harm to husband Harry and to take the property, is there here a robbery? There can be no robbery in this instance because both husband and wife, at least in law, jointly own the keys. Some jurisdictions may allow charges to be brought against the wife for an assault with a deadly weapon, but she cannot rob him of property she already owns partially.

This concept becomes more complex from a law enforcement perspective when partnerships and mutual ownership move outside the sphere of marriage. When several people buy a boat or an airplane "together," the law holds that if any one of the partners takes the entire property from the other property owners, even if by force, there still has been no robbery. Some jurisdictions have statutes that expressly forbid any one owner from such "taking" of the total property from partners, but as a common-law or a case-law matter, mutual ownership precludes the crime of robbery, the civil courts being the remedy rather than the criminal courts, just as in the case of marriage.

In spite of this somewhat complex problem occasionally encountered by law enforcement dealing with reported robberies, property ownership, as already noted, can usually be thought of in the common everyday understanding of ownership. In other words, if the property taken in a robbery appears to police to have been owned by the victim, such ownership in most cases will be sustained by a strict legal analysis of ownership. This brings the discussion to the next factor in larceny as it relates to robbery, the "taking away" of the property from the victim.

Taking Away

Many law enforcement professions are amazed at the depth of detail into which legal scholars can take the discussion of historical common-law interpretation of the "taking away" of property. But the technical ramifications of what "truly" constitutes "taking" and "away" is far beyond the scope of practical police concern with robbery laws. For all intents and purposes, if force or threat of force is intentionally used to deprive an owner of property, that property, if owned by the victim, need only be moved slightly from its location to form the basis of robbery.

In terms of the taking away of property, there is a technical problem somewhat more difficult than the "permanence" issue that is similar to what has already been discussed as mutual ownership under property. This problem relates to the use of force to recover lent property—a situation in which there is not mutual ownership but rather an owner seeking recovery by use of force. Consider this example:

EXAMPLE

Harriet lends her sterling silver tea set to neighbor Nana. Months pass before Harriet asks Nana to return the set. Nana's response is that the set was taken in a burglary for which there was no insurance. Nana's response to Harriet's inquiry as to why Nana failed to inform Harriet of the burglary was a proposal that Harriet indulge herself in an anatomical impossibility.

More months pass and Harriet, while attending a social function in the home of one of Nana's friends, is served tea from what she believes to be her missing set.

Harriet confronts the indignant hostess with the accusation that she, the hostess, is a thief. The hostess' denials of improper ownership infuriate Harriet, who finally arms herself with a cake knife and threatens to cut off the "thieving hands" of the hostess unless the tea set is relinquished post haste.

The set is *not* Harriet's but is instead an identical set. Harriet, nevertheless, believes it is her set.

From the police perspective, this particular set of facts would unquestionably justify an arrest—all things being equal. However, whether the arrest is for robbery is possibly another matter, depending on local law and its allowance for the probability that Harriet did in fact *believe* the tea set was hers.

As a practical matter, the prosecutor and certainly the courts can take Harriet's belief into account if she is charged with robbery by the arresting officers. Her beliefs are perhaps less relevant if she is instead charged with some form of assault, as discussed in the last chapter.

A "version" of this problem of the recovery of lent property emerges in certain jurisdicitons that do not have explicit statutory regulations for repossessing financed properties such as automobiles and furniture. In most jurisdictions, however, this is statutorially regulated in such a manner that the use of force is absolutely precluded unless recognized law enforcement personnel are involved.

This does not preclude the use of force in recovering lent property. Indeed, in terms of taking away, the law permits an owner forcibly to recover lent property, all other things equal.[4] Many jurisdictions partially regulate such force, but as a matter of law an owner is permitted physically to force the return of property he has lent to another. In such cases, some states "allow" one person to do literally everything involved in robbery as long as clear proof exists that the property "taken away" is owned by the "robber."

In housewife Harriet's case, noted above, some states might exempt her from charges of any kind—assault with the cake knife and all—*if* the silver tea set she recovered was in fact her property. Of course, this would have been an extreme in any jurisdiction. A "better case" would have been Harriet "recovered" her set in Nana's home rather than the home of Nana's friend.

Careful scrutiny of local assault law usually establishes alternative charges to robbery when situations of this kind confront police.

In summary, it can be said that the taking-away segment of robbery is constituted as soon as the owner is deprived of direct control of the property—customarily meaning that when the property is moved from its location, it has been taken away.

Permanence

The final factor included in the three segments of larceny as they relate to robbery is the *intent* to fraudulently deprive the owner of property—and to do so *permanently*.[5] The question of whether or not the owner is to be deprived *permanently* can become a technical difficulty in this simplistic explanation of robbery, but in most cases the use of force or the threat of force to remove the property establishes a basis for the assumption that the removal is "permanent," insofar as the law is concerned.

In spite of the use of force establishing a "probability" that there is permanence in the "taking away," the concept of permanence is still worthy of discussion. In other words, the question of for "how long" the robber intends to deprive the victim of the property taken is worthy of discussion. Consider, for example, the prosecution of a "clear-cut robbery" in which all elements, or *nearly* all elements, are factually documented except permanence—and at the conclusion of the trial a defense successfully contending that the robber sought only to deprive the victim of his money "temporarily." The effort to develop proof of "permanence" is the problem area in this regard. In other words, just as *intent* can be the difficult part of proving crime, so also can difficulties arise in proving a victim is deprived of property permanently, unless the evidence clearly suggests that deprivation was not "temporary." Fortunately, the evidence of other crime elements usually suggests such permanence. When violence, or the threat of violence, is involved, the significance of this "permanence" diminishes—the threat of violence more often than not removes the similarity to the crime of "joyriding" a stolen car without intent to deprive the owner *permanently* of his or her property.

Or consider an automobile taken away at gunpoint. It is somewhat easier to delineate this act as robbery, even with the claim of an intent to return the property to the owner, than it would be if the same car were stolen without the owner's knowledge. In other words, while the intent to return is nebulous and subjective, the inclusion of violence or the threat of violence mitigates in the direction of permanent deprivation to the degree that police are able to develop such evidence. The claimed intent to use the car for "joyriding" is far less credible for a robber passing up the opportunity to steal a car without force or violence. Presumably, the theft of money or other property functions along these same rationales. Jurisdictional variations usually make this problem somewhat academic in the statutory emphasis on the intent to "take away" the property through use of force or the threat of force. As an example of how state laws can be structured to emphasize the taking away of property through the use of force, consider as an example, the definition of robbery used in Pennsylvania's Criminal Code: "Robbery is the felonious and forcible taking from the person of another of goods or money to any value by violence or by putting in fear, an offense is complete if there is a taking in presence of, although not from owner's person by putting in fear."[6]

The language of this statute would be difficult to bend in the direction of temporary deprivation once the property has been taken away. The main thrust of this law, and of most state laws on robbery, is to bear down on the use of violence or the threat of violence to deprive someone of property. Of course, every seasoned police officer has witnessed emphasis placed by defense attorneys in criminal courts in areas not emphasized in the law itself. Nevertheless, the permanence of the

robbery is not often a serious problem for police in terms of the statute
—the robbery itself usually remains the paramount consideration for
law enforcement.

Fraudulent Intent

When robbery is strictly interpreted as *larceny* with assault, the technical larceny requirement that the taking away be *permanent* can apply.
As already noted, the use or the threat of force mitigates the credibility
of "temporary deprivation," but it remains *conceivable* in terms of the
robber's "intent" that it is temporary in nature. Most veteran police
officers have heard a claim that property taken in a robbery would have
been returned had the robber not been apprehended. From a legalistic
point of view, successfully arguing this contention in court would
change an armed robbery into something known as "trespass and
temporary conversion." Even though the argument is unlikely in view
of the fact that the victim was assaulted, the nebulous nature of intent
as a state of mind make this area of robbery investigation as significant
as all other areas. Effort in establishing intent of permanence is always
justified from the law enforcement perspective. In other words, effort
invested in developing evidence of intent to deprive the victim of the
property *permanently* is as significant as all other areas of the robbery
investigation. Indeed, as noted throughout this volume, the *intent* of
the accused offender is crucial in all criminal law.

Having examined the relationship of larceny as a segment of robbery, attention can now be directed to the other crucial segment of
robbery—the assault, or the use or threat of force.

FORCE AND FEAR

Legal scholars refer to the kind of threatened violence often involved
in robbery as *constructive violence*—a technical term meaning violence
that places the victim in grave *fear*. Since individuals vary widely on
what makes them afraid, and how much of what makes them afraid it
takes to make them fearful, it is difficult to establish a specific point at
which someone is fearful enough to submit to the will of another on the
basis of fear. As in cases of rape, discussed in the preceding chapter,
many robbery victims might be more angry than fearful at certain levels
of threat.

The *force* either used or threatened in a robbery, as in the case of
rape, is a crucial factor but, in many ways, is more indirect than direct.
For in the crime of robbery, as in the crime of rape, the force need only
be threatened, not necessarily carried out.[7]

The property stolen in a robbery remains the central criterion in
determining the crime of robbery if for no other reason than that *fear*

emerges as an extremely nebulous concept. Nevertheless, the crime of robbery requires either violence or sufficient threat of violence to lead one to "assume" that fear was present—therefore force and fear must be considered.

Again recalling our discussion of the crime of rape, the role of fear remains analogous to the role of fear in the crime of robbery. The woman being raped need not overtly resist the rape to establish that she is fearful. Indeed, her fear presumably is the basis of her *not* resisting. So also in the crime of robbery, the failure to resist the loss of the property being stolen would be based on fear. In robbery, then, as in rape, *resistance* can be assumed once it can also be assumed that the victim was intimidated by and fearful of the offender.

The assumption that the victim is fearful becomes a legal function of examining the accused offender's capability of causing physical harm. It is worth note that the harm threatened must not only be within the offender's capability, but it must also be *physical*. In other words, the offender must be *able* to inflict physical harm, and the harm inflicted must be physical. Threatening the victim with consequences other than physical harm may be a crime such as blackmail or extortion (see Chapter 8). But if the harm threatened is not physical in nature, it cannot be robbery, just as there can be no rape unless physical harm is threatened or done.

Since the harm threatened must be physical if the crime of robbery is to be charged, some consideration should be given to the kind of physical violence that would constitute legitimate fear for the purpose of defining robbery. Clearly a loaded gun or a knife would establish a basis for assuming that the victim failed to resist out of fear.

However, the victim's fear alone is not sufficient to establish a basis for determining that the robbery occurred. A victim might be equally fearful of a threat to disclose some secret love affair as he would be of a beating with brass knuckles. But his fear of the brass knuckles would be the basis of robbery, whereas his fear of disclosure of a secret love affair would, at worst, be blackmail. In some jurisdictions, the physical harm threatened can be such things as burning down the victim's house or otherwise destroying the victim's immediate personal property. But in essence, the law requires that the force or threat of force must be physical harm in order to "convert" the crime of larceny into robbery.

Another interesting similarity between the crime of rape and the crime of robbery exists in the area of *consent*. Rape is constituted by the failure of the victim to grant legal consent, and robbery is technically constituted by the victim failing to give consent to take the property. Of course, this relates to fear in the sense that consent can be assumed in the absence of *resistance*, unless the victim is fearful of physical harm.

A somewhat more practical application of the concept of consent, or more specifically the concept of resistance, is the role that resistance plays in distinguishing between the crime of robbery and crimes such as purse snatching. A woman held up at gunpoint has been robbed, but a woman whose purse has been "snatched" from the car seat beside her has not. Consider the following:

EXAMPLE

Nadine is a street-walking prostitute. While Nadine is still dressing following the provision of sexual services, her customer, who completed dressing first, suddenly grabs Nadine's purse and flees from the hotel, leaving Nadine with neither the fee owed by the fleeing customer nor the fees paid by previous customers.

The customer cannot be charged with robbery because he neither used force on Nadine prior to the theft nor threatened Nadine with force. The question of Nadine's *resistance* is therefore not germane. But since resistance is not germane in this set of circumstances, it is clear that no robbery has occurred. The questions of resistance and consent are always relevant in cases of robbery. In purse snatching it can be assumed that the victim would have resisted if she had been permitted to resist. Indeed, in cases where force is used prior to the actual snatching of the purse, purse snatching *is* robbery.

A slight modification of the example can focus on some of the other complexities of the crime of robbery as opposed to similar crimes.

EXAMPLE

Nadine's customer has a sexual appetite for activities that include what is known as "bondage"—the practice of various sex acts while one partner is tied or handcuffed.

Unlike most professional prostitutes, Nadine has no knowledge of the hazards of this practice and permits herself to be securely tied to the bed while her customer performs various sex acts. At the conclusion of these activities, the customer announces that the previously agreed-upon fee will not be paid. Moreover, the customer announces that unless Nadine discloses the location of her money, the customer will leave Nadine tied up indefinitely without food or water. Furthermore, the customer threatens to gag Nadine during this period.

When stripped of the bizarre circumstances, this situation contains the *possibility* of the crime of robbery. The questionable areas relate to such things as Nadine's vulnerability occurring on a voluntary basis —at least originally—and her *consenting* to place herself in a position where the harm is at least partially without her resistance. This unlikely situation can be brought closer to the realm of robbery, as understood by practicing law enforcement professionals, by simply having the customer produce any type of weapon while Nadine is in her completely helpless state and having him then take away her money—the question of unpaid fee remaining of concern to no one except Nadine.

While this facetious example is by no means "typical," the functions of resistance and consent are nonetheless illustrated. To whatever degree there appears doubt that the absence of resistance is based on fear of physical harm, the case of robbery is weakened. This may be why some jurisdictions have established statutory *degrees* of robbery. Degrees of robbery are based on the principle of *severity*, as are degrees of murder. In jurisdictions that establish degrees of robbery, the first degree is usually when some form of force is actually used, and the second degree is where the victim is "merely" intimidated by the threat of force.[8] In the first-degree situation, the question of resistance and consent is resolved. The problem of resistance and consent emerge only in the second degree, only in cases where the failure to resist is alleged to be based upon fear of the consequences of resistance in terms of physical violence.

Another question relating to the force used with larceny is *when* the force was used or threatened. The law requires that the force be used or threatened prior to the larceny in order to be robbery—the force must be the reason that the victim relinquishes the stolen property. Force used after the larceny is irrelevant. In the example of the prostitute, the customer grabbing Nadine's purse and running would not have been committing robbery even had Nadine chased the customer and been beaten by him upon catching up—that would be "force" occurring *after* theft.

Having considered both the components of larceny and the use or threat of force to induce fear, we can now direct our attention to the *nature* of the force used, a critical factor both from the legalistic understanding of the crime of robbery and as a practical police matter.

To be the basis of robbery, the use or threat of force itself must be of sufficient menace to instill the fear of real danger—danger of great bodily harm, or in some areas, fear of grave injury to immediate personal property—real and genuine fear in any case. The means by which an offender can induce this fear is of considerable importance to police —a submachine gun being quite different from a pair of brass knuckles. Police procedures vary according to the type of threat. The *nature* of the force threatened is an important factor for at least two practical reasons, then—the *evidence* that fear was indeed the basis for not resisting and the assumption that consent was not present, and police procedure.

Weapons Versus Strong-Arm Tactics

Both in terms of evidence and in terms of police procedure, the armed robbery is the more dramatic case of robbery, far more dramatic than a report of a strong-arm robbery. The suspect with the submachine gun in a crowded bank poses a different robbery case both for arresting officer and for court than the neighborhood bully who goes too far by taking the wallet of a man he beats up—although both are robberies.

As a practical police matter, the armed robber, at least while in the act of an armed robbery, poses one of the highest risks in police work. Beyond the obvious hazards involved in attempting to arrest armed suspects, the risks of robberies turning into volatile hostage situations is unusually high during robberies of banks, stores, or even individuals, for that matter. The safety of both the arresting officer and the victim is in great danger when the arrest is attempted during or and immediately after an armed robbery.

Paradoxically enough, the need for adequate court-acceptable evidence does not diminish with these high-risk situations. More often than not, greater care is needed in gathering and preserving the evidence to be presented than in the less stressful, less demanding strong-arm type of robbery. Let it suffice to say that the *nature* of the force remains significant in robberies even when the force is only threatened and not "used."

SUMMARY

This chapter began the section on crimes against property with acknowledgment that many jurisdictions conceive of robbery as a crime against persons rather than a crime against property. Consideration was given to the contention that assaultive force is a prime requisite in defining robbery. The requisite that larceny, or a crime against property, be the primary basis of the crime of robbery was cited as justification for classifying robbery as a crime against property for purposes of discussion. Emphasis was placed on the fact that robbery is in effect two crimes—assault and larceny.

Larceny was defined and discussed as the main part of robbery; then force and the threat of force were discussed.

Intent was presented as a component of larceny. The victim's lack of both consent and resistance was discussed in terms of fear of physical harm, which, in turn, was discussed in relation to physical force as a basis for distinguishing robbery from other crimes. Consideration was also given to the nature of the force used in robberies.

NOTES

1. For law implications, see American Law Reports, 11 ALR, 2d, 862, and 58 ALR, 804.
2. See, for example, case law identified in American Law Reports, 61 ALR, 2d, 993, and 56 ALR, 2d, 1224.
3. Consider, for example, *State* v. *Taylor*, 27NJ117, 72 Am. Dec. 347; and the historical *Reg.* v. *Edwards*, 13 Cox cc 384,36LT, 30 (1877).
4. For more elaboration of this subject, see, for example, N. C. Chamelin and K. R. Evans, *Criminal Law for Police*, 2d. ed. (Englewood Cliffs, Prentice-Hall, 1976), pp. 113–115.
5. See, for example, the case law defined in American Law Reports, 56 ALR, 2d, 1224.
6. Pennsylvania State Police Academy, *Pennsylvania Criminal Law* (Harrisburg, Pa.: Telegraph Press, 1970), Sec. 704, p. 296.
7. See law references in American Law Reports, 11 ALR, 2d, 862 and 58 ALR, 804.
8. See, for example, W. L. Clark and W. Marshall *A Treatise on the Law of Crimes*, 7th ed. M. Q. Barnes, revising ed. (Mundelein, Ill.: Callaghan, 1967), pp. 831–870.

PRACTICAL EXERCISE

1. Sketch a flow chart of the activities involved in a robbery.
   a. Indicate the functions of law enforcement and of prosecution and defense in the courts.
   b. Indicate the involvement of perpetrator and victim.
   c. Show the function of evidence and witness.

ANNOTATED REFERENCES

American Law Reports (ALRs). The footnoted ALR references afford an outstanding collation of relevant legal references to the subject discussed.

Clark, W. L., and Marshall, W. A *Treatise on the Law of Crimes*. 7th ed. M. Q. Barnes, revising ed. Mundelein, Ill.: Callaghan, 1967. An exceptionally comprehensive treatment of virtually all technical detail relevant to criminal law.

Coffey, A. R., and Eldefonso, E. *Process and Impact of Justice*. Encino, Calif.: Glencoe Press, 1975. Affords an overall context for considering armed robbery as an advanced segment of a career in crime.

Chapter 8

EXTORTION AND BLACKMAIL

LEARNING OBJECTIVES

The learning objectives of this chapter are:
1. To recognize the similarities and differences in blackmail, extortion, and robbery.
2. To see the distinction between blackmail and extortion as crimes.
3. To be aware of the significance of the *demand* in the crimes of extortion and blackmail, insofar as *property* is concerned.
4. To understand the significance of *illicit intent* in both extortion and blackmail.
5. To know why extortion and blackmail, as crimes, often remain unreported.

EXTORTION IS THE ILLEGAL DEMAND for money or property by a public official, with corrupt intent. *Blackmail* is the illegal demand for money by a private citizen, using intimidation or a threat that a damaging secret will be revealed.

We can see from these definitions of extortion and blackmail that extortion could easily be classified as an "offense against public justice" (Chapter 12). Consider, for example, this definition of extortion: "At common law, it was a crime for any public officer to corruptly demand money or property that neither he nor his office was entitled to. This crime was called extortion."[1] Case law resulting from court decisions has consistently supported the inference that "public justice" is involved in extortion.[2]

Virtually all states have established statutory law that defines extortion as a crime committable only by public officials—blackmail being considered a "variation." Most such law requires, just as the common law requires, that more than an illegal demand for money or property be made. Statutory law customarily requires that the illegal demand be made by a public official with *corrupt intent* to collect the illegal "fee" of property. Furthermore, statutory law on this subject customarily requires that the illegal fee be collected solely because of the public official's status—the status or public power being the source of intimidation of the victim.

In terms of the manner in which "hush money" is demanded to "protect" the victim, the only difference between extortion and blackmale reduces to the requirement that an elected or appointed public official be involved. Conversely, blackmail is the same crime, but "committable" by anyone with the ability to intimidate another (see Figure 8.1).

Intimidation by status in the crime of extortion is analogous to instilling of fear in the crimes of robbery and rape. Just as the robbery and rape victims surrender what is demanded because they fear the threatened violence, so extortion victims presumably surrender the demanded fee because they fear what the public official might (or might not) do if they resist the demand.

This quality of intimidation forms the basis for discussing extortion and blackmail as property crimes. Fear is induced by the threat or use

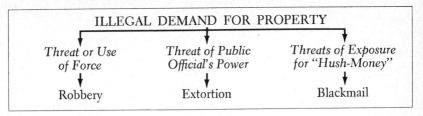

ILLEGAL DEMAND FOR PROPERTY

Threat or Use of Force	Threat of Public Official's Power	Threats of Exposure for "Hush-Money"
Robbery	Extortion	Blackmail

FIGURE 8.1   Illegal demand for property.

of violence in robbery, and fear is induced by other means in blackmail —but fear is an essential part of both crimes.

The fact that extortion involves public officials should not be ignored, however, especially in light of growing concern with cleaning up corruption in government.

Extortion and blackmail are shown in their relationship to robbery in Figure 8.1. Of course, some understanding of the terms *illegal demand for property, power,* and *hush money* are needed to understand the diagram. The phrase *demand for property* is the "illegal communication" that property is required to avoid some undesirable consequence. *Power,* as used in this context, is the official authority of a public official who may abuse the power by "demanding property." *Hush money* has to do with demanding property, usually money, to remain silent. There is often a great similarity in demanding property for extortion and blackmail, and in demanding property in robbery. There is even a similarity in the power a robber has to inflict violence, and the power an extortionist or blackmailer has to inflict the undesired outcome.

In view of these relationships, it should be of no surprise to learn that some of the public, including news media personnel, mix up the crimes of robbery with the crime of extortion and the crime of extortion with the crime of blackmail. Furthermore, it is not uncommon for the entertainment media to present dramas in which gangsters demand protection money from business people and then to label this "extortion." And, as mentioned, many jurisdictions define both extortion and blackmail as exactly the same crime, noting only that extortion by someone other than a public official is blackmail.

The great similarity between some of the components of extortion, blackmail, and robbery may account, in part, for some of the confusion. But in spite of these similarities that in some cases make extortion and blackmail "interchangeable," each will be discussed as a separate crime, mainly because the approach to enforcement of the laws involved is different. We will see that there are yet other differences, besides law enforcement, between extortion and blackmail that justify their separation, at least for the purposes of our discussion.

EXTORTION

In both extortion and blackmail, the purpose is to deprive a victim of something the victim would not have otherwise relinquished.[3]

Ownership

The victim may be the owner of whatever is being demanded, but ownership is not a requisite, as it is in the case of larceny. Common-law definition of robbery requires that the property taken from the victim be owned by the person from whom it is taken. Special statutes and subsequent case law have come to include robberies in which the person from whom the property is taken may not actually own the property robbed. Emphasis in such cases on the fact that the property was not owned by the robber, rather than that it was not owned by the specific person from whom it was taken.

In theatrical drama that includes extortion and blackmail, the victim is often depicted as being forced to acquire, often by illegal methods, property other than his own to satisfy the extortionist or blackmailer. This theatrical representation may not differ significantly from the truth of the matter. Verifiable insight into this segment of the criminal law is impossible, since the criminal law dealing with extortion and blackmail does not emphasize ownership as does the law dealing with robbery, nor is blackmail the type of crime that is always reported.

So in approaching a discussion of extortion as it might be related to robbery, less concern can be focused on ownership of the property illegally demanded. The *illegal demand*, however, for property is just as significant in extortion as it is in robbery.

The Demand

Public officials are constantly "demanding" property from others, and this is not necessarily extortion. A tax collector is a public official, and it is his or her job to demand property in the form of *lawful* tax money. Moreover, tax collectors are entitled to "threaten" the taxpayer with punitive use of the powers of their public office if the taxpayer "resists" the demand.

Of course, the assumption in this case is that the "property" demanded is a lawfully assessed tax. If the demand is not for lawfully assessed tax, the possibility of extortion exists if it can be shown that the tax collector has fraudulent intent in making the illicit demand.

From the perspective of municipal law enforcement, a similar problem with the city mayor may clarify this issue even more—although in a more awkward manner:

EXAMPLE

Mayor Maynard by city ordinance is personally responsible for renewal of all garbage collection franchises within the city. Renewal comes up every six months.

His Honor is empowered to use criteria other than lowest bid to determine to whom franchises are to be awarded—*quality standards* is the term used to describe His Honor's latitude in this area.

The Klank Akan Company wins the franchise formerly held by the Benda Lidd collection firm.

Benda Lidd complains to the City Council that Mayor Maynard not only ignored their low bid but "extorted" them by demanding they buy new garbage trucks.

At this point, the claimed "extortion" has no basis. The mayor is within the lawful rights ascribed to his public office by city ordinance. However, the crime of extortion begins to emerge with this additional set of facts:

EXAMPLE

Upon hearing from the City Council that their complaint was rejected, Benda Lidd produces a letter from His Honor demanding that in addition to the new trucks, it will be necessary for Benda Lidd to "donate" $10,000 to the Municipal Leadership Development Fund, or MLDF, in order to qualify for franchise renewal.

It turns out that the MLDF is merely a bank account in the personal name of His Honor. The City Council turns the matter over to the chief of police, who promptly involves the district attorney.

Where corruption in government exists, more criminal-justice effort will be needed in order to pursue it than is described in this facetious example. For instance, the demand of extortion will rarely be in a written format, available for evidence. In many instances, a blurred distinction between extortion and *bribery* (Chapter 12) may confuse the issue, the difference between extortion and bribery being little more than the nebulous distinction between "implied demand" and "willingness to receive."[4] And even without the delicate implications of the police chief's "boss" being involved, extortion is almost invariably a sensitive matter for criminal justice—sensitive whether handled by police directly, by prosecutors, by attorneys general, or by combinations of all three. Even the involvement of federal investigators, such as the FBI, rarely mitigates the sensitivity of the problem for criminal justice.

This sensitivity of any investigation into corrupt government is one aspect in which extortion and blackmail are clearly discernible, at least for law enforcement professionals. Blackmail, since it does not involve government personnel, lacks this particular type of sensitivity. It will be seen, however, that blackmail is often extremely sensitive for other reasons.

BLACKMAIL

As already noted, some jurisdictions define *blackmail* as extortion by a private citizen. The various definitions of *blackmail* have in common that the victim is in some way threatened by the offender should the victim fail to meet the illegal demand made by the blackmailer.[5]

The most common type of blackmail is the acquisition of some provable knowledge that the victim desires to be kept either secret or partially secret. The acquisition of this guarded information is then translated into a threat to reveal the secret unless hush money is paid —an illegal demand. Consider the following:

EXAMPLE

Gary Goodhouse tires of military service and persuades a group of psychiatrists that he is a homosexual in order to obtain a separation from the military.

Gary attends and graduates from college, gets married, and begins a successful career as a counselor at a boys' academy. Years later, after Gary has raised his children and been promoted to counseling director, an "old army friend" comes to town.

Gary Goodhouse is not long in learning from the "old friend" that financial aid is needed, for which Gary's "old army secret" will be protected.

While this unlikely situation is not typical, it serves to illustrate the ease with which social intimidation is possible. Hush money for the protection of one's reputation may be far more common than those in criminal justice would care to believe.

Intent

The wide variation in state law on blackmailing is fairly consistent on one requirement: the individual doing the blackmailing must have the *intent* to demand and gain property from the individual or individuals being blackmailed. The significance of this intent may be discernible in this example:

EXAMPLE

(A)

Mabel Mobility tires of a successful career as a call girl and moves to a distant city. Mabel gains employment in a department store, joins a church, becomes engaged, and marries a prominent businessman.

Mabel's husband hires one of her former clients, whom Mabel recognizes immediately.

Time passes with no evidence that Mabel has been betrayed, whereupon Mabel contrives a situation to be alone with the former client. At the meeting, Mabel presents the former client a large amount of cash, "in appreciation."

At this point, there is no blackmail, since there was no demand or, for that matter, no promises of continued secrecy. A gift has merely been presented. Consider, however, the added developments:

(B)

Mabel's former client initially attributes the unexplained cash gift to his exceptionally strong masculine charm. On reflection, however, he recalls engaging Mabel's services in the other city.

Mabel's former client contacts Mabel and informs her that an additional gift will be necessary if she hopes to deprive her husband of knowledge of her former occupation.

Probably atypically, Mabel confesses her past to her husband and advises him of the demand made, whereupon the police are contacted. Arrangements are made for Mabel to deliver the money demanded, and the blackmailer is arrested—presumably successfully prosecuted under local jurisdictional requirement.

Of course, the crime of blackmail is far more complex, at least in potential, than is suggested by these simplistic examples. In the sense that virtually any method of intimidating an individual into giving money or property other than through the use or threat of violence, as in robbery, will constitute blackmail, the possibilities of what can be considered blackmail are unlimited.

As a practical police matter, accumulation of evidence is, at best, difficult during the frequent exertion of pressure on police not to reveal the secret even when the blackmail is reported. Other complicating variables often make this a particularly difficult law to enforce—even aside from the fact that it is presumably reported only in rare instances.

SUMMARY

This chapter presented the crimes of extortion and blackmail. Acknowledgment was made that by definition, extortion could conceivably be categorized as a public-justice offense (Chapter 12). However, the main similarity of robbery, blackmail, and extortion—all three are demands based on some form of intimidation—is the dominant feature and classifies them all, for purposes of our discussion, as crimes against property.

It was emphasized that *extortion* can only be committed by public officials, using their public status for fraudulent intent. Blackmail was presented as essentially the same crime, differing only in the fact that private citizens can commit the offense.

Blackmail also has no limits upon the kinds of intimidations that can be used, whereas the threads used in extortion must be some form of application of the power inherent in public office.

NOTES

1. N. C. Chamelin and K. R. Evans, *Criminal Law for Police*, 2d ed. (Englewood Cliffs, N.J.: Prentice-Hall, 1976), p. 185.
2. See, for example, *People* v. *Mahumed*, 381 Ill. 81, 84, 44NE 2d 911 (1942).
3. See, for legal elaboration, *People* v. *Fichtner*, 281, App. Div. 159, 118 NYS, 2d, 392 (1952).
4. See, for example, *People* v. *McLaughlin*, 2 App. Div. 419, 37 Supp. 1005, 11 NY Cr. 97, 73 NY St. Rep. 496, rev'd 150 NY365, 44NE 1017.
5. *People* v. *Mahumed*, 381 Ill. 81, 84, 44NE 2d 911 (1942).

PRACTICAL EXERCISES

1. Sketch a flow chart indicating the activities in the crime of extortion.
   a. Show victim and perpetrator.

b. Show the function of evidence.
c. Show the functions of law enforcement, prosecution and defense, and the courts.
2. Using the state penal code, summarize the sections relevant to the crimes of extortion and blackmail.

ANNOTATED REFERENCES

Clark, W. L., and Marshall, W. *A Treatise on the Law of Crimes.* 7th ed. M. Q. Barnes, revising ed. Mundelein, Ill.: Callaghan, 1967. Sections dealing with the common-law roots of the crimes of extortion and blackmail are presented in exceptional case-law detail.
Coffey, A. R. *Administration of Criminal Justice.* Englewood Cliffs, N.J.: Prentice-Hall, 1974. This book comprehensively addresses what was presented in this chapter as a difficult problem for criminal justice: approaching the existence of corruption in government, the problem of extortion.
Imbau, F. E., and Thompson, James R. *Criminal Law and Its Administration.* Mineola, N.Y.: Foundation Press, 1970. This comprehensive volume provides an excellent general context for the material in this chapter on the relationship between various crimes by virtue of the law enforcement method used.
Lowey, A. H. *Criminal Law in a Nutshell.* St. Paul, Minn.: West, 1978. Section III in this book, addressing the concept of intent, affords a detailed perspective of intent as it relates to extortion and blackmail.

Chapter 9

BURGLARY

LEARNING OBJECTIVES

The learning objectives of this chapter are:
1. To understand the difficulty in establishing the necessary *proof* for each of the six elements of common-law burglary.
2. To recognize that the concept of *intent*, as discussed throughout this volume, is particularly difficult to prove in burglary, because the intent has to exist prior to entering the building.
3. To see the distinction between burglary and trespassing.
4. To know the difference between burglary and breaking and entering.

A CRIME AGAINST PROPERTY OR PERSON?

THE CRIMES DISCUSSED THUS FAR have been introduced with some provision that could account for discussing them in a different context. Robbery, for example, was introduced as being just as much a crime against the person as a crime against property when acknowledgment is given to the fact that it is both assault and larceny. The crime of extortion was introduced as being as much a public-justice offense as it is a crime against property, since only a public official using public office can commit the crime of extortion.

The crime of burglary must also be introduced for discussion as a crime that—by common-law definition, at least—is not "historically" a crime against property. With the concept of property clearly in mind, consider the following definition of *burglary*: "The breaking and entering of the dwelling house of another by night, with intent to commit a felony, whether the intent be executed or not, constitutes the common law felony denoted burglary."[1] From the perspective of considering burglary as a crime against property, as opposed to a crime against the person, consider the implication of the term *felony* in the definition above. Had this "felony" been explicitly identified as larceny, then it could be stated that burglary is by definition a crime against property. Furthermore, we might assume that just as robbery is composed of two crimes—assault and larceny—burglary, if "redefined," would be made up of the combined crimes of larceny and whatever else is involved in the common-law definition of burglary.

But the common-law definition of burglary did not specify *which* felony, even though burglary was defined as a crime. Burglary was defined in common law as a specific, single crime requiring, among several elements, the *intent* to commit another crime, without specifying what the "other" crime might be. Technically it could be *any* crime—perhaps against a person, perhaps not.

If we ignore for the moment the fact that burglary has probably been prosecuted historically as well as contemporarily as a crime against property, the common-law definition suggests that burglary could be constituted by the breaking and entering of a dwelling for the purpose of murdering the occupants. Indeed, as originally conceived, common-law burglary was what will be presented later in this chapter as a crime

201

against the security of a dwelling rather than a crime against either the property or the occupant of the dwelling. Also, as originally conceived, the *corpus delicti* of the burglary crime had to be proved in all six of its elements or parts:[2]

1. *Breaking*, which may be "actual" (via the use of force) or "constructive" (via fraud, trick, or duress).[3]
2. *Entering*, which is simply the physical penetration of the dwelling or its "curtilage," meaning other buildings of the residence.
3. *Dwelling house*, meaning a home for habitation.
4. *Of another*, meaning just that.
5. *In the night*, meaning sunset through sunrise.
6. *Felony intent*, meaning the breaking and entering were intended for the purpose of committing a felony.

Even in cases where the first five elements are "easy" to prove, it has always been difficult to prove felony intent *prior* to the breaking and entering. The point at which the decision is made to commit the felony is at best a nebulous factor—perhaps in some instances nebulous even to the offender. Consider, for example, the possibility that the decision to commit the felony is made *after* entering the dwelling. Common law would hold that this, if true, would be sufficient proof to determine that no burglary exists. As a pragmatic matter, consider the difficulty in proving that the decision was *not* made *after* entry. This particular point will be discussed in more detail later in the chapter.

In view of the difficulty of proving not only intent, as it has been discussed so far in this volume, but specific intent prior to the entry of the dwelling, it should be of no great surprise that statutory law passed by most jurisdictions has modified the crime of burglary considerably. Consider, for example, this definition of *burglary* from Illinois criminal law:[4] "*Burglary.* (a) A person commits burglary when without authority he knowingly enters or without authority remains within a building, housetrailer, watercraft, aircraft, motor vehicle, railroad car, or any part thereof, with intent to commit therein a felony or theft." Of particular note here is that this definition of burglary specifies theft, which is customarily the offense *intended* by the burglar (although the vaguer phrase "intent to commit a felony" is retained).

Some jurisdictions have modified their definitions of the intent element of burglary to include intent to commit either a felony *or* a misdemeanor—in order to make proof substantially less difficult. Another approach adopted by many states in dealing with the problem of proving intent is the establishment of first- and second-class burglary. Just as in the cases of first- and second-class murder, or first- and second-class robbery, burglary in the first or second degree has to do with the severity of the burglary. Severity, or the level of seriousness of the offense, is customarily interpreted by states establishing first- and second-degree burglary as meaning that first degree involves such things as a deadly weapon or an actual assault, whereas the second degree is a burglary without either weapon or assault.

Although the inclusion of assault and use of weapons in the definition of burglary helps to determine the seriousness of the crime, it confuses the issue of whether or not to classify burglary as primarily a crime against property. It is true that prosecutions are frequently based on a complement of numerous charges and a selection of the best combination of evidence and charges, but those within the criminal-justice system need a clear understanding of the primary nature of the crime in order to make intelligent decisions while performing their assigned duties.

In those jurisdictions, then, that establish first- and second-degree burglary in terms of assault or weapons, burglary might be considered, like robbery, to be made up of two crimes—one against the person and the other unspecified but probably against property. Of course, when a home is broken into for the sole purpose of committing a crime against a person, independent of any concern with property, the choice of burglary as the charge obviously has a somewhat weakened rational basis. Since the definitional problem exists only in the first-degree case and not the second-degree case, it might be better to approach the crime of burglary on the basis of breaking into a dwelling to steal something; if a weapon is carried into the home or if an assault is perpetrated after entering the home, the assault or the weapon can be thought of as "incidental" to the property crime of burglary. The "case" for considering burglary as a property crime is made best by the frequency with which larceny, whether grand larceny or petty larceny, serves as the specific crime *intended* at the time the breaking and entering occurs. Put another way, the majority of jurisdictions have statutory law and enforcement programs geared to the assumption that larceny was the crime intended at the time of breaking and entering, and the "first-degree assault or weapon" is germane to the charge only in the sense of increasing the severity of the penalty.

Support for the contention that burglary was a property crime even at common law is gained by closer analysis of the common-law definition of burglary. We have already noted that complete proof of six separate elements is required for conviction of burglary in common law. The third element, defining "dwelling house" as the place of burglary in common law, historically brought into being case law that establishes that the occupants need not be present to prove the house entered was indeed a dwelling.[5] If no resident need be in the dwelling in order for the crime of burglary to be committed, then presumably burglary was not a common-law crime against the person. So while it remains obvious that a crime against the person *could* be committed as part of the burglary, it is also clear that the crime of burglary did not necessarily include a crime against a person in that burglary could occur in an "empty house." While not stressed in case law, the prosecution retained the latitude to satisfy the "dwelling" element even when the "dwellers" were away at the time of the crime, leaving little to refute the argument that burglary was a crime against property—except for the concept of a crime against dwelling security.

Crime Against Dwelling Security

Consider the following: "The house must be the house of another; but, as burglary is an offense against the security of the habitation, and not against the property, occupation, not ownership is the test."[6] The seeming problems posed by adding a third category of crimes (first, crimes against the person; second, crimes against property; and now third, crimes against dwelling security) is a problem that is certainly far more apparent than real.

Statutory modifications[7] to the common-law definition of burglary include in all jurisdictions the complete elimination of the requirement that a dwelling be involved: most jurisdictions explicitly include all buildings and, in some cases, all forms of vehicular transportation as well, as applicable to the crime of burglary. Mitigating against the common-law concept that a third category of crime against dwelling security exists is the further elimination of the requirement that a burglary be committed at night—burglary thereby moving from the arena of stealthy invasion of a secured dwelling to a general category of breaking into any structure for the purpose of theft. Jurisdictions that have added such categories as burglary "using explosives" usually specify some relationship to "safe-blowing," or "safe-cracking," which clearly defines an assumption that a crime against property is involved —"safe-cracking" having nothing to do generically with either crimes against the person or crimes against dwelling security.

In effect, the statutory removal of the "dwelling" restriction, or rather the addition of virtually all buildings, day or night, changes the crime "against dwelling security" to a crime either against the person or against property, with the overwhelming weight of the existing influences on the side of burglary as a crime against property.

Of course, burglary statutes, by and large, still allow for conviction of burglary without larceny. It is not being suggested here that statutes have generally evolved to the point of explicitly isolating larceny as a component of the crime of burglary. But the point is that the requirement to prove *intent* is now most often satisfied in terms of the intent to steal *property*—a persuasive factor in trying to assess whether burglary is thus perceived as a crime against property or the person.

BURGLARY VERSUS TRESPASS

While by no means a technically accurate comparison in criminal law, the following somewhat simplified comparison of burglary to trespass may help to clarify further the *nature* of the crime of burglary. It will also afford a partial background for the comparison, later in this chapter, between the specific crime of breaking and entering and the specific crime of burglary when the two are distinctly different crimes.

Since it is true that a burglary case can be prosecuted successfully without larceny, a practical question for law enforcement is: What is the difference between the crime of burglary and any other crime involving illicit entry into a building? For the purpose of exploring this hypothetical abstraction, the question can be rephrased into: What is the difference between the crime of burglary and the crime of trespass.

Of course, the answer derived through analysis of the criminal law emerges as a matter of the provable *intent* of the individual entering a building illicitly. One who enters with the *intention* to steal upon entering is the burglar, whereas one who does not intend to commit *any crime* upon entry may be considered a tresspasser when certain other legal variables are "adjusted."

Variation in statutes between jurisdictions makes impossible a definitive statement of all of the problems associated with using the intent of the accused to determine whether or not the accused is a burglar or a trespasser. But as a practical police matter, there are some universal "indicators" having to do with intent that may help to clarify the hypothetical distinction between trespassing and burglary.

Before consideration is given to any of these "indicators" that a burglary rather than a trespass exists, it should be pointed out that the problem of proving intent is not a minor problem in any crime and is exceptionally difficult when intent most be proved as existing prior to the breaking and entering rather than after. The crime of shoplifting is at least partially a statutory concession to the fact that proving the intent of someone prior to entering a building can in many cases be impossible—particularly in instances where the shoplifter may not *consciously* know his intentions at the time he enters the store. Indeed, most apprehended shoplifters claim "spur-of-the-moment" influence from the enticing displays. The insurmountable barriers to *proving* that this is not the case no doubt have influenced shoplifting legislation.

As we return to the discussion of certain indicators of intent prior to entry, we should recall that this volume is addressed to criminal law rather than to police investigation, patrol procedures, or crime prevention. These indicators are discussed merely to establish in a passing manner a rather difficult area in applying certain segments of the criminal law.

Intent Indicators

By far the most obvious indicator that someone had illicit intentions prior to breaking or entering a building is the possession of burglary tools. Certainly, the comparison between burglary and trespass would bring the significance of possessing burglary tools into focus.

Burglary tools can be any mechanical contrivance that facilitates access to otherwise secure areas. There are, however, certain legislative descriptions that tend to narrow the definition of burglary tools; these restrictions can be found in virtually all criminal codes. As examples, consider the criminal codes of Pennsylvania and California as they relate to burglary tools.

PENNSYLVANIA

Possession of burglary tools: Whoever has in his possession any tool, false-key, lockpick, nippers, fuse, forcescrew, punch, drill, jimmy or any material implement, instrument or other mechanical device, designed or commonly used for breaking into any vault, safe, railway car, boat, vessel, warehouse, store, shop, office, dwelling house, or door, shutter, window of a building of any kind . . .[8]

CALIFORNIA

Burglars' tools possession: Every person having upon him or in his possession a picklock, crow, keybit, or other instrument or tool with intent to break or enter into any building.[9]

Such burglary tools, then, when in the possession of someone illegally in a building, obviously increase the probability that the entry was intended for criminal purposes rather than being mere trespassing. Since the toughest test in all cases is proof of intent, the possession of burglary tools is extremely significant—as suggested by the legislative effort to define the possession of burglary tools as a crime.

In terms of indicators that might delineate the specific ramifications of intent, there are certain less tangible but nevertheless valuable indicators associated with what might be called "circumstances." Just as "state of mind" can be extremely vague when practical law enforcement application is necessary, so also can "circumstance." Without any effort to present all of the confusing ramifications of utilizing "circumstance" to suggest "state of mind," a facetious yet germane example may assist in clarifying this otherwise nebulous concept.

EXAMPLE

Patrolman Sharpeye covers a walking beat as part of his swing-shift patrol. Part of his duty is "doorshaking" to ensure that businesses have been locked up for the night. Thursday nights are "open 'till 9" for several of the businesses. Sharpeye has had to advise people of this from time to time when they mistakenly came by on other nights.

Sharpeye has advised Larry Locklift of this "mistake" on two different occasions when Sharpeye found Larry trying the door of a radio repair shop after hours—Larry claiming the belief that he believed the shop open every night.

Sharpeye notes that Larry drives a van truck, apparently full of radio equipment.

On the third occasion, Sharpeye finds Larry *inside* the repair shop. The owner is called, states that nothing is missing, and concedes that he may have left the door unlocked. Larry insists it was an innocent mistake because he found the door unlocked, and though unlighted, believed the shop open for business on a Wednesday night.

Larry's lawyer insists that this, at worst, is an "unintentional trespass."

Here the intent is clear from the repeated tries, and does not have to be sought after by the police, as evidenced by the radio equipment in the truck, the wrong night, and the unlighted shop—all in the context of a policeman being a witness to the fact that the suspect knew Thursday was the only evening for legitimate business.

This example contained indicators obvious enough to persuade many prosecutors in most jurisdictions that Officer Sharpeye took into custody a burglar, at least if local jurisdictional rules permit "breaking" to be proved as "constructive breaking" on entry alone. With certain latitude allowed, it could be burglary even though the owner verified no loss and even though the door was apparently left unlocked by the owner.

Lest this example prove misleading, it should be stressed that this facetious situation is not presented as a typical case in which intent can be proved. The situation is presented merely to clarify the distinctions between an individual illegally in the building with no criminal intent and an individual who has criminal intent. It is cited to show some indicators that theft is intended.

This, then, brings us to a more relevant police concern, a distinction between burglary and breaking and entering.

BURGLARY VERSUS BREAKING AND ENTERING

The modifications in statutes in many jurisdictions have had the effect of making crimes out of what were, at common law, simply "elements" of burglary. The wide variation between jurisdictional definitions of "statutory" burglary is so extreme that it becomes safe to say that in one place or another there is criminal penalty for "breaking and entering with intent to commit a misdemeanor instead of a felony," no other elements required; "entering without breaking" with *intent* the only other element required; "daytime-only burglaries," and a host of "special burglaries" fitting various jurisdictional philosophies.

While the purpose of most of the legislation is to remove the many barriers to successful prosecution of the cumbersome six-element common-law burglary, these "statutory" burglaries have created a confusion of terms in some cases, and as a basis for ineffective investigation and prosecution in others. This is particularly true when burglary is considered to be exactly the same as the statutory crime of breaking and entering, as is common in many jurisdictions. Depending on what the person using the term means by *breaking and entering*, this confusion of terms can cause a number of problems.

If breaking and entering is used as a *category* of crime that encompasses *all* offenses associated with burglary, then no problem exists. It is when the term *breaking and entering* jurisdictionally identifies the specific statutory offense that *differs* from another offense identified as burglary that the problem begins to emerge. Investigating officers who are not attuned to clear distinctions between statutory crimes, and who use terms that fail to draw attention to the distinctions, run a much higher risk of believing they have satisfactorily proved a serious level of crime when in reality they may have gathered evidence sufficient only to prosecute a minor crime. Chamelin and Evans provide an excellent example of this type of problem:

> The distinction might be important in a felony-murder case. Suppose a state statute provides that homicide occurs during commission of or attempt to commit a burglary. Does this mean burglary as the crime was defined as common law, or does it include all the breaking and entering offenses?[10]

Of course the criminal courts of each jurisdiction can unravel this as a judicial process through case law whenever statutory law remains vague. From the law-enforcement perspective, however, the problem being unraveled by the courts has already occurred: prosecution for a more serious crime may, of necessity, be reduced to insufficient evidence, which could conceivably be based upon an officer's not distinguishing between one level of severity and another through using what he believes to be "generic terms." When the term *breaking-and-entering* refers to a specific statutory offense rather than to all the burglary-related offenses, effort is needed to keep the distinctions between the specific crimes clear. Perhaps an example of the applications of distinctions would prove useful— again a facetious example intended merely to clarify concepts rather than to be a definitive basis for enforcing burglary-related laws:

EXAMPLE

(A)

Burglar Ben operates in a jurisdiction that defines breaking and entering as one crime and burglary as another crime. The technical difference is that the crime of breaking and entering has occurred when the first two elements of common law have been accomplished, regardless of *intent*, whereas the crime of burglary requires all six elements.

Burglar Ben notes that the penalty imposed for breaking and entering is probation under the supervision of a young female criminology intern from the local university and the penalty for burglary is bamboo splinters under the toenails while being stretched on the rack. Ben, makes the pragmatic choice as to what he prefers the police to be able to prove should his luck fail.

In this example the stage has been set for what has been discussed earlier in this volume as plea bargaining. It also shows how important it is for the police to distinguish clearly between specific crimes.

(B)

Burglar Ben is professional enough about his career to know that the most difficult evidence is that of intent. Accordingly, Ben has developed skills in unlocking without tools. Moreover, his "casing jobs" and otherwise sizing-up work carefully circumvent discernible patterns where witnesses can testify to his probable knowledge of, interest in, access to, or plans for any of his work locations.

Ben is quite proud of his professional acumen and confides to his friend Lil that he has become increasingly successful. She expresses doubt, whereupon Ben boasts of the location of his next job, the size of the take, and the method he will use.

Fortunately, police detectives later interivew Lil following a dispute with Ben over a paternity matter.

Yes, she had heard Ben had been caught inside someone's house, but no, she hadn't mentioned he *intended* anything.

Physical evidence satisfies the statute on breaking and entering— but intent?

Bail releases Ben only to generate yet another dispute with Lil regarding a paternity matter. The fortunate police detective receives a call from irat Lil. Burglar Ben is now charged with burglary rather than breaking and entering.

Of course, the "convenient" statutes and circumstances in this example do not fit the reality of day-to-day law enforcement in *any* jurisdiction. Again, however, the example does put into perspective the importance of retaining clear distinction between each category of burglary. Taking the example seriously for the moment, we can see that the lucky detective may not have been so lucky had he not clearly understood the distinction between the breaking and entering and the burglary as separate levels of offense or had he believed that all breaking and entering is the same and that the investigative job is over as soon as the breaking and entering has been satisfied.

SUMMARY

This chapter introduced the crime of burglary in terms of the complexities of the common-law definition, which established six separate crime elements to be proved. Each one of these elements was examined in terms of the legal requirements of the common law and subsequently recompared to the legislative modifications that have occurred.

It was noted that the legislative intent is primarily concerned with removing the insurmountable barriers to proving intent prior to breaking and entering.

The problems of identifying burglary as a crime against property were examined in the context of reference only to *felony* in common law, combined with the necessity of establishing proof of intent prior to entering.

Other modifications, such as legislatively expanding the definition of burglary to encompass more than dwellings, were examined, and the original "third category" of crime, the crime against dwelling security, was briefly discussed.

Burglary and trespassing were compared, and it was seen that the distinction between them is based on burglary tools.

Finally, burglary and breaking and entering, as specific crimes, were compared. It was pointed out that certain problems are posed when law enforcement personnel fail to keep the distinctions between the two crimes clear.

NOTES

1. W. L. Clark and W. Marshall A *Treatise on the Law of Crimes*, 7th ed. M. Q. Barnes, revising ed. (Mundelein, Ill.: Callaghan, 1967), p. 983.
2. For case-law collection, see *American Law Reports*, 93 ALR, 2d, 525.
3. For case-law collection on constructive breaking, see American Law Reports, 79 ALR, 2d, 286.
4. Illinois Criminal Code, S.H.A., Chapter 38 (1961).
5. Clark and Marshall, A *Treatise on the Law of Crimes*, p. 989.
6. *Ibid.*, p. 991.
7. See Note, "A Rationale of the Law of Burglary," 57 *Columbia Law Review* 1009 (1951).
8. Pennsylvania State Police Academy, *Pennsylvania Criminal Law and Criminal Procedure* (Harrisburg, Pa.: Telegraph Press, 1969), p. 372, Section 904.
9. California Penal Code, CPC, Sec. 466.
10. N. C. Chamelin and K. R. Evans, *Criminal Law for Police*, 2d ed. (Englewood Cliffs, N.J.: Prentice-Hall, 1976), p. 157.

PRACTICAL EXERCISES

1. Sketch a flow chart indicating the activities involved in the crime of burglary.
   a. Emphasize evidence.
   b. Show the functions of law enforcement, prosecution–defense, and the courts.
2. Using the state penal code, summarize the sections relevant to the crime of burglary.

ANNOTATED REFERENCES

Chamelin, N. C., and Evans, K. R. *Criminal Law for Police*. 2d ed. Englewood Cliffs, N.J.: Prentice-Hall, 1976. Chapter 13 of this text offers the reader an interesting alternative approach to much of the same material presented in this chapter.

Coffey, A. R.; Eldefonso, E.; and Hartinger, W. *An Introduction to the Criminal Justice System and Process.* Englewood Cliffs, N.J.: Prentice-Hall, 1974. This book elaborates the involved relationship between criminal justice functions as noted in this chapter in terms of police and prosecutor relationships.

Eldefonso, E.; Coffey, A. R.; and Grace, R. C. *Principles of Law Enforcement.* 2d ed. New York: Wiley, 1974. Segments of this book dealing with police procedure afford in-depth consideration of what this chapter presented in that subject area.

Inbau, F. E., and Thompson, J. R. *Criminal Law and Its Administration.* Mineola, N.Y.: Foundation Press, 1970. Sections addressed to burglary afford outstanding reference material from case law on burglary.

Chapter 10

ARSON, EXPLOSIVES, AND INCENDIARIES

LEARNING OBJECTIVES

The learning objectives of this chapter are:
1. To recognize the distinction between crimes involving explosives or incendiaries and other forms of property crimes.
2. To learn the early common-law similarities between the crimes of burglary and arson.
3. To become aware of the statutory modifications that have occurred in the common-law crime of arson.

ARSON AND CRIMES INVOLVING EXPLOSIVES and incendiaries have become more significant in recent years, partly because of modern technology and advances in military weaponry. Just as the emergence of firearms modified the earlier crime of highway robbery, explosives and incendiaries have now modified the crime of arson. Accosting an ancient caravan with bows and arrows or swords no doubt flowed from the same criminal motivation that train robbers of the last century experienced. But with the introduction of gunpowder in weapons that were so efficient that balking at the robber risked nearly certain death, the crime of highway robbery required fewer robbers and afforded better chances of cooperation from the victims. Modern chemistry has produced a similar effect on the crime of arson.

There are two additional reasons that the significance of crimes involving arson and explosives has increased. From a local-jurisdictional point of view, arson for profit became profitable with the emergence of fire insurance. From the perspective of law enforcement over all—including federal law enforcement—the increase in terrorism also accounts for the increased significance in crimes related to explosives. Put another way, the "arson of old," which will be described shortly in terms of the common law, is increasingly a criminal-law problem in terms of arson for profit—even now evolving from the relatively modern phenomenon of a desperate business owner using arson as a last-ditch effort to cope with disastrous indebtedness to the organized effort to defraud insurance companies. With regard to explosives and incendiaries, their increased use, or at least the increased threat of their use in terrorism, as will be discussed later in this chapter, places even greater significance on statutory laws that have been created since common-law definitions of arson.

The increase in significance of these kinds of crime is worth note even in a book devoted to criminal law, rather than to criminology or to police procedures. It is worth note because of the possibility that both terrorism and arson for profit are of such a nature that legislative changes in at least the penalties for these crimes are conceivable should the incidence of these crimes continue to rise. Indeed, it is conceivable that in addition to changes in penalties, there may be extended definitions of the crimes related to arson, explosives, and incendiaries.

214

With the possibility of considerable change in the criminal law in this area, the crimes of arson, explosives, and incendiaries will be presented primarily as crimes against the property, but with the recognition that in the cases of terrorism, crimes against the person are indeed a potential.

ARSON

The crime of arson is and always has been deemed a very serious crime, although for different reasons at different times. The old common law defined arson as the "willful and malicious burning of the house of another either by day or by night." Later in this chapter, a similarity to this common-law definition will be drawn in the discussion of explosives. But in terms of approaching a discussion of the crime of arson, there is a similarity in common law between this definition and the definition already presented earlier of burglary—in both there are multiple elements to be proved. In contrast to the six elements old common-law burglary required, arson required "only" four to be proved:[1]

1. Dwelling defined the same way as common-law burglary.
2. Dwelling belonging to someone else but not necessarily occupied by the owner—occupied by anyone, just as in common-law burglary.
3. Actual burn, however slight, rather than "scorch."
4. Willful and malicious, which is a matter of proving intent.

This interesting comparison through "multiple elements" of common-law burglary and arson can also be drawn into the area of a "third category of crime"—the category of crimes other than those against the person or against property. Just as burglary was considered a crime against the "security of a dwelling," common-law arson was considered a crime "against habitation"—neither a crime against the person nor a crime against property.[2]

Subsequent statutory modifications in contemporary criminal law have changed this clear distinction and, as in the case of burglary, tended to establish arson as a crime against property. It is worth note, however, that many jurisdictions define some arson offenses in a manner that would make a convincing argument in favor of calling arson a crime against a person.

Technical questions about the elements of common-law arson have always been a matter of criminal law. These technical questions usually have to do with such things as the difference between a "burn" and a "scorch," but there are technical ramifications for each of the four elements involved—the element known as "dwelling," the element known as "of another," the element of "burn," and the element of "maliciously willful," which will be cited later in this chapter in relation to statutes dealing with explosives.

Dwelling

A dwelling for the purpose of defining arson at common law is, just as in the case of common-law burglary, a house that must be occupied, rather than "owned."[3] In other words, it was critical not that the *owner* be occupying the house but rather that the house be occupied if arson was to be charged.

In precisely the same manner that a dwelling had to be "lived in" to be burglarized at common law, it also had to be "lived in" for arson to be charged, although the occupant did not have to be at home at the time of the arson. Temporary absences in both cases were permitted by the common law.

In the modern integration of common law and statutes, the technical question of how long an occupant can be "temporarily" out of the house is customarily answered in terms of the *intent* of the occupant: if the occupant intends to return, the house is a dwelling because it is "legally" occupied. For example, the occupants of a dwelling could visit friends in another country for months on end, but the empty house remains a dwelling by common-law definition as long as the occupants plan to return.

Property of Another

By establishing the requirement that the building be owned by someone other than the individual charged with arson, early common-law definition virtually precluded a charge against an owner except in cases where she had clearly rented it out or in some other way given over the occupancy of the house to another. The owner could be charged with arson if she burned the building knowing it was occupied by someone else—the key being the occupancy rather than the ownership whenever both variables are involved.

Technically, evidence was needed that *either* the burned building was not owned by the accused arsonist, *or*, if owned, that the burned building was indeed occupied by someone else—even if occupied without the owner's knowledge (trespassing).

Burned

The crime of arson at common law required a "burning" to occur in order for the crime to exist.[4] Considerable opinion has been expressed for hundreds of years regarding the distinctions between such things as a "burn" and a "scorch." Essentially, the burning has to do with physical damage to the building and its structure rather than to its furnishings, and to do with the degree of damage done. While no blaze, as such, was required in common law, the *burning* element of arson could be satisfied only if there was destruction to wood fibers in the structure, independent of the furnishings within the structure. Smoke damage or "blackening" was not adequate satisfaction of this element— actual fire damage to the structure was required.

The evolution of the specific crime of *attempted* arson in many jurisdictions removed the critical nature of this element of common-law portion, although the difficulty in gathering evidence overall still remains.

Maliciously Willful

Throughout this volume, emphasis has been placed on *intent* in criminal law. In some ways, it was less difficult to prove intent in common-law arson than it is in modern statutory criminal law, with its various specialized and expanded definitions. Arson at common law defined *maliciously willful* in a manner that required no evidence that the arsonist was *necessarily* trying to hurt either the owner or the occupants. Proof was needed only that the arsonist intended to burn the dwelling of another; if it was someone else's house and it was occupied, the intent was malicious by definition.[5]

The voluminous legislation that has been passed in various jurisdictions to clarify and remedy problems posed by common-law definitions has, in some instances, increased rather than decreased the problems of producing evidence of intent. Of course, there are many instances in which the statutory modification of common-law arson has relieved the problems of establishing evidence of intent.

Modern Arson

As already noted, criminal statutes have been expanded to encompass a much broader definition of arson in virtually all jurisdictions.[6]

A major area of change has been the statutory inclusion of property owners attempting to defraud insurance companies.[7] This is significant for many reasons, not the least of which is the elimination of the requirement that the property belong to someone else—the focus here being on the fraud rather than on either occupancy or ownership.

Virtually all jurisdictions have made some statutory modification in the common-law requirement that arson be restricted to dwellings. Buildings in general and even the burning of personal property have been defined as arson by some states, most retaining the common-law element of "of another" as a continuing basis for defining arson.

In terms of the technical question having to do with what constitutes "burning" as opposed to "scorching," it has already been noted that some jurisdictions have statutes defining *attempted* arson as a separate crime, and this tends to provide an alternative in prosecuting arson cases in which the arson "was not successful."

By and large, the elements to be proved at common law for arson are still required in one form or another in most statutory modifications, even in those broader modifications having to do with changes brought about with the advent of fire insurance and the incentive of arson for profit.[8]

Statutory modifications geared to coping with "arson for profit" of course include the burning of *any* building when there is intent to defraud. Whether calling this particular crime "arson" or not, most jurisdictions that define this crime established as an element the necessity to prove *intent to defraud*—more or less replacing the common-law "maliciously willful" element.

Recalling earlier discussions of first- and second-degree murder, robbery, and burglary, some jurisdictions have established a similar concept in matters involving arson for profit—the first degree being reserved for charging those who will profit directly from such crime, the second degree being less severe forms of arson.

In these arson statutes geared to a profit motive and oriented to defrauding, the *intent* to defraud is usually more important that the "possibility" to defraud. Put another way, the defense that the crime was not possible does not apply in this particular case because of the specific intent component. Unlike "crimes" that cannot be crimes if they are not "possible," statutory arson for profit can be a crime even if the profit and defrauding is not "possible."

EXAMPLE

Tom Torch has accumulated overwhelming debts from gambling on horses, poker, and sports events. Tom's ability to meet the demands of his many creditors has suffered so severely that he can no longer obtain refinancing loans.

Tom's recall of paying fire insurance premiums is faulty in that he believes his modest home is insured when it is not—and has not been for a long time.

After carefully removing and storing all of his furniture and personal property, Tom pours gasoline throughout his home and burns it to the ground. Tom is dismayed when the insurance company advises him that this is so obviously arson that they wouldn't pay even if his insurance were still in force.

Tom is even more dismayed when the local fire marshal obtains an arson complaint from the local prosecutor. "No one was defrauded because I wasn't even insured," objected Tom. "But you filed a claim with the insurance company; that proves you intended to defraud," retorts the prosecutor.

This example illustrates the increased significance of *intent* insofar as modern arson is concerned. To illustrate the complexity of variation between jurisdictions, however, consideration might be given to a definition of arson for profit that does not create the significance for intent reflected in this example. With respect to a different concept for intent, consider the following statute defining as crime the "burning to defraud insurer":

> *Burning to Defraud Insurer:* Whoever willfully and with intent to
> injure or defraud the insurer, sets fire to, or burns, or causes to be
> burned, or who aids, counsels or procures, the burning of any goods,
> wares, merchandise, or other chattels, or personal property of any
> kind, whether the property of himself or of another, which, at the time,
> is insured . . .[9]

This contrasts with the example given in that the insurance, and the law cited, must be enforced at the time of the burning—independent of the intent to defraud. The effect of the fact that the insurance was not in force at the time of the "arson" would be that there was no crime, whether it be called arson or "burning." This "difference," as in the case of all crimes with great variation in jurisdictional definition, is resolved simply by consulting the criminal code for the jurisdiction in question.

EXPLOSIVES AND INCENDIARIES

Were this volume addressed to police procedures rather than criminal law, the category of explosives and incendiaries might better be appended to a discussion of machine guns, automatic rifles, and hand grenades instead of being appended to the crime of arson. For indeed, concern with explosives and incendiaries is a rapidly expanding concern—a concern expanding to encompass what will be described later in this chapter as terrorism. It is not uncommon for a terrorist to employ automatic weapons in combination with at least the threat of explosives and incendiaries.

Although terrorism remains largely a problem for national and international enforcement, there is sufficient increase in worldwide terrorism to justify emphasis on terrorist use of explosives and incendiaries in a discussion of criminal law. Certainly, the problem at the federal level is reason enough for all jurisdictions to at least be cognizant of a "broader context" of crimes using explosives and incendiaries.

Local jurisdictions can begin by assuming that criminal groups with exotic names who then employ automatic firearms to enforce their doctrine will also turn to explosives. A kind of systematic relationship between terrorism and "local" crimes of this nature can thus be established.

Most technical advances in the design of military weapons tend to make their presence felt in law enforcement as well as the courts in one form or another, sooner or later. From this source of influence on criminal law, terms such as *destructive device* emerge. Although such a term is not common to the common law, the term is nevertheless increasingly common to the criminal law evolving from common law. This evolution has established statutory modifications to common law that encompass virtually all the weaponry associated with the term *destructive device*. Although not created as "counterterrorism," there nevertheless appears to be an evolution toward a relationship between statutes geared to controlling explosives and incendiary devices in possible future statutes geared to controlling terrorism.

Statutory variation between jurisdictions is such that it might be useful to establish four basic distinctions between weapons and weaponry associated with explosives and incendiaries. Hopefully, some form of common terminology will permit a general discussion without a great deal of confusion with local statutory provisions for control.

The four general categories that will be defined are neither universal nor comprehensive but are intended merely to clarify concepts relevant to any meaningful discussion of explosives and incendiaries.

BOMB: Any device that can be detonated either to cause an explosion as such, or to cause an incendiary reaction, upon detonation.

DESTRUCTIVE DEVICE: As already suggested in the narrative above, a destructive device includes incendiaries and explosives. For purposes of this discussion, it also includes caustic chemical substances, large projectiles and missiles, bombs, grenades, and weapons of extra-large bore, including cannons and mortars.

EXPLOSIVES: For purposes of discussion, explosives are any material that can be detonated to blow up with violent physical impact and concussion accompanied by loud noises.

INCENDIARY DEVICE: Any device, including a bomb, designed or capable of rapid incineration of comparatively large areas upon detonation.

Obviously these definitions are anything but "mutually exclusive": each relates to the other three, either directly or indirectly. This overlap is necessary to encompass the wide variations in statutes between jurisdictions. Nevertheless, in spite of overlapping definitions, each of these four can be considered separately. As a matter of fact, each *must* be considered separately because of the wide variation in the jurisdictional definitions of the crimes related to each. An additional factor in many cases—the factor of automatic weapons—suggests the criminal link between these four when terrorism is involved. This is not to say that criminal use of automatic weapons is confined to terrorism, but terrorists conceive of automatic weapons in much the same manner as they conceive of bombs, destructive devices, explosives, and incendiary devices. With regard to these four "weapons," most jurisdictions divide the related crimes into two broad categories—burglary and blackmail–robbery.

Since criminal codes have not generally addressed themselves to terrorism, statutes against automatic weapons are different from statutes against explosives and incendiary devices. But as both crimes occur for the single purpose of terrorism, it is conceivable that legislation will ultimately be modified.

It is common to pass legislation that makes it a crime to possess a machine gun. It is also common to pass legislation against explosives and incendiaries, but often in terms of the *use* of explosives rather than the possession of explosives. Perhaps, this has to do with the legitimate use that the construction industry has given dynamite and TNT. Nevertheless, automatic weapons tend to be illegal to possess, whereas explosives are many times simply illegal to use. Exceptions will be noted during the remainder of this chapter.

By and large, statutes were designed for the general broad category of explosives with burglary or with blackmail/robbery-type crimes—not for the purpose of controlling radical groups willing to employ both automatic weapons and explosives or incendiaries to achieve various social and political goals.

To clarify this further, it might be useful to treat separately such crimes as safe-blowing and using a bomb to rob a bank—the kinds of crimes currently covered by local jurisdictions. Once this variety of crime is removed, it becomes easier to see the relationship between terrorist use of automatic weapons and explosives, and the inadequacy of many statutes to cope with the terrorist type of crime. Put another way, most criminal codes are simply not structured to cope with the use of automatic weapons, explosives, and incendiaries for the sole purpose of *terrifying* rather than for actual kidnapping, maiming, and murder.

When explosives and incendiaries are not used simply to blow open a safe, or to intimidate for the purpose of general blackmail, the remaining *terrorist's* "application" focuses on two things: first, the much higher risk to life and property, and second, the inadequacy of most statutory laws to focus on this specific variety of crime.

In a sense, this terror can be thought of as the crime of blackmail. The similarity between terror and blackmail exists in that the terrorist quite frequently is creating intimidation, which can be removed only if his demands are met. Unlike the ordinary crime of blackmail, terrorists quite frequently proceed with the kidnapping, maiming, and murdering and pose a threat in terms of its continuation if the demands are not met. And their demands are quite frequently associated with massive social or political changes rather than the profits sought by ordinary blackmailers. It is not uncommon for terrorists to include in their demands the release from custody of other terrorists.

These kinds of differences with other blackmailers create a salient characteristic with regard to the terrorist's use of explosives and incendiaries. Other criminals, seeking merely to gain illegal profit, at least initially, exercise great care to create the belief that a kidnapped victim will not be harmed. Terrorists, conversely, ordinarily regard the murder and maiming of their helpless victims as a part of the blackmail scheme. In other words, initial failure to meet the demands is less likely to produce a change of heart on the part of the terrorists in their threats to murder or maim the helpless victims. More often than not, terrorists are devoutly fanatical in some cause, quite willing to take their own lives in order to further the cause—the risks in terrorists' use of automatic weapons, explosives, and incendiaries thereby escalating dramatically. Paradoxically, the expressed goals of many terror groups who kidnap, murder, and maim their victims are expressed in terms of "human freedom."

The use of explosives and incendiaries by terrorists may still be largely a federal matter, evolving slowly through the international effort to come to grips with politically complex crimes such as skyjacking. Nevertheless, the worldwide incidence of terror is likely to modify the legal structure of many jurisdictions if such terror continues to rise.

A final comment on the potential significance of the terror-type of crime: The "ultimate" terrorist weapon is the portable atomic bomb with its awesome capability to destroy an entire city. This exact same massive threat, if developed, is equally inviting to any large-scale blackmailer.

RELATED CRIMINAL LAWS

Against this background of a somewhat specialized emphasis on terrorism, the general discussion of criminal law relating to arson, explosives, and incendiaries can be concluded by examining an example of the way in which a given jurisdiction writes its laws relating to the subject. With particular regard to the wording of the code, consider the following:

> *Carrying Bombs and Explosives:* Whoever possesses or carries on or about his person or in a vehicle, with intent to use the same unlawfully against the person or property of another, any bomb, bombshell, grenade, or other explosive device or explosive substance, except fixed ammunition, or any noxious liquid gas or substance, is guilty of a felony.[10]

With regard to the wording of this code, two criminal-law factors are of particular interest—the first having to do with intent, or the *mens rea* factor. In this regard, this particular jurisdiction follows the "rules" discussed earlier for arson, by establishing intent in terms of "someone else's" property. Also of interest is the probability that the wording of this particular statute would enable prosecution of terrorists, as already discussed.

Of further interest in this same particular criminal code are a series of related statutes declaring it a crime to carry explosives on trains, explosives to maim, explosives for "malicious mischief," and the manufacturing, storing, selling, or even possessing of explosives.[11] This code also defines as a particular crime the use of explosives to commit a burglary:

> *Burglary With Explosives:* Whoever, at any time, willfully and maliciously, enters any building, with intent to commit a felony by use of an explosive, is guilty of burglary, a felony.[12]

In terms of the relationship between arson and explosives, note here the wording "willful and malicious" in terms of its obvious similarity to arson law as discussed early in this chapter. As a practical police matter, an "attempted" burglary, when all other elements are settled, would probably encompass this element of "willful and malicious" intent with regard to burglary with explosives—would satisfy this statutory requirement if the "attempting burglar" had a bomb or "nitro" in his possession while "attempting." Of course, there is a world of difference in an arrest inside a building and an arrest subsequent to a burglary in terms of establishing the maliciously willful intent to use the explosives, the evidence that the explosives were in the offender's possession at the time the burglary was attempted being a key factor.

But all other factors being equal, jurisdictions that define burglary with explosives in terms of willful and malicious intent would be likely to have the element satisfied if there is a justifiable cause of attempted burglary.

ARSON, EXPLOSIVES, AND INCENDIARIES AS CRIMES AGAINST THE PERSON

Although arson, explosives, and incendiaries have been classified for discussion in this volume in terms of crimes against the property, the brief discussion of the terrorists' use of explosives and incendiaries brings into focus the reality that these same crimes can indeed be against the person: arson and explosives can indeed be used for the specific purpose of murder. Many jurisdictions have adopted statutes that take this into account by explicitly citing homicides involving explosives, incendiaries, or arson. While this is, of necessity, a very serious felony to be considered in any discussion of the criminal law, the majority of arson and crimes involving explosives, as well as incendiary devices, remain against property.

SUMMARY

This chapter introduced the discussion of crimes involving arson, explosives, and incendiaries in terms of an increasing significance due to both an increase in the crimes of arson for profit and the increase in terrorism worldwide. Early common-law definitions of arson were developed in terms of the original four elements, with comparisons made to common-law definitions of burglary—both were originally identified as neither crimes against persons nor property but, instead, crimes against habitation.

Modern statutory modifications of arson were discussed: the expansion of the definitions of arson to encompass buildings other than homes and dwellings, and finally the focus on the specific crime of arson for profit.

Explosives and incendiaries were discussed both in terms of their statutory definition and the increasing significance of terrorists' use of explosives or incendiary devices. Discussion of terrorism was related to the general common law, and attention was drawn to the vast differences in statutory regulation of explosives between jurisdictions.

The chapter closed with examples of a criminal code relating to explosives, and the acknowledgment that even though the majority of crimes involving arson and explosives have to do with property, these crimes nevertheless can be crimes against the person.

NOTES

1. See, for example, W. L. Clark and W. Marshall, *A Treatise on the Law of Crimes*, 7th ed. M. Q. Barnes, rev. ed. (Mundelein, Ill.: Callaghan, 1967), Sec. 1309, pp. 1009–1019.

2. *Ibid.*, p. 1010.
3. Case law bearing on arson definition is collected in American Law Reports, 44 ALR, 2d, 1449.
4. *Ibid.*
5. *Ibid.*
6. See American Law Reports, 76 ALR, 2d, 524.
7. *Ibid.*
8. *Ibid.*
9. Pennsylvania State Police Academy, *Pennsylvania Criminal Law and Criminal Procedure* (Harrisburgh, Pa.: Telegraph Press, 1979), Sec. 906, p. 374.
10. *Ibid.*, pp. 212, 213.
11. *Ibid.*, pp. 260, 303, 377, 428.
12. *Ibid.*, Sec. 902, p. 372.

PRACTICAL EXERCISES

1. Sketch a flow chart depicting the activities in the crime involving either explosives or incendiaries.
2. Using the state penal code, summarize the sections pertinent to crimes involving arson, explosives, or incendiaries.

ANNOTATED REFERENCES

American Law Reports, 76 ALR, 2d, 524. Comprehensive collection of case law relevant to this chapter.

Belli, Melvin M. *The Law Revolt.* Vol 1: *Criminal Law.* Belleville, Ill.: Lawyers Service Company, 1968. An excellent discussion of the changes that are needed in the law to cope with terrorism.

Eldefonso, E.; Coffey, A.; and Grace, R. C. *Principles of Law Enforcement.* 2d ed. New York: Wiley, 1974. Segments of this book having to do with police procedures are particularly relevant to the material presented in this chapter on the growing use of military weapons in crime.

Fox, V. *Introduction to Criminology.* Englewood Cliffs, N.J.: Prentice-Hall, 1976. Excellent theoretical discussion of the various motivations for crime.

Chapter 11

CRIMES
OF THEFT

LEARNING OBJECTIVES

The learning objectives of this chapter are:
1. To understand larceny as a crime, in contrast to larceny as part of the crime of robbery.
2. To recognize larceny and similar crimes of fraud and embezzlement.
3. To learn the distinction between taking property as a crime of theft and the crime of receiving stolen property.
4. To become cognizant of the differences and similarities between the crimes of forgery and counterfeiting.

PUBLIC INTOLERANCE OF THEFT

CHAPTER 6 INTRODUCED THE DISCUSSION of various specific crimes in terms of public tolerance—in terms of how willing the public is to tolerate law violation. The major differences in criminal law between various jurisdictions were presented and subsequently used as a rationale for limiting the discussion of law violation to crimes that are generally *not* tolerated by the public and are more or less universally recognized as crime. In our discussion of sexual crimes, we found, paradoxically, that certain crimes, although nearly universally considered to be crime, are tolerated by a vast majority of the public—indeed, possibly practiced by the majority of the public. It was conceded that *inconsistency* exists not only as variation between the statutes of different jurisdictions but as variation in public tolerance as well—and the public is frequently very tolerant of certain "crimes."

The public's tolerance, however, does not extend to all crime that is widespread. For example, the crimes to be presented in this chapter are indeed widespread, but the general public shows little tolerance for these crimes: the public remains quite willing to complain about violation of theft laws regardless of how discrete the public may be about certain sexual practices that violate law.

These crimes of theft that will be presented in this chapter are *larceny, embezzlement, fraud, "receiving," forgery,* and *counterfeiting.* Larceny will be presented in essentially the same context as that in the previous discussion of burglary and robbery (Chapter 9). Each of the other theft crimes will be dealt with in relation to this fundamental theft concept of larceny. This suggests the need for a preliminary definition of *theft.*

THEFT DEFINED FOR DISCUSSION

Theft as the "common denominator" for the crimes to be covered in this chapter is simply what the dictionary defines as *stealing:* to steal is to take or appropriate without permission, dishonestly or unlawfully."[1] The term *appropriate* perhaps describes some of the crimes discussed in this chapter better than other crimes to be discussed. Regardless of the degree to which the term *appropriate* will apply to any particular crime, each of the crimes of theft have in common a factor that can be thought of as "unlawfully taking."

Earlier discussions of property, and more important, of ownership might be useful in drafting a tentative definition of theft.

First, let us examine the concepts of *possession*[2] and *custody* of property. Chamelin and Evans summed this distinction up: "A man has possession of property when he may exercise his discretion in the use and handling of that property. . . . One may be in physical control of an article without necessarily having possession of it."[3] A definition of theft that can be used for a meaningful discussion then must incorporate the concept of possessing property owned by another, rather than simply merely having such property "in custody."

Of course, the point here is that the mere "holding" of something— or as many prefer to state, the mere *control* of something—may not permit its *use*. For purposes of discussion, then, theft cannot be defined as a situation in which the "thief" has "merely" acquired property over which he had no discretion. Put another way, when there is no discretion, control of property is not the same as the possession that is needed to constitute theft.

The concept of ownership, of course, is the key to establishing a concept of theft. An owner can be *assumed* to have possession in this technical sense, whereas the accused thief has possession only when he has demonstrable discretion over the use of the property. A discussional definition of theft, then, reduces to the unlawful possession of someone else's property. The concept of intent will be established in the following discussion of the theft crime known as larceny.

LARCENY

Chapter 7 discussed robbery as a crime made up of two separate crimes —larceny and assault (refer to Figure 7.1). In that discussion, larceny was presented as having three major parts:

1. a victim's property "taken away"
2. an actual "taking away" of the property
3. an intent to deprive the victim of the property

Since we were discussing larceny as only one segment of another crime, these three parts were satisfactory. In the present discussion of larceny as the major crime of theft, however, a bit more elaboration is needed.

The *corpus delicti* of the crime of larceny at common law could be simplified even more than it was in our previous definition—at least in cases where there was a confession. The *corpus delicti* of larceny at common law had only two elements in cases that were confessed— the first element being an owner losing property by felonious taking, and the other element a confession.[4] Of course, when one removes the element of confession, common-law larceny must have six distinct parts:

1. A trespassory
2. A taking
3. A carrying away
4. A property
5. Property owned by another
6. Intent to deprive the owner permanently[5]

Trespassory

The term *trespass* is ordinarily understood in terms of an encroachment of some type—trespassing often thought of or defined by "no trespassing" signs posted on land that an owner wishes to keep free of uninvited visitors. As used in common-law larceny, *trespass*, or the *trespassory*, means taking the property from the *possession* of another.[6] In other words, from the common-law perspective of larceny, there is a significant difference between simply being unwelcomed on someone's land and unlawfully taking possession of the property of another— possession again being a critical factor.

Rather than emphasizing the "unwelcome" interpretation of trespass, common law emphasized *possession* of another's property.

The degree to which the concept of possession was emphasized at common law is illustrated by the reality that one could be convicted of larceny by taking unlawful possession from another thief. This brings into focus the second element of common-law larceny—taking.

Taking

While the concept of possession is critical to the element of trespassing, the actual taking is perhaps even more critical in establishing the common-law crime of larceny.[7] Though critical, the taking was a relatively simple matter established by virtually any former proof that the "taker" has obtained illegal possession—*illegal* meaning the property was owned by someone else, and *possession* defined in terms of the taker's discretion to control or use the property at his own will. Beyond the trespass in which possession was taken, common-law larceny required a "carrying away."

Carrying Away

The term that legal scholars apply to the element of carrying away in common-law larceny is *asportation*, meaning the illegal removal of the property after taking possession.[8] Of course, the evidence that possession had been taken would, in most cases, be the asportation: the carrying away would demonstrate that possession had been taken.

The carrying away must be complete enough to remove any doubt that the property taken is in a different location than it was before it was taken. The taking away can be satisfied only when the property has been carried away to a point other than its original location.[9]

Common-law larceny, then, required three elements to be considered before concern was even directed to what most would agree is the critical factor in theft—the property.

Property

In our discussion of robbery in Chapter 7, in which robbery was discussed as being made up of the two crimes of larceny and assault, property was defined as requiring legally recognized *ownership*— ownership subject to certain legalistic constraints. In most cases, this concept of property reduces simply to the old cliché "possession is nine-tenths of the law." In other words, in many cases, the mere possession, as already defined, virtually satisfies all constraints of the law—whoever has legal possession has ownership in most cases.

A more definitive examination of the common-law notion of property is possible by making a distinction between, say, *personal property* and *real property*—"real" referring to land and structures, "personal" referring to anything else that can be *owned*.

Insofar as larceny at common law is concerned, however, ownership was customarily personal property "of another."

Property of Another

Of course, *ownership*, as defined earlier, can be assumed on the basis of possession but was nevertheless a separate element of common law.[10] Ownership is, then, a crucial factor in larceny. As already noted, the owner, or legal possessor, could also be a thief. The owner *legally possesses* the property before theft, and the thief *illegally possesses* the property after the theft—possession remaining significant primarily in terms of ownership.

Intent

The significance of intent in criminal law has been repeatedly established throughout this volume. The intent element is even more significant in common-law larceny than in certain other crimes, because the intent in larceny must be to *permanently deprive* the owner of possession.[11]

The permanence of the deprivation of the owner's property was critical to the crime of larceny at common law. In discussing the larceny segment of robbery, the implication of *force* or the threat of force creates situations in which the permanence can be more readily presumed; at least the use of force creates situations in which, circumstantially, permanence can be assumed.

But in terms of larceny as a specific crime, the intent to deprive the owner permanently becomes, in most cases, a matter somewhat more difficult to prove, and when proof is forthcoming, it is usually a combination of facts and circumstances rather than a clearly established situation. Consider this example:

EXAMPLE

(A)
Stanley Stealer covets his neighbor Buzz's chain saw. Buzz makes the mistake of leaving his prize chain saw in the back of his pickup truck, which he has unwittingly parked in front of Stanley Stealer's home. Stan sees and takes the chain saw.

Stan has now (1) trespassed as defined in our discussion of larceny, (2) taken as defined, and (3) carried away as defined—the (4) property, and (5) "of another." Five of the six elements have already been established in the setting of this situation. Now the question of intent to deprive permanently comes into focus. With regard to the permanence of the intent to deprive Buzz of his chain saw, consider this:

(B)
Stan uses the unlawfully obtained chain saw to saw a cord of firewood. He then hides the chain saw in his basement, awaiting Buzz's reaction. Buzz suspects Stan and announces the intent to report the theft to the police. Stan returns the chain saw forthwith.

This is now a difficult situation because it can be argued *either* that Stan intended to keep the chain saw permanently or he wouldn't have hid it, *or* Stan intended merely to borrow it, as demonstrated by its return. In other words, "If Stan were going to return it, why did he hide it," versus "If Stan were going to keep it, why did he return it?"

In this particular situation, Stan's hiding of the saw after using it weighs on the side of permanent intent. This becomes clear if we change the story to have Stan return the saw immediately after cutting the firewood—the situation is now conspicuously different.

The critical factor is intent rather than *time*, so no clear case emerges in any event. But from the frame of reference of evidence, the nature of the problem should be clarified by this facetious situation. Needless to add, had Stan required Buzz to *pay* for the return of the chain saw, particularly under any pretext that someone else had stolen it, a much clearer case of larceny is established.

Statutory Modification

As with most crime definitions, there is a great deal of variation between jurisdictions in defining larceny, at least in the wording of the statutes. As a practical police matter, most jurisdictions retain the basic common-law approach to larceny—that it is a crime of parts that includes to some degree each of the six larceny elements at common law.

While variation in statutory penalty does exist, most jurisdictions are consistent in defining *petty larceny* as a misdemeanor and *grand larceny* as a felony—some jurisdictions preferring to use other terms but nevertheless having the same implication. Grand larceny, of course, is a theft of something of considerable value; petty larceny being a theft of lesser value.

This concept of value has led to establishment in some cases of first- and second-degree larceny—certain jurisdictions holding that first-degree larceny involves the theft of extremely valuable property and that second-degree involves the theft of property of lesser value.[12]

Many jurisdictions have established statutes that virtually combine larceny with embezzlement in a category of crime known as *obtaining property by false pretenses*. This category actually forms a rather broad "family" of crimes having to do with theft. Regardless of local-jurisdictional variation, however, one must understand common-law larceny to understand crimes of theft in general—crimes of theft that include embezzlement.

EMBEZZLEMENT

The crime of embezzlement[13] was acknowledged in England long before American statutory law defining *embezzlement* emerged. (By "acknowledged" is meant the very loose and informal recognition in feudal England that the concept of *ownership* was sufficiently clear in titles or possession that "wrong" could be done to ownership, as well as to the owner and the owner's property.) But though embezzlement was acknowledged, it was not a common-law crime. Embezzlement, then, is a statutory crime posing a somewhat different problem for discussion in that there is no common-law definition on which to draw. But in spite of the absence of a common-law definition, there is a great deal of consistency in the way various jurisdictions define embezzlement.

Definition

Returning to the broad distinctions between crimes against the person and crimes against property, we recall that there are yet other broad categories of crime—for instance, crime against habitation, as defined in early common-law definitions of burglary and arson. While it was argued that the modifications in early common-law statutes against habitation or against occupancy have modified the law in the direction of increasing the crimes against property, the additional category was nonetheless acknowledged. In much the same way, an additional category is created by the crime of embezzlement—embezzlement being a crime against *ownership*.[14]

Of course, this additional category will also be presented in the context of a crime against property. But conceiving of embezzlement as a crime against ownership permits a clearer picture of what the crime of embezzlement is all about. Consider the following definition of embezzlement: "The fraudulent conversion or appropriation by a servant, clerk, agent, bailee, officer of a corporation, public officer, or other person specified in the statute, of money or property."[15] Note, in particular, the similarity of this crime to the crime of extortion. Just as extortion requires that a public official be involved, embezzlement requires that other particular individuals be involved. Put another way, the most pertinent similarity between extortion and embezzlement is that both have requirements that someone in particular be involved— public officials in the cases of extortion and those listed in the above definition in the case of embezzlement.

Another similarity is the *assumption* that the individuals be *trusted* —at least in theory. For, indeed, if the persons specified were not trusted, they could not embezzle—at least in theory.

As a practical police matter, many jurisdictions define embezzlement in a way that puts it in the same classification as larceny, or they make the embezzlement definition so similar that the evidence required is virtually the same. Nevertheless, the specific crime of embezzlement requires that a specific individual be responsible for the crime—otherwise it is another crime, if a crime at all. Indeed, what distinguishes embezzlement from larceny is the requirement that the "converter" be in an entrusted position, so that the crime does not require a trespassing as in the case of larceny. Consideration of the concept of conversion is therefore worthwhile at this point.

Conversion

Conversion, as related to embezzlement, is the converting of *possession* of property from its owner to someone other than the owner. In a sense, being able to convert possession illegally and do so without trespassing is the only functional difference between larceny and embezzlement—except perhaps in jurisdictions that broaden the definition of larceny so broadly that it encompasses what is being discussed here as embezzlement. In this regard, some jurisdictions have broadened the embezzlement definition to the point of including the finding of lost property and converting it.*

Except for these variations between jurisdictions, there is a rather consistent approach to embezzlement, whether it is incorporated within the category of larceny or not. The consistency in most statutory law has to do with the conversion, which can only be accomplished by someone entrusted. Whether or not the accused *could* convert possession of the property is usually the distinction between larceny and embezzlement as it is being discussed in this chapter, regardless of what either is called or how they are combined in statute. Put another way, most jurisdictions acknowledge that embezzlement is not possible unless the individual is in a position sufficiently entrusted to convert possession of property without trespassing as is required in larceny. Except for this difference, both crimes require essentially the same variety of evidence to prove.

FRAUD

The crime of fraud, like embezzlement, is without a common-law basis —fraud is a completely statutory crime. Even though common-law elements cannot be discussed for this crime, an understanding of the elements of larceny affords a good background for considering the statutory nature of fraud. Statutes have a certain consistency in defining fraud, even though there is a great deal of variation in jurisdictional definitions for the punishment of this crime.[16]

---

* Examination of local, specific embezzlement statutes from any jurisdiction in question is the only effective method of determining whether "found" property can possibly be encompassed within the definition of "entrusted" property.

The *Treatise on the Law of Crimes* breaks out eleven factors involved in fraud:

1. There must be some form of pretense.
2. The pretense must be more than withholding facts.
3. There must be a representation of something that exists or did exist other than a forecast, an intention, a promise, an opinion, or bragging.
4. The representation must be a lie.
5. The lie must be intended to deceive.
6. The liar must be aware that it is a lie told for the purpose of illegally gaining property.
7. The deception must be successful.
8. The deceived person may or may not be negligent.
9. The property must be taken away.
10. The victim must be "injured."
11. The property must be defined in the written law of the jurisdiction.[17]

Careful study of these eleven factors will clarify the significance of the term *false pretenses* in fraud matters.

False Pretenses

The term *false pretenses* is used in many jurisdictions to identify what is being discussed here as the crime of fraud, but it usually has a somewhat broader definition than will be discussed here. In the present context, the term *false pretense* is used to help clarify some of the characteristics of fraud rather than to identify a particular crime. In other words, the term is being used here to emphasize the "pretense" nature of fraud rather than to replace the term *fraud* as identifying a particular crime. This is done because of the importance of recognizing the difference in evidence involved in theft by fraud—*pretenses* are the prime requisite.

Of course, in jurisdictions where the term *false pretenses* is the actual name of the crime being discussed here, this discussion is directed to false pretenses as a crime. However, the term applies to what will be discussed here in terms of differences with other forms of theft. In that context, the eleven factors involved in fraud, noted above, become relevant in terms of pretenses, *false pretenses* in this case describing theft by a different means—theft by means of pretenses.

Fraud, then, differs from robbery in that there is no effort to fool the victim in most robberies. In the case of fraud, the victim must be fooled for the crime to be successful in most cases. One of the unique characteristics of fraud is that effort must be exerted to prevent the victim from being clear on the purpose of the crime. Consider this example:

EXAMPLE

Timmy Truthful buys wholesale used automobiles from a car dealer friend and resells them as a private "original" owner.

Timmy not only fails to reveal the car's history, but he also pretends that he is the original owner, certifying that often faulty cars are in good repair. He often confides that the "original-owner sham" is the most effective method to convince the buyers that a bad car is good—a deception successful in repeated instances.

Tim claims the prices he charges are based on professional appraisals, which his victims rarely check before giving Tim the money requested—money quite often beyond many of the victim's ability to comfortably pay.

Tim lives in a state that specifies automobiles as property subject to *fraud*, or "false pretenses," law.

Of course, this example fits hand-in-glove with the eleven factors of fraud. But slight alteration of the example can serve to clarify the unique characteristics of "false pretenses" insofar as criminal law is concerned. Suppose Tim does not pretend the appraisal occurred. Then he is merely offering an *opinion* of the car's worth, not grounds for fraud as defined. Certainly, Tim's withholding of facts about the car cannot be proof of misrepresentation when all he need do is simply claim he failed to recall the facts that were not reported. Consider this "lost-memory defense" in terms of the eleven factors noted for the crime of fraud.

Tim did fail to acknowledge that the car was used by *pretending* he was the original owner, but this omission would be a difficult basis for fraud if it were the only misrepresentation involved. The case would obviously change even further if the state in which Tim operated did not identify automobiles as property in fraud cases. Since fraud cases often develop in a less classic manner than presented in the example, further consideration of misrepresentation is worthwhile—misrepresentation, swindles, and other tricks involved in false pretenses.

Misrepresentation, Tricks, and Swindles

Although many jurisdictions make provisions for separating fraud as a specific crime from the false-pretense crimes of misrepresentations, tricks, and swindles, all four of these false-pretense crimes are very similar. Methods of false pretenses vary, but as applied to the statutory crimes of misrepresentation, trick, or swindle, they are essentially the same as the false pretenses involved in the crime of fraud. The con game approach to swindling may depend more on the victim's greed than on the perpetrator's skill at misrepresenting, but the con game is, nevertheless, "falsely pretending" in the same sense that fraud in general is.

Were this a text on criminology or police investigation, the examples would, of necessity, dramatize the similarity of all crimes involving false pretenses—they would emphasize the similarity regardless of jurisdictional variations in statutes.

Of course, intent remains critical, even though it varies widely depending on the false pretenses involved. Just as *false pretenses* can actually be a term identifying a specific crime as well as a description of the nature of the crime, so also the term *misrepresentation* can be either. But in both cases the intent is to fool the victim, as in the brief example cited for the crime of fraud. In other words, the misrepresentation of the con game may differ somewhat from the fraud example, but false pretenses are essential to both—and in both cases, the *intent* to defraud must be present.

RECEIVING STOLEN PROPERTY

Early common law identified "receiving stolen property"[18] as a misdemeanor, if the receiver knew that the property he was receiving was in fact stolen. This misdemeanor at common law was made up of four parts:

1. *received*, made up of the accused actually taking *possession*
2. *stolen*, made up of evidence that the property received was unlawfully taken from the owner
3. *aware*, made up of the receiver's knowledge that the property was stolen
4. *intent*, existing when the purpose of receiving is fraudulent

In brief elaboration of these four parts of the crime of receiving, it is worth note that this crime is usually described in conjunction with concealing the stolen property. In most jurisdictions, both receiving and concealing are crimes, and the two are distinguished in terms of minor technicalities. This is reflected in the statutory law in terms of what has been discussed earlier as possession. If the receiver simply aids someone else in concealing stolen property, many jurisdictions will hold this aid in concealment as much a law violation as being the actual receiver of stolen property. Even when the aid in concealing is nothing more than the space to hide the stolen property, the concealing is, in these jurisdictions, as much a crime as actual fencing.

As for what constitutes *stolen*, it is generally held that property unlawfully acquired by way of *any of* the crimes of theft will constitute a basis for the crime of receiving. Court decisions buttress this legislative structure when they identify property taken in *any* unlawful manner as a basis for the crime of receiving.

With regard to being *aware* that the property is stolen, most statutes are satisfied with proof that the receiver *had knowledge* that the property received was stolen—that the property either received or concealed was stolen. In most cases, the burden of proof usually rests upon the accused he must prove that he was *not* aware that the property he received or concealed was in fact stolen. The variation between jurisdictions usually exists in areas having to do with whether the accused "should have known," but in most cases the burden of proof is on the receiver regardless of the wording of various statutes.

In cases where a statute requires proof of actual knowledge, the case is more difficult, in that beyond unlawful possession the accused has wide latitude to explain how possession occurred without his knowledge of stolen property. This, of necessity, brings police, in many cases, face to face with the specific task of proving intent—intent being essential in all crime definitions.

Intent in these crimes differs little from the intent in other crimes. In the case of receiving, intent involves the receiver or concealer *intending* to keep the rightful owner deprived of the stolen property—or in some cases, intending to force the owner to pay for the recovery of the stolen property.

As a practical police matter, cases of receiving usually align with such crimes as burglaries, which are best controlled when the fence, or receiver, is apprehended—fencing being a crime that, of necessity, requires a crime of theft to precede it.

FORGERY

Early common law recognized forgery as a crime. However, as an early common-law offense, forgery was in many ways restricted to what was then a somewhat limited concept of "writing" and of "documents."[19] Forgery was at common law a misdemeanor and merely one of several minor offenses known as "cheats"—the term *cheat* evolving to encompass a broader range of crimes of theft since early common law.

The advent of banking and checking accounts probably had much to do with vast statutory expansion of forgery beyond this limited common-law definition. Contemporary statutory laws regarding forgery encompass virtually any fraudulent alteration of writing, as well as any "misrepresentation" or alteration. Perhaps the expansion is best clarified by a brief review of the original concept of forgery in common law:

1. making a false instrument
2. the false instrument itself
3. alteration
4. alteration sufficient to defraud, or cheat, the victim
5. intent to defraud the victim

Statutory expansion throughout virtually all jurisdictions has focused on number 2, the false instrument.

False Instrument

As a practical police matter, *paperhanging*, which is writing checks without enough money on deposit (that is, insufficient funds), is the most common form of the modern statutory crime of forgery. Although stolen credit cards and forged signatures have increasingly been incorporated into this "family" of crime, "bad checks" remain the major problem area. Increasing electronic security and various other safeguards may modify this in years to come.

The segment of the crime known as the instrument is the critical factor in understanding the crime of forgery. The bad check is often the instrument, but virtually anything that, when forged, will yield unlawful payment is an instrument. In other words, if altering or creating something in writing could lead to unlawful payment, a case for forgery could be based on what has been forged.

A majority of jurisdictions will identify for purposes of defining forgery *any* instrument that acquires this form of written misrepresentation—whether it be a bill or a check or any similar instrument.

Also in relation to the instrument of forgery, it was noted that there is a requirement that the instrument be "sufficient to cheat." This sufficiency comes down to pinpointing what was just mentioned as "leading to unlawful payment." If the instrument does not have the capacity to produce a false payment, then there can be no forgery. *Payment*, of course, must be broadly defined but usually reduces to the legal liability to deliver money. For example, since a "good check" carries legal liability to make payment, so a *forged* check presumably acquires capability to rate payment.

Statutory law generally allows any method of forgery to stand as the act—whether it be pencil or printing press.

Uttering

A crime related to false instrument, considered by many to be simply another form of forgery, is uttering. Common law allowed for uttering as well as passing false instruments.[20] In essence, this is a crime in which the individual passing or uttering the false instrument is not the actual forger. The law required, of course, that the utterer or passer be aware that the instrument was false. The term *utter*, then, when beyond the question of who did the actual forging to the actual defrauding involved. Law, in this regard, sometimes includes the *attempt* to utter or to pass a false instrument, or to *offer* a false instrument.

COUNTERFEITING

Counterfeiting is an offense closely related to forgery. At common law, counterfeiting evolved in relation to forgery cases in which the forgery was something other than a false instrument as described above. In a sense, then, counterfeiting became a crime to fill in certain loopholes in the common law crime of forgery.

Such things as fraudulent copies of famous paintings and statues emerged as a separate category of crime simply because forgery did not encompass the specific crime of *copying the authentic original*. In other words, forgery may not be a copy of an authentic original and may be contrived without any authentic basis, the false pretenses being the only critical variable. Conversely, counterfeiting requires the existence of an original to copy. The federal crime of counterfeiting U.S. currency is perhaps the most dramatic illustration of counterfeiting. Police also encounter the unlawful duplication of authentic ID cards, drivers' permits, and similar instruments—these are customarily defined in statutes as crime. Situations and statutes vary to the point that nothing definitive can be said about an absolute distinction between forgery and counterfeiting in all cases, since *either* charge is, in many cases appropriate.

SUMMARY

This chapter presented a variety of crimes known as crimes of theft, beginning with a basic definition of larceny. Earlier discussion of larceny as one segment of the crime of robbery was elaborated in terms of both its common-law origin and its subsequent statutory modification. The extended discussion of larceny, in turn, provided a background for a discussion of embezzlement and fraud as statutory crimes—both having in common the requirement of false pretenses as a basis. Misrepresentation, tricks, and swindles were also discussed.

The crime of receiving stolen property was presented, along with the crime of forgery and counterfeiting.

NOTES

1. *Webster's New World Dictionary of the American Language*, s.v. "steal."
2. See, for example, C. W. Clark and W. Marshall A *Treatise on the Law of Crimes*, M. Q. Barnes, revising ed. (Mundelein, Ill.: Callaghan, 1967), pp. 819–870.
3. N. C. Chamelin and K. R. Evans, *Criminal Law for Police* (Englewood Cliffs, N.J.: Prentice-Hall, 1976), p. 210.
4. Clark and Marshall, *Treatise on the Law of Crimes*, p. 798.
5. American Law Reports, 88 ALR, 2d, 674.
6. American Law Reports, 82 ALR, 2d, 863.
7. *Ibid.*
8. American Law Reports, 56 ALR, 2d, 1149, and 82 ALR, 2d, 863.
9. Clark and Marshall, *Treatise on the Law of Crimes*, p. 832.
10. American Law Reports, 71 ALR, 2d, 605; 82 ALR, 2d, 863; and 56 ALR, 2d, 1149.
11. American Law Reports, 88 ALR, 2d, 674, and 82 ALR, 2d, 863.
12. See, for example, J. C. Klohel and C. L. Meick, *Criminal Evidence for Police*, 2d ed. (Cincinnati: Anderson, 1975).
13. See, for example, American Law Reports, 56 ALR, 2d, 1149, and 36 ALR. 373, 366.
14. Chamelin and Evans, *Criminal Law for Police*, p. 129: embezzlement defined as a crime against ownership.
15. Clark and Marshall, *Treatise on the Law of Crimes*, p. 898.
16. See, for example, M. McKay, "Fraudulent Transactions in the Criminal Law," 3 *Western Ontario Law Review* 10 (1964).
17. Clark and Marshall, *Treatise on the Law of Crimes*, p. 921.
18. For background, see American Law Reports, 82 ALR, 2d, 863; 56 ALR, 2d, 1149; 36 ALR, 373, 366; and 71 ALR, 2d, 605.
19. Clark and Marshall, *Treatise on the Law of Crimes*, p. 953.
20. *Ibid.*, pp. 966, 967.

PRACTICAL EXERCISES

1. Select any *one* of the crimes of theft discussed in this chapter and sketch a flow chart reflecting all the activities involved in this crime.
   a. Emphasize the activities of the perpetrator.
   b. Reflect the functions of law enforcement, prosecution–defense, and the courts.
2. Using the state penal code, summarize the sections pertinent to all the crimes of theft that were discussed in this chapter.

ANNOTATED REFERENCES

Bassioni, M. C. *Criminal Law and Its Processes.* Springfield, Ill.: Thomas, 1969. This book affords a somewhat different approach to contrasting crimes against property than does the present chapter.
Ehrlich, J. *Ehrlich's Criminal Law.* Albany, N.Y.: Mathew Bender,

1970. An interesting looseleaf "how-to" format; includes illustrative cases.

Eldefonso, E.; Coffey, A.; and Sullivan, J. *Police and the Criminal Law*. Pacific Palisades, Calif.: Goodyear, 1972. Chapter 6 affords a general common context in which to consider the contents of the present chapter.

Perkins, R. M. *Criminal Law*. Mineola, N.Y.: Foundation Press, 1969. A classical book of definitions for evaluating the terms used in the present chapter.

Chapter 12

OFFENSES AGAINST PUBLIC ORDER AND PUBLIC JUSTICE

LEARNING OBJECTIVES

The learning objectives of this chapter are:
1. To understand the concept of "peace" as it relates to offenses against public order and public justice.
2. To recognize the significance of "public fear" in relation to the concept of disorderly conduct.
3. To become aware of the distinction between crimes such as vandalism and trespassing and other crimes such as gambling or unlawful assembly.
4. To learn the significance of "status" offenses.

IN A SENSE, ALL THE CRIMES AGAINST the person and against property have already been presented in previous chapters. In this chapter and the remaining chapter, crimes involving public order, public justice, and juveniles will be presented. Although many of these remaining discussions of crime will deal with what amounts to both crimes against the person and against property, the crimes to be discussed in the remainder of this volume are, nevertheless, "specialized" and differ somewhat from previous discussions.

This is not to suggest that these crimes are any less "criminal" than the crimes already discussed. Indeed, the "technical" definition of crime can be distinguished in severity only by penalty or the misdemeanor-felony distinction—crime is crime. But for purposes of discussion and clarity, it might be well to recognize something of a contrast, or at least a "difference," in the *nature* of the crimes being discussed for the remainder of the volume as opposed to crimes already presented.

To assist in conceptualizing this contrast, refer again to Figures 6.1 and 7.1 in Chapters 6 and 7. These two figures are not intended to provide a definitive elaboration of these crimes, but to refresh the memory of the reader before we proceed with a discussion of offenses against public order and public justice. From these two figures, a kind of picture should emerge of the basic classifications of crime. Most citizens would acknowledge that there are other kinds of crime confronting the police—the crimes that will be discussed in this chapter as crimes against public order and crimes against the government process.

Review of the crimes already discussed may serve as a foundation for considering such crimes as disturbing the peace, vagrancy, gambling, vandalism, trespass, and crimes against the government process. The criminal element of intent as related to crimes previously discussed will remain germane to the offenses presented for the remainder of this chapter. In other words, these crimes, though somewhat different in some respects from the crimes against property and persons as already discussed, can be best understood in terms of the same *mens rea* principles used to develop understanding of crimes against people and property.

The extremely wide variation in statutes from one jurisdiction to the next precludes any particular unifying influence. It is suggested that readers consult the criminal codes of their own jurisdictions in relation to each of the crimes to be presented in this chapter.

DISTURBING THE PEACE

A kind of parallel can be drawn between the discussion of indecent exposure in Chapter 6 and the crime being presented here, disturbing the peace. Both crimes have to do with disturbing the public. Both crimes also involve a somewhat subjective notion of what offends the public and *where* the public might be offended. A nude on a nude beach may not be offensive to the very same public who may complain vigorously to police about a nude standing on a street corner. Similarly, a loud band concert in an auditorium may not be offensive to the very same public who might vigorously complain to police of a loud stereo music system next door late at night.

It should not then be surprising that a wide variation exists in the statutes that each jurisdiction chooses to adopt in coping with this rather nebulous problem. Perhaps consideration should be given to the concept of *peace* before any further attention is directed to *disturbance*.

The significance of the concept of peace, as related to crime in the criminal law, is suggested in many ways, not the least of which is implied in the term *peace officer*. The term *keeping the peace* is often used to encompass all that police officers are responsible to achieve. In a general sense, using the term *keeping the peace* to encompass all police responsibility is not totally accurate, in that it would imply that no crime existed. The term *keeping the peace*, then, is of little value in fully understanding the crime of disturbing the peace. Further consideration of *peace* is indicated.

With respect to the concept of peace, it is worth note that at common law the crime of disturbing the peace evolved out of offenders that tended to blur the distinction between ecclesiastic religious law and the criminal law. The peace that was being kept, of necessity, became somewhat ambiguous when it related to profanity, blasphemy, and witchcraft. Integrating these offenses against peace with such peace violations as a noisy shotgun in the dead of night was not difficult in a land dominated by a national church.[1] American criminal law has no such national church and has, of necessity, legislated laws more closely aligned to nonreligious disturbances of the peace.

In terms of retaining the influence of common law, however, it is worth note that whether religious or civil, disturbing the peace as a crime had to do with "shocking the public." Put another way, whether the public was shocked at some gross insensitivity to religious protocol or shocked at loud unexplained noises, the public's peace was disturbed.

As will be noted shortly, then, the concept of peace has much to do with "peace and quiet." Setting this observation aside for the moment, we can now direct our attention to consideration of the "disturbance" segment of disturbing the peace.

American criminal law, without an established national church, has nevertheless adopted some of the early common law peace disturbances that were more religious than civil.* For this reason, it might facilitate understanding the crime of disturbing the peace to consider the term *disorderly conduct*. At least in its semantics, the term *disorderly conduct* fits what is customarily involved in the crime of disturbing the peace better than the term *disturbing the peace*, which can be either religious or civil.

Disorderly Conduct

The public could be just as shocked by conduct that violated religious mores as any other behavior. But in a land where a national church does not establish clear definitions of religious disorder, the term *disorderly conduct* can be applied more readily to a concept of public order.[2]

Public order can, in turn, be related to a general "peace-and-quiet" standard in any given community—and this standard be used to determine if conduct is disorderly.

While examination of various criminal codes from various jurisdictions showed a great deal of fluctuation in defining *disorderly* even within this context, there is sufficient consistency to take a general position that disorderly conduct is what is considered disorderly in a given locality. There are, nonetheless, certain consistent ramifications of laws having to do with disorderly conduct, one of which is fear.

Fear. In most jurisdictions, whatever is believed to generate fear on a wide-scale basis within a community would constitute a disturbance of the peace, and hence disorderly conduct. Therefore, in spite of major variations and specific definitions of what constitutes disorderly conduct, there are certain consistent variables assumed to generate fear. Consider, for example, unlawful assembly, lynching and rout, riots, and nuisances.

Nuisances. Before examining some of the more dramatic situations in which public fear would presumably be generated, it might be well to address one of the more common problems facing police patrol. Most communities establish statutes that define as crime peace disturbances such as dog owners failing to keep their dogs from barking at night, parties not ending by a "reasonable hour," being excessively noisy, and a host of other nuisance disturbances with which police must deal. As a practical matter, police process these kinds of complaints more by warnings than by summons or arrest. Other forms of disturbances are more significant than nuisances and often entail arrests.

* Random samples of five or more state criminal codes usually produce discernible evidence that religious-based law has influenced the statutes.

Unlawful assembly, rout, riot. The *Treatise on the Law of Crimes* depicts the common-law crime of unlawful assembly as an "incipient state of riot," adding that the unlawful assembly also has the potential to "breach the peace."[3] This same source defines *rout* as a "perpetuating action" of an unlawful assembly, and defines *riot* as an unlawful assembly with "overt acts of violence." In effect, this establishes a continuum of behavior, increasing in severity toward actual violence. Variations between jurisdictions notwithstanding, this continuum of increasing severity is generally adopted into statutes as the varying degrees of disturbing the peace—riots exceeded only by lynching as the severist crime of this nature.

VAGRANCY

Laws governing disturbing the peace can draw on common-law roots for clarity, but the crime of vagrancy—loitering, usually because of being broke and having nowhere to go—is entirely statutory and without common-law background.

There is some question of whether vagrancy statutes are constitutional, being that the crime of vagrancy is a status or condition rather than a behavior or act as called for in the concept of *mens rea*.[4] It should not be surprising, then, that many jurisdictions have no vagrancy law. Those jurisdictions that do retain vagrancy laws may someday encounter a U.S. Supreme Court decision that such laws are totally unconstitutional should a test case be brought before the highest court of the land. In essence, vagrancy as a crime permits being jailed for the "status of being broke" rather than for any criminal act. Some would argue that the "status of being drunk" establishes the concept of "status offender," but most would argue that being broke is somewhat less criminal than drinking to the point of violating the law.

At a practical police matter, the laws on vagrancy usually afford an expedient for law enforcement that is difficult to do without. Public complaints of "nuisances" that are not covered by ordinance can often be dealt with through vagrancy statutes. In spite of the trend toward urbanization throughout the nation, the "stranger in town" is more likely to generate suspicion that leads to complaints to the police. Vagrancy laws frequently permit police response in that no other crime fits the nature of the public's concern.

Essentially the purpose of these laws is prevention of loitering, which presumably will in some way prevent crime. In practice, these laws reduce to legislating against being broke in a strange city—scarcely a model of criminal justice in a democratic society.

GAMBLING

Anyone who has visited the state of Nevada presumably knows that gambling is not illegal in all jurisdictions. Gambling was not crime at common law, and it is only "partially crime" in most jurisdictions under statutes.

In states that do identify gambling crimes, the offenders often have to do with when and where the gambling occurs, or perhaps with the type of gambling, rather than outright prohibition of gambling. Even in states where gambling is illegal, some form of licensed horse betting or lottery is often permitted.

Statutory variations between jurisdictions include different approaches to licensing lotteries, horse races, card houses, bingo games, and a host of advertising promotions. Licensing enforcement ranges from none at all through rigid, stringent monitoring by gambling commissions or other forms of governing bodies. Some states go so far as to out-and-out run the gambling insofar as certain enterprises are concerned, such as horse racing or paramutual betting.

Gambling—including the booking of bets and illegal gaming tables and houses—is not as much of a concern to the police as is the connection of these activities to organized crime. Like prostitution, gambling is a minor crime problem until "organized"; then it often becomes a major enforcement problem.

Perhaps more than any other crime that varies between jurisdictions in terms of statutes, gambling requires careful review of the local criminal statutes for full comprehension of the enforcement obligation.

VANDALISM

The term *vandalism* is often used interchangeably with *malicious mischief*, a common-law misdemeanor involving damaging someone else's property maliciously.[5] Technically, if arson is committed for the sole purpose of damaging the property rather than for any mercenary motive, it is malicious mischief in the sense that this crime is being presented in this section—the fact that arson is a more serious crime and likely to be the charge instead of malicious mischief notwithstanding.

All jurisdictions recognize vandalism and malicious mischief and have established statutes that have a great deal of similarity, varying only in specified punishment for these crimes. This similarity is probably due to the common-law requirement, adopted into all the statutes, that the *intent* of this particular crime be willful and malicious damage of another's property. Of course, the *mens rea* concept further requires that actual damage to the property be done for the crime to be complete. In most jurisdictions, virtually any form of damage constitutes a basis for this element of the crime.

Police involvement in these cases is often in conjunction with what will be presented in the next chapter—juvenile offenses. This is not to say juveniles are the only vandals with whom police must deal: vandalism and malicious mischief are common occurrence during labor disputes, labor strikes, and a host of other disagreements that get out of hand and require police intervention.

TRESPASS

The technical definition of *trespass* used thus far in this volume encompasses a broad range of behaviors, all of which function as one element of other crimes. As an offense in and of itself, *trespass* has to do with going onto someone else's land or premises without their permission— or more specifically going onto their land against their wishes.

All jurisdictions permit "remedy" for the offended property owner in the civil court, removing this offense somewhat from the sphere of criminal justice. However, many jurisdictions define such trespassing as a crime, which, in turn, introduces potential intervention of criminal justice. Insofar as the criminal law is concerned, statutes are customarily geared to forbidding unauthorized hunting, fishing, poaching, and so on, with control of recreation activities—camping, hiking, and boating— also included in some jurisdictions. The key, of course, remains *ownership* of the land and, more particularly, the trespassers' intent to violate the owner's wishes that they stay off the land.

As a practical matter, these cases, when they involve police, often focus on the presence or absence of *proof* that the trespassers were *aware* they were trespassing and *intended* to do so. Signs and other forms of "advisories" are usually called for in criminal codes that contain statutes against trespassing.

GOVERNMENT-PROCESS CRIMES

The remaining crimes to be discussed in this chapter have to do with government process—with crimes involving judicial process and other forms of government responsibility. The crime of extortion, presented in Chapter 8, is, in all respects, in this same classification; it was presented in Chapter 8 merely because of its conceptual similarity to the crime of blackmail.

As was acknowledged in Chapter 8, some have expanded the concept of extortion to encompass any form of crime that uses a threat of force, thereby making extortion a form of robbery. However, from the perspective of the common-law definition that extortion can only be committed by a public official, the previous discussion of extortion can be integrated in the present discussion, the tremendous similarity to blackmail notwithstanding. For, indeed, extortion is in many ways just as similar to the first crime to be discussed in this section, bribery.

Bribery

The common-law definition of *bribery* was the giving of anything of value to a public official with the intent to influence the official.[6] The relationship between bribery and organized crime has been noted in the literature.[7] Were this volume addressed to criminology, this relationship between bribery and organized crime would be pursued in depth. For our present purpose, examining the criminal law, the crime of bribery will be discussed only as a crime.

Virtually all jurisdictions define bribery as a crime that differs somewhat from other crimes in terms of the *act*. Recalling the concept of *mens rea* presented throughout this volume, the act in bribery is in a sense only partial. By *partial* is meant that most statutes require that the act of giving something valuable to a public official is required, but the public official is not actually required to act to complete the crime of bribery; she need merely "agree" to be influenced by the bribery gift—and not necessarily influenced in her public office. Put another way, the public official's "half" of the act is merely to agree. Aside from the "attempted bribery" statutes, which will be noted in a moment, bribery has occurred when the public official agrees to be influenced by th gift, *even if she fails to keep her illegal promise.*

Bribery differs from extortion in most jurisdictions in that bribery does not require the promise to be made in relation to the public office, nor for the promise to be kept—merely to be made and be based on the gift.

Examination of various criminal codes suggests that legislative changes to common-law bribery are being made in the direction of preventing the "agreement," as well as preventing the agreement from taking effect, as shown, for example, by the following: "Whoever shall . . . by means of . . . any promise or agreement, for the payment . . . of any money, goods, or other thing in order to obtain or influence the vote, opinion, verdict, award, judgment, decree, or behavior of any [public official] . . ."[8] Now, in terms of structuring the law toward preventing even the effect to bribe, consider this example: "Every person who gives or *offers* any bribe to [a public official] of this state, with intent to influence him . . . is punishable by imprisonment [italics added].[9]

This same penal code contains additional sections identifying a host of various public officials to whom even the *offer* of a bribe is a crime.[10]

When enforced in terms of "offering," the concept of *attempted* crime as previously described would encompass the charge—also, presumably, excluding prosecution of the official who reported the attempt unless additional evidence that she agreed to bribes was available.

Some jurisdictions have chosen to expand the concept of "public official" to include in their bribery statutes "athletes." Not surprisingly, these same codes that include athletes often include athletic officials, which would again broaden the concept of "public officials." In jurisdictions with these broader definitions of who may be bribed, the significance of bribery customarily expands damatically for law enforcement.

Of course, the concept of intent is as relevant to bribery as it is to all other crimes—*intent* as related to common-law bribery reducing to evidence that either the "offer" or the "agreement" or both are *corrupt*. The "agreed-upon outcome" between the official and the briber need not favor the briber. This differs somewhat from extortion—discussed in Chapter 8—in which the "outcome" must favor the "extorted" victim. And in bribery, as already noted, the public official who "agrees" need not necessarily agree to utilize his public office in order to complete the crime.[11]

Nonfeasance and Misfeasance

Extortion and bribery are the serious offenses related to public office. However, there are other crimes in most jurisdictions that are criminal only when a public official is charged—these crimes are nonfeasance and misfeasance.

NONFEASANCE: In most jurisdictions, if it can be proved that a public official *deliberately* failed to perform any function of his office that is specified by statute, a charge of nonfeasance can be made. Punishment for this crime varies greatly between jurisdictions, but it is nevertheless commonly recognized in criminal statute that direct failure to perform legally mandated duties of an accepted office constitutes crime. The case, in most instances, must be blatant in that the *intent* segment of this crime is singularly difficult in many instances.

MISFEASANCE: There is a crime in many jurisdictions that is very similar to nonfeasance, known as misfeasance. This is a kind of "abusive power" crime in which the jurisdiction has legislated parameters on the use of authority and power in a public office. The crime involves abuse of this statutorially defined authority.

Jury Tampering

The term *tampering* is defined in different ways in different jurisdictions in part because "protection of juries" is approached in different ways. For instance, many jurisdictions specifically cite juries or jury members in statutes dealing with bribery—a juror, in such instances, is identified in the same manner as a public official was identified in the discussion above. For, just as only public officials can be prosecuted for extortion, as defined by many jurisdictions, so also do many jurisdictions restrict the definition of "jury tampering" to the activities of a juror receiving a bribe, or the act of trying to bribe a juror.

For purposes of discussion, tampering can be thought of as some form of bribe, as some form of threat, or as both. In other words, if either threats or bribes are used to influence a jury, tampering has occurred. Most jurisdictions legislate against illicit efforts to influence juries.

As a practical matter for criminal justice, either a bribe or a threat that can materially alter a trial can nullify exhaustive investigation and even skillful prosecution of a case. It is, then, in the interest of criminal justice that local jurisdictions regard jury tampering as serious crime. In other words, criminal justice should emphasize enforcement of laws designed to ensure that a criminal trial is tried by "twelve jurors who will be fair to both sides of the case."[12]

It is a wise investment of time and effort to examine the criminal code of the immediate jurisdiction to determine how clearly the statutes attempt to control jury tampering. Jury trials that can be manipulated by either bribes or threats are a major discredit to the entire criminal justice system—a major discredit in exactly the same sense as are bribes or threats that can control the judiciary, the prosecution, or the police.

Perjury

The common law crime of perjury is also known as false oath, and was defined as willfully taking a false oath in any judicial process.[13] While it will be noted shortly that the perjury concept has been expanded beyond the judicial process in many jurisdictions, it is the judicial process to which criminal justice must direct its concern with the overall problem of perjury. Nevertheless, it is worth note that expansion of the perjury concept of crime has reached a point that perjury can be declared if there is "false swearing" in obtaining a marriage license.[14]

Insofar as the criminal-justice system is concerned, perjury is primarily a crime related to the judicial process. Witnesses who lie can totally destroy carefully investigated and even skillfully prosecuted criminal cases in much the same way as a threatened or bribed jury, as discussed above, can destroy criminal justice effort.

As a technical matter, the "oath" segment of "false oath" has been legislated in many jurisdictions to permit affirmation (declaration that the witness will tell the truth) but not under oath, of testimony—the swearing of an oath being offensive to many on religious grounds. The "affirming," from the criminal justice frame of reference at least, provides the same basis for establishing perjury as a crime. And in any event, whether the witness is swearing an oath or "affirming" testimony, the purpose of both is to establish the basis for holding a witness accountable to the judicial process. Both the common law and statutes approach the crime of perjury on this basis; the witness is accountable for his testimony once he has sworn an oath or affirmed his testimony.

As with all crime, the perjurer must intend to commit the crime or it is not a crime. Intent here incorporates knowledge in that the testimony being given must be *known* not to be true.

As a practical matter, perjury laws allow for witnesses to *believe* virtually anything they choose to believe, even in the face of demonstrable evidence that they should not believe. Charging a witness with perjury entails acquisition of evidence that the witness was *aware* that he was not telling the truth, and this, in turn, entails the necessity to analyze carefully the entire context of the trial. It often leads to close collaboration between thorough police investigation and skillful prosecution of the perjury charge. The integration of related facts and testimony must be combined to establish a clear indication that the witness was aware that under oath, or after affirmation, he was not telling the truth. Perhaps an example will help clarify this concept.

EXAMPLE

(A)

Henry Hired is a key witness engaged by the defendant, Sidney Stickup. Sidney offered Henry a substantial amount of money to testify that Sid was not one of two men that robbed a store. Unfortunately for Sidney Stickup, his instructions to Henry were to claim that he was an eyewitness to the robbery, whereas Henry was actually in another town.

Henry so testifies, elaborating the reasons he is certain that it was not Sid who was in the store at the time of the robbery.

The prosecutor becomes suspicious, investigates, and develops evidence that Henry was in another town at the time the robbery occurred. A perjury charge is filed.

Of course evidence that Henry was not where he said he was after he swore to tell the truth established the case of perjury in this facetious case. But consideration of a slight alteration in the situation provides some clarification of the complexity usually involved in perjury cases —the difficulty of proving the *intent* to lie under oath or affirmation.

(B)
Henry testifies that Ed was with him in the other city at the time of the robbery.

Proving that Henry was aware he was lying under oath with this modification in the situation becomes more difficult. It is relatively easy to produce evidence that Henry was in a physically different location than he testified. It is somewhat more difficult to prove Henry was aware he was lying when *time* is the only variable. Henry could be simply "confused" about time, but being in a different city is a different credibility matter. A tougher burden of proof is clearly established whenever the perjurer can claim confusion and there is no overwhelming evidence to demonstrate that this is merely a deceptive maneuver.

In any case, false testimony *is* serious crime from the frame of reference of criminal justice. This is born out by its felony status in most jurisdictions.

Materiality

The judicial rules governing evidence must, of course, prevail in approaching perjury as a serious crime. With respect to perjury, the main concept in judicial rules governing evidence is the concept of *material evidence*. The term *material evidence* refers to evidence that demonstrably affects the outcome of a trial. The very existence of such a concept shows that a great deal of evidence presented in many trials has little demonstrable effect on the outcome. In perjury the perjured testimony must be evidence that does, in fact, affect the outcome of the trial. In other words, in much the same manner that there must be *knowledge* on the part of the perjurer, as well as *intent* to form the crime of perjury, so also must the perjured testimony be "material"[15]— at least perjury within the judicial process as being discussed in this section. In those cases of perjury outside the judicial process, the significance of materiality varies from one jurisdiction to another.

SUMMARY

This chapter introduced offenses against public order and public justice with a brief graphic review of all the crimes discussed earlier as crimes against either persons or property.

The unique characteristics of crimes against public order and public justice were presented in the context of sharing the same *mens rea* requirement as other crimes.

Disturbing the peace and disorderly conduct were discussed in terms of differences between early common-law concepts that were quasi-religious and modern statutory law geared more to behavior that generates public fear. Unlawful assembly, lynching and rout, riots, and nuisances were also presented in this discussion.

Vagrancy was identified as a crime that some jurisdictions retain even though it is more of a *status* than an act of crime as discussed throughout this volume in terms of *mens rea*.

Gambling was presented as a widely varied statutory crime—the variation being in terms of the degree gambling is permitted from one jurisdiction to the next and its relationship to organized crime.

Vandalism and malicious mischief, along with trespass, were also discussed as crimes against public justice.

Crimes against government process were discussed as bribery, nonfeasance, misfeasance, jury tampering, and perjury. It was noted that bribery, like extortion, along with nonfeasance and misfeasance, are crimes committable only by public officials. Jury tampering was shown to be similar to perjury in that it is difficult for the criminal-justice system to achieve convictions for these crimes, even with conscientious police investigation and skillful prosecution.

NOTES

1. W. L. Clark and W. Marshall *A Treatise on the Law of Crimes*, 7th ed. M. Q. Barnes, rev. ed. (Mundelein, Ill.: Callaghan, 1967), pp. 96–100.
2. *Ibid.*, p. 97.
3. *Ibid.*, p. 588.
4. *Ibid.*, p. 204.
5. *Ibid.*, p. 978.
6. *Ibid.*, p. 1032.
7. See, for example, N. C. Chamelin and K. R. Evans, *Criminal Law for Police* 2d ed. (Englewood Cliffs, N.J.: Prentice-Hall, 1976), p. 187.
8. Pennsylvania State Police Academy, *Pennsylvania Criminal Law and Criminal Procedure* (Harrisburg, Pa.: Telegraph Press, 1969), Section 303, p. 190.
9. California Penal Code, Sec. 67.
10. California Penal Code, Sec. 67½, 68, 85, 86, 92, 93, 133, 137, 138.

11. Clark and Marshall, *Treatise on the Law of Crimes*, p. 1035.
12. F. E. Inbau and J. R. Thompson, *Criminal Law and Its Administration*, (Mineola, N.Y.: Foundation Press, 1970), p. 5.
13. Clark and Marshall, *Treatise on the Law of Crimes*, p. 1038.
14. See, for example, American Law Reports, 101 ALR, 1259.
15. Clark and Marshall, *Treatise on the Law of Crimes*, p. 1043.

PRACTICAL EXERCISE

1. Compare the statutes of any two jurisdictions for differences in terms of crimes against public order and public justice.

ANNOTATED REFERENCES

Clark, W. L., and Marshall, W. A *Treatise on the Law of Crimes*. 7th ed. M. Q. Barnes, revising ed. Mundelein, Ill.: Callaghan, 1967. This classic treatise affords the reader a scholarly, in-depth analysis of the common-law basis of many of the offenses presented in this chapter.

Coffey, A. R. *The Prevention of Crime and Delinquency*. Englewood Cliffs, N.J.: Prentice-Hall, 1976. Elaboration of the influences of a justice system that is *just*, as opposed to the system that remains when government-process crimes are tolerated.

Inbau, F. E., and Thompson, J. R. *Criminal Law and Its Administration*. Mineola, N.Y.: Foundation Press, 1970. A scholarly review of pertinent case law relating to many of the offenses discussed in this chapter.

Prussel, F. R. *Criminal Law, Justice and Society*. Goodyear Publishing co.: Santa Monica, Calif., 1979. Discussion of many of the subjects of this chapter on a somewhat different format.

Chapter 13

CRIMES INVOLVING JUVENILES

LEARNING OBJECTIVES

The learning objectives of this chapter are:
1. To develop an understanding of the recent rapid change that continues to occur in juvenile justice.
2. To recognize the distinction between adult responsibility and juvenile accountability in terms of differences in adult and juvenile crime.
3. To know what status offenses are.
4. To understand the difference between juvenile delinquency, in which a child is a perpetrator, and crimes in which the child is the victim.
5. To see child abuse as a justice problem overall.

IT COULD BE ARGUED THAT JUVENILE law violation is irrelevant to a discussion of crime and unnecessary to an understanding of the criminal law. This argument might include a contention that many jurisdictions define juvenile offenses as something other than crime—usually something vaguely referred to as "delinquency," delinquency therefore being different from crime. Moreover, in the jurisdictions that recognize juvenile offenses as *crime*, the argument could be made that the crimes have already been discussed in this volume.

In point of fact, offenses involving juveniles are *both* crime *and* what is generally accepted as delinquency by most jurisdictions. Moreover, there are crimes committed *against* juveniles that are unique in criminal law and worthy of discussion outside the specific context in which crimes have been discussed in previous chapters. In short, a discussion of criminal law is not complete without discussion of crimes involving juveniles.

Parens Patriae

Crimes involving juveniles suggest the need for defining *juvenile*. For purposes of our discussion, a *juvenile* is any person below the age that a given jurisdiction uses to define *adult*. From a criminal law point of view, a juvenile has traditionally required special criminal justice treatment.

This special treatment in criminal justice evolved in large measure from early English law and is most commonly known by the term *parens patriae*. The *parens patriae* concept means, among many other things, that an informal approach is adopted by the courts in dealing with juvenile offenders. England established special courts for various matters, including juvenile offenses.

As will be noted shortly, juvenile justice is undergoing a significant change that modifies this concept of *parens patriae*—another good reason for including juvenile offenses in our discussion of criminal law.

Discussion of crimes involving juveniles can be divided into two parts (1) offenses by juveniles, and (2) crimes against juveniles. For the purposes of our discussion, it is important to substitute the term *offense* for the term *crime* in cases where the offense is by a juvenile. The reason for this substitution will become clear during the course of the discussion.

OFFENSES BY JUVENILES

In view of the many differences between jurisdictions in their statutory approach to dealing with juveniles who violate the law, it might be useful to establish a conceptual framework for distinguishing between *crime* and *delinquency,* as implied in the modification of the term *offense.* Laws differ so much from one jurisdiction to the next that virtually no assumption can be made without qualification—the distinction between crime and delinquency then becoming more functional than may appear at first.

Recalling the *mens rea* concept of crime, a definition of delinquency might be tentatively formed on the basis of law violation without the *capability* of *intent*—the lack of capability having to do with chronological age, or a minor child's immaturity.

Jurisdictions vary on defining the age at which a juvenile can "intend" to commit the act he may have committed. Furthermore, most jurisdictions recognize various degrees of intent, even though these degrees are usually subtle and rarely explicit. A conceptual framework that facilitates understanding these various "degrees" can be formed by comparison of *accountability* for one's behavior with *responsibility* for behavior—substantially more than a mere semantic difference.

Juvenile Accountability

If the distinction between accountability and responsibility[1] appears to be "a distinction without differences," it may be because the variation in justice procedures has not been examined in relation to the age of the offender. Take any of the crimes already discussed as examples— robbery, burglary, battery, arson, or any other crime. Under certain circumstances, the *act* of most of these crimes could be committed by a young child. But immediately the question arises of whether a young child, at least a *very* young child, could *intend* to commit the crime as required in *mens rea.* Some jurisdictions contend that certain *crimes* can be *intended* by a 16-year-old. Other jurisdictions contend that a 16-year-old is a minor child not yet capable of forming "criminal intent" —at least until some juvenile court finds that the 16-year-old is "unfit" for juvenile court by virtue of his "sophistication." The problem is complicated somewhat by the fact that even when children are "too young" to form intent, they may nevertheless be "too old" to ignore totally.

The example of *arson* has been cited to illustrate a kind of "graduated accountability."[2] Most states would hold that an 18-year-old setting neighborhood homes on fire was old enough to "form the criminal intent" needed to constitute the *crime* of arson. However, many states would contend that a 16-year-old setting fires deliberately is "too young" to be prosecuted in adult criminal court but is nevertheless "old enough" to "account" for his law violations. Furthermore, many states would enpower a juvenile court to take jurisdiction over a 12-years-old setting such fires, even though they may deprive the court of the option of finding the 12-year-old "unfit" and *remanding* the 12-year-old to an adult criminal court. The example of arson perhaps becomes even clearer when a 5-year-old presumably recognized universally as incapable of forming the "criminal intent" ascribed to adult crime.

A kind of continuum of accountability, with responsibility, emerges when the various practices of juvenile justice in different jurisdictions are examined. This continuum ranges from no accountability of any kind for the very young, to increases in accountability for older youngsters, up through out-and-out responsibility for juveniles found to be "unfit" for juvenile court and remanded to adult criminal court.

The accountability, or "accounting," takes many forms but customarily can be measured in terms of punitive consequences for older, "more accountable" juveniles.

Adult Responsibility

Beyond providing a conceptual framework, the distinction between juvenile accountability and adult responsibility makes possible an important distinction between *crime* and *delinquency*: crime involves adult responsibility for law violation and delinquency involves varied degrees of accountability depending on the age of the juvenile.

From a philosophical standpoint, adult criminal justice can be thought of as being based on concern for *what* the offense is, in contrast with juvenile justice, which addresses concern to *why* the offense was committed. Though somewhat oversimplified, this philosophical orientation permits clearer understanding of the criminal-justice system in relation to the juvenile-justice system.

This philosophical distinction, however, is gradually diminishing in clarity. Well over a decade ago, the Supreme Court set in motion a major change in this philosophical position with the first of many influences toward basic changes in how juvenile offenses are to be handled.* This decision, now commonly known as the "Gault decision," effected a major change throughout juvenile justice—a change that has gained strength from subsequent court decisions and subsequent legislation in many jurisdictions. The Gault decision has had profound influence on what was presented in the beginning of this chapter as the *parens patriae* concept of "special treatment" for juvenile offenders.

* *In re Gault*, 377 U.S. 1, 87 S. Ct., 1428, *Gault v. Arizona*: May 16, 1967, the U.S. Supreme Court rules that Gerald Gault was not afforded *due process* in the juvenile court process. The Court held that juveniles, like adults, have the *right to* legal counsel, to refuse to self-incriminate, to confront their accuser, to cross-examine, to get a transcript of the hearing, and to have appellate review.

Indeed, the Gault decision and subsequent influences have moved the juvenile-court process much closer to the adult criminal-court process, even though a clear distinction still exists in all jurisdictions between juvenile accountability and adult responsibility.

While the seeming transition from traditional juvenile court to adult criminal court is likely to end well short of demanding full adult responsibility from children, it is nevertheless clear that the trend is toward *increasing* the juvenile *accountability* for answering to offenses committed by the juvenile.

For this reason, it can be assumed for purposes of discussion that in most jurisdictions, acts defined as crimes for adults can at least be brought to the juvenile court's attention, with insistence that the juvenile be held to "account" for his behavior—to answer for his behavior in terms of possible punitive consequences. In effect, this permits law enforcement to relate to juvenile offenses in at least a *similar* manner as to adult offenses, even though law enforcement and justice in general must continue to acknowledge that children cannot be held fully responsible for delinquent acts.

This need not be confusing. Consider the following example:

> Any person who is under the age of 18 years when he violates any law
> of this state or of the United States or any ordinance of any city or
> county of this state defining crime other than ordinance establishing
> a curfew based solely on age is within the jurisdiction of the juvenile
> court, which may adjudge such a person to be a ward of the court.[3]

In this example, statutes also permit the juvenile court to find youthful offenders over 16 years old "unfit" for juvenile court, and the offenders may subsequently be transferred, or "remanded," to adult criminal court. From the point of view of practical police procedures, this legislative possibility permits the perception of "crime" to remain essentially the same regardless of the age of the "criminal," the determination of which court a young offender should face being made by the juvenile court.

Moreover, this practical police perception of juvenile justice remains intact even in cases where the juvenile court retains jurisdiction of the case, approaching the case with alternatives that are essentially the same as the options available to the adult criminal court and merely geared to juvenile offenders:

1. summary probation
2. supervised probation
3. specific-term detention
4. state-operated correctional institutions and parole

262 CRIMES INVOLVING JUVENILES

These options may gain clarity if considered in the context of how juvenile-justice systems usually work in most jurisdictions—work in terms of police, probation, courts, and juvenile institutions.

Juvenile Justice

Juvenile offenses cut across nearly all the adult crimes discussed thus far. Many police officers would support contention that juveniles may be more involved in vandalism (at least of schools) than adults, and it is certain that veteran police officers have encountered juveniles who have committed all of the crimes noted thus far in this volume.

Police. Whether the particular jurisdiction approaches law enforcement on the basis of "juvenile specialists" or on the basis of "general law enforcement," the fact remains that police are the primary *intake* of juvenile justice. This should come as no surprise, since police are in fact the primary intake of adult criminal justice, carrying the major responsibility of determining when an arrest is necessary for enforcement of law.

Perhaps some confusion is generated in jurisdictions that empower school truant officers to arrest children, or welfare social workers to "bring" children to the juvenile court. But in terms of understanding juvenile justice as it relates to criminal law, the police are the primary intake for the juvenile justice system. Just as criminal courts rarely try cases not dealt with by police, so also are police the major source of juvenile court work. Police determination of when further referral is necessary, however, is customarily through some form of juvenile probation.

Juvenile probation. The "classic" concept of juvenile probation that prevailed prior to recent modifications of *parens patriae* philosophies is undergoing substantial change throughout most jurisdictions. The resources provided by the probation officers of the jurisdictions, however, remain. That is, the juvenile court in most jurisdictions has access to probation officers who can investigate the legal and social segments of juvenile offenses referred by police. Moreover, the probation officers make recommendations to the court in terms of what is needed to resolve the matter, and further provide probation supervision should the court so order.

There are two terms that, because they are used as nouns rather than as adjectives, tend to confuse the two major approaches to juvenile probation: these two terms are *social work* and *probation services*.

Some jurisdictions provide juvenile probation as a social-work process, in which the emphasis is placed upon *why* an offense was committed in contrast to emphasis on the offense itself. This orientation is obviously more attuned to the *parens patriae* philosophy currently in transition. In contrast to this orientation, the *probation-service* process emphasizes the protection of the community. Each orientation has some influence from the other—the social-work approach acknowledging the danger to the community of a violently assaultive youth, and the probation-services approach acknowledging the value of counseling in correcting a youthful law violator.

In spite of whatever confusion exists in these two separate orientations for juvenile probation, there was until recently a unifying force that kept perspective in the area of juvenile justice, excluding excessive concern with psychiatric and sociological variables. That unifying force was the traditional function of juvenile probation to screen police referrals. This screening placed the primary responsibility of determining whether or not matters went to juvenile court in the hands of probation officers, and it also held probation officers responsible for any unfortunate consequences of the failure to bring youthful offenders before the court. This traditional screening role is now being modified as an increasing number of jurisdictions approach juvenile court on an adversary basis. By *adversary* is meant the "bifurcated" juvenile-court hearing in which there are two parts: The first is a prosecution–defense approach replacing the former informal atmosphere called for by *parens patriae*. The second part is what is often called the "dispositional half" —the court dispositions are increasingly focused on a conviction, analogous to the focus of adult criminal trials. In jurisdictions adopting this approach to the juvenile court, the traditional screening role played by probation officers is being absorbed by the prosecutor, bringing juvenile court process even closer to an actual criminal court.

Regardless of the degree to which prosecutors assume the screening function, probation generally remains the primary disposition for the juvenile court, a disposition that by itself retains a considerable degree of influence for juvenile probation officers. "Home on probation," under the supervision of the probation officer, is usually attempted by the juvenile court before considering committing a juvenile to a correctional institution.

Juvenile court. The rapidly accelerating transition already noted engulfs the juvenile court process itself, changing juvenile court from the once *informal*, nonadversary *parens patriae* atmosphere to a stern, adversary trial court atmosphere, with a corresponding demand for all of the rules of evidence of criminal court. Although the transition is not complete, virtually all police have experienced in recent years an increased demand for more "hard evidence" in juvenile-court cases that were once handled so informally that evidence was more apparent than real. An execption to this transition for law enforcement and dealing with juveniles is the status offender.

Status offender. Police matters involving juveniles, juvenile probation, and juvenile courts in most jurisdictions deal with three varieties of juvenile problems—crimes *against* juveniles, offenses *by* juveniles, and yet another category that is frequently called "status offender."

A *status offender* violates laws that would not be crime if committed by an adult. Typical of these offenses are curfew violations and truancy from school in those cases where school attendance is required by law. Jurisdictions that legislate against disobeying parents and guardians increase the variety of status offenders and in the process increase the complexity of the juvenile-justice system where the system is required by law to intervene.

In a volume addressed to the *criminal* law, elaboration of these status offenses cannot be justified. However, it is worth note that these offenses constitute a tremendous burden on police resources in that they frequently involve extremely complex family problems, often reaching the point of parents attempting to force police or juvenile probation to "take" a child that they declare "beyond control." Needless to add, juvenile court is similarly taxed attempting to deal with these particularly vexing problems.

Juvenile institutions and parole. Ordinarily, the juvenile court has already ordered juvenile probation supervision and it has proved unsuccessful before the juvenile is ordered removed from his home and placed in a correctional institution. The determination that probation supervision has failed is usually made on the basis of additional offenses on the part of the juvenile on probation. Exceptions generally are made for children "in trouble"; in these cases the children are placed in the home of a relative, in a foster home, or in even in certain schools as an appropriate alternative to correctional institutions. In such cases the juvenile court is usually convinced that the environment of the juvenile is such that it remains likely that the juvenile need only be placed in a different environment to avoid further difficulties.

If the court decides that the juvenile needs correctional treatment, a correctional institution is ordered. Correctional institutions for juveniles range from minimum-security "ranches" through maximum-security "prisons"—the same continuum along which adult correctional institutions vary. The program provided by the institution usually includes parole supervision after release, just as in the case of adults.

To sum up law violation *by* juveniles, the juvenile-justice system is acquiring more and more of the trappings of criminal justice while retaining a distinction between the juvenile's *accountability* for his offenses and an adult's *responsibility* for crime.

CRIMES AGAINST JUVENILES

In the discussion of crimes against the person in Chapter 6 there was a brief discussion of the crime of child molesting. Child molesting was presented as a serious crime requiring felony punishment in most jurisdictions. The purpose in discussing child molesting in Chapter 6 as a crime against the person rather than in the present section as a crime against juveniles was to discuss all sexual crimes together.

If one is to understand the nature of crimes against children, child molesting is a particularly significant crime to begin with in that it demonstrates clearly the rationale for legislating protection for children. Most children are both physically and mentally unable to defend themselves against abuse of any kind—whether the abuse be by their own parents or by other adults. Crimes against juveniles are for this reason a special category of crimes against the person.

Child molesting, unfortunately, is only one of the many crimes perpetrated against children. Most jurisdictions define as crime any form of *serious* abuse of children. Out of deference to the reality that even a poor parent customarily does a better job of rearing a child than the best of government-operated facilities, most jurisdictions structure the laws protecting children in such a manner that only *gross* abuse or neglect constitutes the basis for criminal-justice intervention. Examination of the criminal codes and other relevant statutes in the particular jurisdiction usually clarifies the degree to which the laws of any given state structure intervention into family life. In examining various penal codes, it becomes clear that most jurisdictions define as crime *parental abuse or neglect* of children but vary in their criteria for defining what constitutes abuse or neglect. In general, some degree of failing to feed and clothe a child is usually defined as crime, along with some degree of failing to provide adequate shelter. Many jurisdictions establish discretionary or judgmental statutes with respect to the degree of cleanliness in homes for children. While at times vague, these statutes are intended to ensure that responsibility for rearing children is not ignored.

Review of various penal codes also indicates that most jurisdictions define as crime the *beating* of children—beating as contrasted with "normal" parental discipline. The distinction between beating and whipping is not consistently defined and frequently requires medical opinion. Physical trauma—bruises and so on—is frequently photographed as evidence.

Other forms of child abuse vary in definition from one jurisdiction to the next, but there is one "category" of abuse that most jurisdictions recognize having to do with a child's home being *unfit*—a term generally applied to a filthy environment that is neither sanitary or conducive to child rearing by some local jurisdictional standard.

Not surprisingly, from the frame of reference of *mens rea* as discussed throughout this volume, the establishment of parental *intent* to commit these crimes is difficult to prove. The state is quite often at a tremendous disadvantage in attempting to impose a standard of cleanliness on a family—particularly in situations in which seemingly "filthy homes" rear well-adjusted, normal children. For this reason, only the more appalling, dramatic cases of "unfitness" make their way to the court in most jurisdictions—at least make it to the adult court as a crime.

Another manner in which the child's welfare can be brought to the attention of the court is a referral to the juvenile court—a referral "on behalf of the child" rather than "against the parents." Because of the difficulty in proving parental *intent*, even when a child is physically abused, most jurisdictions provide for petitioning the juvenile court to declare an obviously abused child a dependent child of the court. This justice procedure allows for court jurisdiction to be established in protection of the child without the necessity of filing criminal charges against parents—the status of the dependent child of the court is much the same as wardship. In this approach, the proof need only be that the child *was* in fact abused or neglected in some manner, whether or not the parents are charged with an adult crime in the case.

The juvenile court in these dependency matters, then, is permitted to function as it once did in all juvenile matters—*on behalf of the child*—the *parens patriae* concept from early English law still prevailing in dependency matters. What was discussed in the first section of this chapter as a transition toward adversary hearing is not applicable to dependency matters in that the juvenile-court atmosphere in dependency matters remains informal and geared to achieving a safe, healthful environment for the child rather than to achieving a conviction.

Dispositions in these matters frequently are the return of the child to the parents' home under probation supervision—the parents are actually on probation rather than the juvenile in these matters. Of course, the alternative of a relative's home or even a foster home are available to the court once the dependency has been established. The availability of alternatives, however, is diminishing in many jurisdictions because of the alarming number of young victims of incest, beatings, starvings, and other forms of gross neglect. The problem of child abuse and neglect is an increasing challenge to America justice.

CONTRIBUTING TO THE DELINQUENCY OF A MINOR

In addition to these tragic dependency matters, there is a category of offenses "against" juveniles that are actually in a "gray area" fluctuating between offenses *by* juveniles and offenses *against* juveniles. This category is best known in most jurisdictions as the crime of *contributing to the delinquency of a minor*.

The statutes in most jurisdictions view this crime as clearly *being against* the child. But as a practical matter, many juveniles have become so sophisticated in their delinquent behavior that it is not exaggerating to state that they frequently influence the adult to violate a law far more than the adult influences them—a contradiction of the premise that the child is helpless and vulnerable. But since this point is too sociological for a volume addressed to criminal law, this seeming paradox will not be pursued. It should be noted, however, that as a practical police matter, many jurisdictions deal with a situation in which a crime has been "mutually" committed by both an adult and juvenile by sending the adult to adult criminal court and the juvenile to juvenile court. The juvenile court is then left with the task of determining the level of juvenile accountability.

In the more common "contributing crimes"—involving sexual activities, alcohol, and narcotics—police usually perceive the child as the victim and deal only with the adult. In other words, from the perspective of criminal law, in the statutory crime of "contributing," in most jurisdictions the adult is held responsible; in the "vice" type of case, police practice usually functions in this manner. But it remains clear that in many "marginal" cases juveniles had achieved a level of delinquent sophistication long before the contributing adult arrived on the scene—a possible rationale for future modifications in these contributing laws. Veteran police officers who have observed immature 19-year-olds virtually dominated by 17-year-old delinquent sophisticates usually advocate such modification.

SUMMARY

In this, the concluding chapter, crimes involving juveniles were overviewed. Crimes were divided into three categories: crimes by juveniles, crimes against juveniles, and a "gray area" known as contributing to the delinquency of a minor. The term *offense* was used, instead of the term *crime*, to accommodate the reality that juveniles by definition cannot be held criminally responsible in the same sense that an adult can.

Juvenile accountability and adult responsibility were presented as two ends of a continuum that corresponds to the age of the offender.

Comparisons were made between the juvenile-justice system and the adult criminal-justice system in terms of police, correctional institutions, and parole.

A special category of *status offender* was discussed: juvenile crimes that would not be crime if committed by an adult—truancy, curfew, and behavior beyond parental control.

Crimes against children were presented in terms of various forms of abuse and neglect.

Finally, attention was given to laws defining as crime "contributing to the delinquency of a minor."

NOTES

1. One of the present authors has dealt with this subject in greater depth in two volumes devoted to juvenile justice: A. R. Coffey, *Juvenile Justice as a System: Law Enforcement to Rehabilitation*, (Englewood Cliffs, N.J.: Prentice-Hall, 1974), and A. R. Coffey, *Juvenile Corrections* (Englewood Cliffs, N.J.: Prentice-Hall, 1976).
2. Coffey, *Juvenile Justice as a System*, p. 3.
3. California Welfare and Institutions Code, Sec. 602.

PRACTICAL EXERCISES

1. Sketch a flow chart of the entire juvenile-justice system in your jurisdiction.
2. Prepare a three-page synopsis of the juvenile-court law in your state.

ANNOTATED REFERENCES

Coffey, A. R. *Juvenile Justice as a System: Law Enforcement to Rehabilitation*. Englewood Cliffs, N.J.: Prentice-Hall, 1974. A full volume on what was surveyed in this chapter.

———. *Juvenile Corrections*. Englewood Cliffs, N.J.: Prentice-Hall, 1976. A full volume on what was presented as juvenile court alternatives in this chapter.

Eldefonso, E. *Law Enforcement and the Youthful Offender*. 3d ed. New York. Wiley, 1977. Emphasis on what this chapter noted as police responsibility in juvenile offenses.

Eldefonso, E., and Hartinger, W. *Control, Treatment, and Rehabilitation of Juvenile Offenders*. Encino, Calif.: Glencoe Press, 1976. Further elaboration of the material in this chapter.

Appendix A

CRIMINAL PROCESS AND COURT STRUCTURE

A police officer should have a general idea of the various steps in the criminal process. The following outline is a simplification of these steps and also a brief survey of the major rules pertaining to the protection of the defendant in criminal cases. Although California's State Constitution is often cited as an example, most state constitutions are similar.

Also included in this outline is a brief description of the various courts, their makeup, and their function.

CRIMINAL PROCESS AND PROCEDURE

The following steps take place in the criminal process:

I. Arrest

    A. There is no difference between the right of a private citizen and a police (peace) officer to make an arrest without a warrant (with one exception).

    B. Both may make an arrest when a misdemeanor is committed in their presence. A private citizen may make an arrest when a felony has in fact been committed, and it is reasonable to believe the arrested party did commit the felony. A police officer may make an arrest when he has reason to believe (not that it actually has been committed) a felony has been committed and reason to believe the arrested party was the offender.

C. Note that neither a peace officer nor a citizen has the right to make an arrest without a warrant for a misdemeanor unless it is committed in his presence.

II. Complaint

A. An accusation in writing filed before a magistrate.
B. A private citizen may go before the district attorney and swear to facts indicating that the defendant has committed a crime against him. The district attorney may then have a judge issue a warrant for the defendant's arrest.
C. A citizen or peace officer making an arrest without a warrant must then file a complaint before the district attorney.

III. Arraignment, Lower Court

This is held in the lower court to inform the defendant of the charges made against her, presenting her with a copy of the complaint against her, to advise the defendant of her rights, to get her plea, and to set a date for trial.

A. Following arrest, the defendant must be taken before the court for arraignment within a "reasonable" length of time, generally 48 hours.
B. The court reads the complaint, identifies the defendant by asking her name, informing defendant of her right to counsel and setting bail if such has not been done.
  1. If the Offense Is a Misdemeanor
    a. At the arraignment the defendant may plead guilty to the charge and be sentenced at this time.
    b. The defendant may request continuance before entering her plea to obtain counsel, or a continuance for a valid reason.
    c. The defendant may plead not guilty. A date may then be set by the court for trial. This may be by jury or by judge. The defendant has a right to have the trial in 30 days; if not then, the charge is dismissed. The defendant may waive this 30-day requirement.
  2. If the Offense Is a Felony
    a. At the arraignment of the lower court, defendant may plead guilty to the felony charge.
    b. The lower court has no jurisdiction to hear or to sentence in the felony matters.

    c. The lower court in not less than 2 or more than 5 days must order the defendant to appear in the superior court for sentence. Reason: lower court cannot sentence for felony.

    d. The defendant then appears in superior court to be sentenced.

    e. If the defendant pleads not guilty, a date is set for preliminary examination.

IV. Preliminary Examination

  A. At arraignment in the lower court, the defendant may enter a plea of not guilty. The magistrate must then have the preliminary examination within 5 days. Postponements may be allowed at the defendant's request.

  B. The defendant must then have a preliminary examination in the lower court. The purpose is to determine if there is reasonable grounds to believe the offense committed is a felony, and if there is reason to believe the defendant committed it. However, the defendant may waive right to preliminary examination and be sent direct to superior court.

  C. This is not a trial, and the district attorney need not give her case away by presenting all her evidence. Just enough evidence is presented to "tie the defendant" with the felony. This preliminary is a "screening" of cases so that the superior court will not waste its time hearing cases where it is obvious that the prosecution does not have a case, or where in fact the offense is not a felony.

  D. The lower court may dismiss the case against the defendant if there is not sufficient evidence to indicate a felony has been committed, or if there was a felonious act, but the defendant cannot be connected with its commission.

  E. At this preliminary examination, it may be discovered that the offense is really only a misdemeanor. The defendant may then be ordered to stand trial for this.

  F. If at the preliminary examination, the judge finds a felony has been committed, and there is reason to believe the defendant may have been the culprit, the defendant is "held to answer," which merely means that the defendant will go into the superior court for trial. The defendant cannot be deprived of this preliminary examination.

  G. In some jurisdictions, the custody of the defendant is transferred from the city jail to the county jail. The reason is that lower courts (municipal courts) are in large areas city counts under the city police, while the superior court is a state court and the county sheriff has jurisdiction over the prisoner.

Note: At this point, the law provides that persons awaiting trial (not convicted of anything at this point) are not placed in custody with persons serving sentences for conviction of crimes.

V. Filing Information

A. The written accusation charging a person with a crime, the jurisdiction of which lies in the Superior court, is signed by the district attorney after examination (the lower court discussed) and is committed by the magistrate.
B. This is simply the transcript of the testimony of the preliminary examination held in the lower court signed by the district attorney. The defendant is charged with a felony.
C. This "information" must be filed in the superior court within 15 days after the preliminary examination or the case is dismissed. The offense charged must be stated and signed by the district attorney.

VI. Arraignment, Superior Court

A. The information (transcript from the preliminary examination in the lower court) is filed in the superior court.
B. The defendant is then again arraigned in the superior court. The charges are read to her, she is informed of her right to counsel, and the day for trial is set.
C. The defendant, of course, may plead guilty at any point, and receive her sentence, or ask for continuance.
D. The defendant has a right to be brought to trial within 60 days after the arraignment in the superior court, unless she requests continuance and waives this right. The date for trial is set.
E. At every stage of the proceedings, the defendant is entitled to counsel of her own choice and, if she can't pay for counsel, the court must provide her with appointed counsel.

VII. Trial in the Superior Court

A. If the defendant pleads guilty at the arraignment in superior court, her case is normally continued for 2 to 4 weeks for the probation officer's report. The date set for sentence is set at this point.
B. If the defendant has a trial (by judge or jury) and is found guilty, again date for sentence is put over 2 to 4 weeks for the probation officer's report. The date is set for sentence.

C. The defendant is then sentenced when probation officer's report submitted to the court.

VIII. Information and Indictment

A. All offenses must be prosecuted in the superior court by indictment or information except:
1. Removal of state officers
2. Offense in the militia.
3. Misdemeanor for which jurisdiction has been conferred upon superior courts sitting as juvenile courts.
Thus, there are only two methods to get most cases before the superior court.
B. *Information:* As previously discussed. Merely, the transcript of the preliminary examination is signed by the district attorney, and an order of the examining magistrate, is presented, clearly stating the offense.
C. *Indictment:* An accusation in writing presented by a grand jury to a competent court charging a person with a public offense.

IX. Grand Jury

A. Each county has a grand jury of nineteen citizens, drawn from the jury panel.
B. They may inquire into all public offenses committed, which may be tried, within the county and present them to a competent court by indictment.
C. They are not responsible to the courts or the district attorney and may make their own investigations. They may also inquire into all county officers and county expenditures. They may examine all accusations made to them by private citizens, public officials, and their own members.
D. The district attorney usually presents the cases to the grand jury when she seeks an indictment. Twelve of the nineteen jurors must concur.
Note: When there is a felony indictment against a defendant, the first court proceeding is the arraignment in the superior court. There is no arraignment or preliminary examination in the lower court. At the arraignment, the defendant must be presented with a copy of the grand jury's transcript.

X. Why Grand Jury Indictment Instead of Complaint—Information Procedure:

A. When the defendant is "missing," indictments may be made without defendant being present. He must be present in a preliminary examination in order to file the information.

B. When there are many defendants involved, if the prosecution starts charging or trying some of them, others may flee. It is best to secretly indict them all at once.

C. No complaint is necessary. No complaining witness is necessary.

D. The prosecution may wish to avoid "tipping its hand" in the preliminary examination. Thus, it is best to get the indictment and avoid the preliminary.

E. It is sometimes easier to get grand jury indictment than to withstand a preliminary examination. The defendant need not be present at grand jury but must be at preliminary.

XI. Distinction Between Felony and a Misdemeanor

A. Penal Code Section of Respective State Defines Distinction
   1. A felony is a crime punishable by death (if falling within the January 1, 1974, "guidelines" of acts that may carry the death penalty) or confinement in a state prison.
   2. When a crime is punishable by state prison OR county jail, it is deemed a misdemeanor for all purposes after a judgment other than imprisonment in the state prison.
   3. If committed to the Youth Authority, the crime is a felony.

B. A commitment to the Youth Authority is a felony unless
   1. After the ward is discharged from the Youth Authority, she has not been placed in a state prison by the Youth Authority (D.V.I. is not a state prison).
   2. The committing court, on the person's application, makes an order determining that the crime for which she was convicted was a misdemeanor. Section 1772 W&I Code provides the same procedure except that the defendant must have an honorable discharge (meaning good record on parole), and then the court may set aside the verdict of guilty and dismiss the accusation or information and release her from all penalties and disabilities. Thus there is no conviction at all. PRACTICE: This may be done by the probation department, the district attorney, the public defender, a private attorney, or the ward herself by obtaining:
      a. A certified copy of her discharge.
      b. An affidavit reciting that the subject was not placed in a state prison, signed by the clerk of the Youth Authority.
      c. Placed on the calendar of the committing court.
      d. Oral or written notion made praying that the offense

be declared a misdemeanor; or under 177 W&I that the verdict of guilty be set aside.

3. The implication of the above section seems to mean that if the Youth Authority places a ward in a state prison during its control, that the ward, like an adult authority felon, must meet the requirements of Penal Code Sections 4850–4853 (California) in order to have his commitment set aside through pardon.

SUMMARY OF COURT STEPS

I. Arrest, Complaint

II. Arraignment, Lower Court

    A. Misdemeanors
       1. Sentence if guilty plea to misdemeanor.
       2. Not-guilty plea—trial for misdemeanor.
    B. Felony
       1. Guilty plea—referred to superior court for sentence.
       2. Not-guilty plea—put over for preliminary examination.

III. Preliminary Examination, Lower Court

    A. Guilty plea at this time—put over for sentence.
    B. Finding a felony committed and reasonable grounds that defendant committed it. Defendant held to answer in superior court.

IV. Arraignment, Superior Court

    A. Guilty plea—put over for sentence.
    B. Not guilty plea—put over for trial.

V. Trial, Sentence

DEFENDANT'S CONSTITUTIONAL AND STATUTORY RIGHTS WHEN CHARGED WITH A CRIME (GENERAL)

The person charged with a crime has certain protections set up by the Constitution and by code provisions. The United States Constitution is the protector of the people against the federal government, and generally the first ten amendments (known as the Bill of Rights) do not apply against the state. The "due process" clause of the United States Constitution is what gives the people their rights against the state.

Thus, it is necessary to look to the state constitution, which is the document that gives the people right against their own state legislative acts, to determine what these protections are. Various code sections and common-law rules of evidence also give the defendant every guarantee of a fair trial.

An officer of the law should have a general knowledge of these rules so that he is not placed in a position whereby misunderstanding occurs. The following are a few of these major rules.

I. Right to a Jury Trial, State Constitution

    A. Every defendant may have a common-law jury of twelve to decide the disputed facts of his case. The defendant may waive a jury trial, if he fully understands the nature of the waiver. He may also waive the number and be tried by less than twelve in misdemeanor cases.

    B. To sustain a conviction all jurors must agree. If less than all agree, then it is a hung jury and defendant may be tried again. There is no limit to the number of times the defendant may be tried.

    C. The defendant can have the judge hear the case without jury.

II. Double Jeopardy, State Constitution

This simply means no one can be tried for the same crime more than once.

    A. A hung jury is not an acquittal, and a retrial for the same offense is not double jeopardy.

    B. The same act may be an offense under two jurisdictions and thus may be tried for both.
EXAMPLE: Auto theft in San Francisco. Drove car to Nevada. Two crimes.
      1. State law violation.
      2. Federal law violation, Dwyer Act. Defendant may be charged and convicted of both, one in state court, the other in federal court. This is not double jeopardy.

    C. The same act may be more than one crime. Unless the two are merged, the defendant may be tried on both.

III. Right to Bail—No Excessive Bail—State Constitution

    A. Prior to conviction the defendant always has a right to bail.

    B. Capital offense. Discretionary with judge and not a right. Any offense punishable with death is capital.

    C. After conviction and pending appeal, bail is discretionary with the judge and not a right. Same rule applies to Youth

Authority commitments from superior court; the judge may allow the defendant out on bail pending acceptance of case.
D. If the defendant does not have the funds to put up for bail, he may be retained in custody but cannot be put in with those convicted of a crime.

IV. The Right to Speedy Trial—State Constitution

A. The right to be brought before a magistrate after arrest in a reasonable time, 48 hours.
B. The defendant entitled to have his case adjudicated in an expedient manner. He may always waive this right in an open court.
C. In superior court, the defendant must be brought to trial in 60 days after indictment by grand jury or filing of information by district attorney. If he is not brought to trial, there is a dismissal and a bar to further prosecution for that offense.

V. Right to Counsel—State Constitution

A. The defendant has a right to counsel of his own choice at every stage of the proceedings.
B. California Constitution: "If defendant desires counsel and cannot pay a fee, the court must appoint counsel to defend him. Court should so inform defendant of his right."
C. The defendant may always waive his right to counsel. Court cannot force counsel on defendant, as he always has the right to act as his own attorney.

VI. Right Not to Testify Against Self—Self-Incrimination—State Constitution

A. The defendant need not testify against himself. There is always the presumption of innocence, and he need not declare such. The burden of proof is always on the prosecution. The defendant need not sign or make any statement to the police.
B. The defendant never needs to take the stand and declare his innocence or to answer any question at all. The rule applies to "testimony" and does not apply to fingerprinting, standing to be identified by witness, putting on coat, hat, etc., worn by culprit.
C. California allows judge and district attorney to comment to jury that defendant has not taken the stand to deny the charges or to offer testimony as to his innocence (contra rule in most states).

D. The district attorney cannot mention defendant's prior felony conviction unless the defendant takes the stand. If the defendant does, the district attorney may impeach his credibility as a witness by showing a prior felony conviction.

VII. Right to Be Confronted by Accuser—State Constitution

A. The defendant always has a right to have a witness against him testify in his presence.
B. The defendant, or his counsel, has a right to cross-examine the witness against him, to seek the truth, and to impeach the witness to show he may be lying, mistaken, hostile, prejudiced, etc. The jury must weigh the credibility of the witness.

VIII. Statute of Limitations

These statutory requirements simply mean that within the prescribed period of the statute, an indictment, a complaint, or information must be filed. The time requirement does not run when the defendant is out of the state. The purpose is to allow a defendant to get his defense together, and it would be unjust not to set some limitation on the time that a person could be charged with a crime. This rule is, of course, meant to protect the innocent but is many times an asset to a clever criminal. His crime may be outlawed by that time and then there is nothing the police can do if he subsequently admits it.

A. Felonies: Crimes so specified have a three-year statute of limitations from the time information is filed, *not* from the filing of the complaint.
B. Misdemeanors: There is a one-year statute of limitations the commission of the crime.

When these time limits have expired, the defendant cannot be tried for the committed offense. This is jurisdictional, and a conviction after statute has run is void, even if the defendant does not plead this as a defense. The time starts to run from date of the commission of the crime.

C. Acceptance of bribe by a public official or employee—six years.
D. No statute of limitations for murder, embezzlement of public money, or falsification of public records.

IX. No Common-Law Crimes in Some States (e.g., California)

A. There can be no crime committed unless such is so designated by statute and a penalty is prescribed.
B. The statute must be clear and not vague as to what is prohibited. The statute must be in plain English (no Latin

medical terms). People must be able to understand what the statute means.

X. No Cruel and Unusual Punishments—State Constitution

A. Prisoner must be treated as a human being.
B. Interpretation of "cruel and unusual" changes with the time and the sociological makeup of the Supreme Court. The death penalty by hanging, shooting, or gas held *not cruel*. Beating not permitted in California now, but is in Southern states.

RULES OF EVIDENCE THAT PROTECT THE DEFENDANT (GENERAL)

The purpose of the rules relating to presentation of evidence is to get to the truth—to exclude testimony or demonstrative evidence that confuses the issue and to admit that which seeks to show the true facts. Obviously we can only discuss a few of the major highlights with which the police officer should be familiar.

I. Establishing the Corpus Delicti

In every criminal case the corpus delicti must be proved before any other evidence as to guilt may be presented.
A. Corpus delicti—the elements of a crime; called the body of the crime." It must be shown that a criminal act took place—e.g., a car was stolen, a store was burglarized, a person was robbed.
B. The identity of the person committing the crime is not a part of the corpus delicti.
C. Hollywood leads you to believe one cannot prosecute for murder without "producing the body." Corpus (body) delicti has nothing to do with production of a body. You can show the corpus delicti of a homicide by circumstantial evidence.
D. Thus, usually if one cannot get the complaining witness in robbery, burglary, etc., to testify, there is no proof of corpus delicti and no prosecution.
E. Proof that a crime has been committed must be shown before the extrajudicial confession or admission of the defendant are admissible in evidence. However, admission in open court is enough.

II. Competency of Witness

A. Every witness may be competent except a young child or someone who is insane or feebleminded. All witnesses may be cross-examined to test their credibility or competency.

B. A wife is not a competent witness against her husband. Not so when the crime the husband is charged with is against wife or child. Merely old common-law rule that husband and wife are one. Neither husband nor wife alone can waive this rule of competency, and thus one cannot testify against the other. After divorce, each may testify against the other, subject to the rules of privileged communication discussed below.

III. Privileged Communications

A. Certain communications are privileged, and the defendant can refuse to waive. Thus the other party cannot testify against the defendant.
1. Husband—Wife. Not to be confused with competency of husband or wife to testify against each other. Privileged communication is only that which took place during the marriage, not any communications that took place before marriage. Thus, once divorced, a witness may testify to anything communicated prior to marriage. However, during a valid marriage husband or wife cannot testify at all against one another.
2. Attorney—Client
3. Clergyman or Priest-Confessor
4. Newspaper reporter may refuse to disclose source of information.
5. No such privilege between doctor and patient in criminal case.
B. No privileged communication between probation and parole officer and client. A duty of parole or probation officer as a peace officer is to disclose any information he has about a crime commission to proper authorities.

IV. Illegally Obtained Evidence

A. Federal courts will not admit evidence against a defendant that has been obtained illegally—e.g., unlawful search without search warrant, stolen evidence, wire tap.
B. California and 22 other states will admit any evidence regardless of how obtained if it is otherwise admissible.
C. Defendant may civilly sue the police officers, but evidence will still be admitted.

V. Hearsay Evidence Rules (At Least 20 Exceptions)

A. Simply means that the testimony offered rests on the veracity of some person other than the witness.
B. The law requires that the witness testify only to those facts that

he gained by his own perceptions—not what some one else has told him.

C. The law demands that the person who actually saw the act, or heard it (if that is the fact to be proved), testify, not the third person who gained the information from someone else.

D. Exceptions are numerous. A few important ones in criminal cases are:

1. The witness refuses to talk, or the witness has taken flight and cannot be located. A third person may then testify to knowledge of the incident (but it need not be accepted by the court if challenged).

2. Confessions must be freely and voluntarily given.

3. Dying declaration may only be used in connection with naming the person who killed the dying victim.

E. Testimony to facts only, not opinions. Exceptions are numerous.

1. Expert witnesses (medical, scientific), blood test, handwriting, etc.

2. Opinions as to color, height, speed, weight, etc., and imperfectly describable event.

VI. Conviction with Only Uncorroborated Testimony of Accomplice

A. An accomplice is one who may be prosecuted for the same offense as the defendant.

B. Someone who merely has knowledge of a crime is not an accomplice.

C. A child under 14 cannot be an accomplice, because the law presumes that one under 14 is incapable of committing a crime unless *clear proof can be shown that he knew the wrongfulness of the act.*

D. Parties to a crime.

1. Principal: One who participates in a crime directly, or who aids and abets, or who, not present, advises and encourages its commission. The act of one principal is the act of them all. The same rule applies to conspirators.

2. Accessory: Every person who conceals or aids a person after a felony has been committed, with the intent to help him escape, is an accessory. This means more than mere silence; there must be some overt act to make one an accessory.

COURT STRUCTURE (EXAMPLE: CALIFORNIA)

I. Supreme Court

Chief Justice, six associate justices. Two departments, three in each. Appointed by governor with approval of judicial council.

They are then elected for 12-year terms. No opposition, but running on their record. A yes or no vote.

A. Highest court of appeal in the state.
B. Cases come up from district court of appeal or superior court. All death cases reviewed.
C. May order any case in district court of appeal up to them on questions of law alone. No jury.
D. Issue writs of habeas corpus everywhere in state (except federal cases).
E. Final review unless U.S. constitutional question involved.

II. District Court of Appeal

There are four district courts of appeal with each district, having at least one division (court).

San Francisco—two divisions
Los Angles—four divisions
Sacramento—one division
San Bernardino—one division

There are three justices to each division, including a presiding justice. Three justices sit on each court. No jury.

A. Same procedure for appointment and term of office (12 years) as in supreme court.
B. Appellate jurisdiction on all criminal cases in their district prosecuted by indictment or information (felonies), except where judgment of death rendered.
C. Issues writs of habeas corpus for persons in custody within the district.

III. Superior Court

Number vary in different county—set by legislature.

A. Elected for six-year term.
B. Highest trial court—tries all feonies. May issue writ of habeas corpus in respective county.
C. Accepts appeals from lower, inferior courts.
D. Juvenile court—original jurisdiction for 702 W&I cases even if only a misdemeanor.

IV. Municipal Courts (Court Reorganization January 1, 1953)

Each county divided into Judicial Districts by Legislature; court tries misdemeanors.

A. Over 40,000 population—municipal court formed.
B. Under 40,000—justice court.
C. Where municipal court exists, there are no justice courts.

D. Justice court is a court for a township—a political subdivision of a county.
E. Police court is a city court.

V. Judicial Council

A. Composed of chief justice of supreme court, one associate justice, three justices of district court, four judges of superior court, one judge of municipal court, and one judge of inferior court, all chosen by chief justice for two-year term.
B. FUNCTION: Advising and coordinating body for improvement of the administration of justice. Assigning of judges from one county to another when calendars heavy. Prescribes rules for practice and procedure on appeals. Makes recommendations to governor and legislature regarding improvement in the judicial branch of government.

Appendix B

PURPOSE OF THE DISTRICT ATTORNEY'S OFFICE*

THE PURPOSE OF THE DISTRICT ATTORNEY's office is to carry out the duties imposed by law upon the district attorney [1]. The principal functions of the district attorney's office are as follows:

Public Prosecutor

The district attorney is the public prosecutor.

Preparation and Trial of Criminal Cases

The district attorney prepares complaints upon which warrants are issued for the arrest of people charged with or reasonably suspected of committing public offenses. He draws all indictments and informations, and conducts the trial of criminal cases. He may grant immunity to witnesses. After felony conviction, the district attorney files with the clerk of the superior court his views with respect to the defendant and his crime for transmittal to the Department of Corrections, and he assists the attorney general on appeals from criminal convictions. He obtains civil judgment against bonding companies arising out of bail forfeiture. The district attorney investigates and reports to the superior court on all applications for rehabilitation and pardon.

---

* Adapted from California Criminal Justice Cost Project, Phase I. Prepared by Public Systems, Inc., Sunnyvale, California, August 1971 (mimeograph). For California Assembly Rules Committee, Sacramento, California.

Advisement Grand Jury

The district attorney is the legal advisor to the grand jury.

Trial of Accusations Against Public Officials

The district attorney conducts the trial of accusations against public officials.

Conducting of Civil and Criminal Actions for Nonsupport of Children

The district attorney is specifically required to prosecute criminal violations for nonsupport of children. In nonsupport matters, he also brings civil actions to determine paternity and conducts civil actions for nonsupport under the Uniform Reciprocal Support Act.

Abatement of Public Nuisances

The district attorney conducts civil and criminal actions to abate public nuisances.

Commitment and Trial of Mental Illness, Drug Addiction, and Inebriacy Cases

The district attorney prepares commitments for the mentally ill, the mentally deficient, and the feebleminded, narcotic addicts, and persons addicted to habit-forming drugs and inebriates. He also conducts the trials of these cases.

The district attorney prosecutes all violations of state law and county ordinances. He does not prosecute violations of federal statutes or violations of city ordinances.

To assist the district attorney in performing these functions, he has a staff of assistant and deputy district attorneys, criminal and nonsupport investigators, clerical personnel, and the Laboratory of Criminalistics.

PREPARING COMPLAINTS

Requirements

As public prosecutor, the district attorney prepares complaints for the arrest of people charged with or reasonably suspected of committing public offenses. In addition, he draws all indictments and informations. There are four tests that should be applied in every case before a criminal complaint is prepared. They are as follows:

1. Has a public offense been committed?
2. Is the identity of the perpetrator known?
3. Can the offense be proved beyond a reasonable doubt?
4. Should there be a prosecution under all the circumstances?

No complaint should be authorized unless each of the above four questions is answered in the affirmative.

While the prosecutor owes a duty to the people of the State of California to prepare complaints in proper cases, he also owes a duty to the accused to prove his case beyond a reasonable doubt. The prosecutor should never forget that an arrest is a serious matter, particularly to the individual arrested. Every arrest constitutes a criminal record, which, in most instances, will remain with the arrested person for life.

When a complaint is prepared, the proper ultimate charge should be selected at the outset. The practice of authorizing one charge and later reducing the case to a lesser charge or increasing to a greater charge should be studiously avoided.

Authority

Misdemeanors. All deputies are authorized to prepare misdemeanor complaints when the basic requirements for a criminal complaint have been met.

Felonies. In California, the assistant district attorneys and attorneys IV and III (more experienced senior D.A.) are authorized to prepare felony complaints.

The senior deputies assigned to courts (municipal) may authorize felony complaints for the respective police department in each jurisdiction. When the deputy assigned to these courts is not a senior attorney, he should, insofar as is practicable, review each felony complaint prepared with an assistant district attorney.

Drafting

In general. Complaints may be stated in the ordinary and concise language of the statute. The time at which the offense was committed may be pleaded at any time within the statute of limitations before filing the complaint. A single complaint may include two or more different offenses of the same class of crimes or two or more different offenses connected together in their commission.

Signing and Filing

Complaints may be sworn to on information and belief in both misdemeanor and felony cases. All felony complaints should be signed by a peace officer. Misdemeanor complaints should be signed by a peace officer whenever possible. Deputy district attorneys should not sign complaints except in instances where a stipulated reduction complaint is filed in a municipal or justice court.

Generally, complaints should be filed in the municipal or justice court having jurisdiction of the place where the offense was committed. An exception may be made in certain nonsupport cases and certain cases involving state regulatory agencies where all of the parties involved in the action is not residing in the place where the officer was committed.

When misdemeanors committed in another judicial district are filed in the county seat, the complaint should show on its face where the offense occurred.

Citizen Complaints

Felonies. All citizen complaints concerning the commission of felonies should be referred to the police agency having jurisdiction of the place where the offense occurred. A felony complaint requires preliminary examination, production of witnesses at preliminary and trial, and extensive investigation, which a private citizen is not able to perform. In addition, court notices for preliminary examination and trial are sent to the parties signing the complaint. Peace officers know what to do upon receipt of these notices, whereas private citizens usually do not.

Misdemeanors: investigated complaints. Where the police have investigated the commission of a misdemeanor and a citizen appears in the office with a copy of the police report seeking a complaint, he should be fully questioned to determine if the four requirements for preparing a complaint have been met. If it appears that a complaint should be authorized, and if the police report contains a statement of the accused regarding his side of the matter, then deputy district attorneys may prepare a complaint.

When it appears that the four requirements for preparing a criminal complaint have been met, but the police report contains no statement from the accused as to his side of the matter, a complaint should not be prepared until the deputy district attorney has given the accused a chance to state his side of the case. The complainant should be advised that the accused will be given an opportunity to state his side of the matter, and a future date should be set when the complainant can be informed of the results of the deputy district attorneys' interview with the accused and what action they then propose to take.

Prior to preparing a complaint, the complainant should be informed of the seriousness of a criminal action. He should further be clearly informed that once the action is instituted, only the district attorney can move the court to dismiss it: he cannot drop charges after the action has begun.

It is generally better practice to move slowly in authorizing citizen complaints. Trials are usually conducted many months after a complaint is issued. Most citizen complainants will no longer wish to come to court over the matter after a few weeks' time has elapsed. Deputy district attorneys should be particularly cautious about approving criminal complaints where family or neighborhood disputes are involved. Many of these disputes are primarily civil in nature, and a separation, divorce, civil injunction, or move away from the undesirable neighborhood is the only real solution to the problem. A criminal complaint rarely solves the basic problem in these cases. Usually, the citation method of handling the dispute will be more successful than authorizing a criminal complaint.

Misdemeanors: noninvestigated complains. In cases where there has been no police investigation in the citizen's complaint, except for very minor criminal matters, the complainant should be referred to the police department having jurisdiction of the offense so that the complaint may be investigated. When the investigation is complete, the case should be handled as an investigated complaint described above. The district attorney's office is not an investigative agency and has neither the personnel nor authority to conduct investigative work that should be done by police agencies.

Minor criminal complaints involving only the complainant and the accused may be investigated by the deputy district attorney, using the citation method. A deputy district attorney should never authorize a noninvestigated citizen complaint without first hearing what the accused has to say.

Police Agency Complaints

Complaints prepared for police agencies must meet the same four requirements as any other complaint outlined in requirements above. Before authorizing the complaint, the deputy district attorney should assure herself that all necessary police investigation has been completed. If the investigation necessary to prove the case beyond a reasonable doubt has not been completed, the complaint should not be authorized until such investigation is complete. The fact that a person is already in custody is no justification for issuing a criminal complaint where, because of incomplete investigation, the case cannot be proved beyond a reasonable doubt.

If a complaint meets the four requirements and is authorized for a police agency, a copy of the complete police report should be attached to the office copy of the complaint. At the time the complaint is authorized, the officer in charge of the investigation should be clearly advised of any follow-up investigation that will be required prior to trial.

At the time the complaint is authorized, the officer should be advised which witness and what evidence will be required for the preliminary examination. The officer should further be advised that the preliminary examination will be held within five days and that the witnesses and evidence must be present in court at that time.

Deputy district attorneys should resist any tendency to authorize a complaint either greater or lesser than the planned ultimate charge and disposition of the case. The practice of filing a greater charge with the idea in mind of taking a reduction at a latter date is not acceptable.

GLOSSARY
OF LEGAL TERMS

Abet. Encouraging or inciting a crime. Abet usually applies to aiding an individual in the violation of a law.

Accessory. Person who has knowledge of a law violation (felony) that has been committed and assists the perpetrator to avoid arrest, trial, or punishment.

Accomplice. Individual who is *equally* responsible for an offense considered a violation of a law.

Accused. Term for a defendant in a criminal case. Often used interchangeably with *prisoner* or *defendant*.

Admission. Acknowledgment of the existence of an act or a fact.

Affiant. Refers to a person who constructs and signs an affidavit.

Affidavit. A written statement made under oath, usually before a notary public or another authorized person.

Affirmation. Positive declaration or assertion, but not under oath, that the witness will tell the truth.

Aggressor. One who aggresses; a person who initiates a quarrel or fight, making an unprovoked attack.

Aid and abet. Any assistance rendered by encouraging words, acts, support, or presence.

Alias. Fictitious name sometimes used by fleeing felons.

Alibi. Excuse; the accused person was elsewhere than at the alleged scene of the offense with which he is charged.

Alien. Foreigner; a foreign-born resident of this country who has not become a naturalized citizen.

Allegation. An assertion that is without proof but that its advocate proposes to support with evidence.

Amicus curiae. Friend of the court. Usually an attorney who volunteers to assist the court in whatever manner deemed necessary.

Anarchist. Although philosophically speaking, an anarchist is someone who believes that the best government is no government at all, in criminal law it is a person who proposes the overthrow of the government by creating disorder and violence.

Animus. State of mind, intention, and will.

Animus furandi. Fully intending to commit a theft (state of mind at the time the theft is committed).

Annul. Invalidate; void and cancel. Commonly used in annulment of marriage.

Anonymous. No name known or acknowledged; unsigned letter, note, etc.

Anthropometry. Having to do with the measurement of the human body to determine differences in races; comparison with corresponding measurements of other individuals.

Appellate. Relating to appeals; person who appeals to a higher court; appeals from the decision of the lower court to a higher court.

Appellate court. A court that has the power to review appeals from another jurisdiction and affirm or reverse the decisions of lower courts.

Appellee. Person appealed against; often referred to as the *respondent*.

Arraignment. Bringing a person before a court of law to answer an accusation.

Asportation. Taking away; moving of items from one place and transporting them to another. Removal of such goods is extremely important when considering any offense of larceny.

Attainder. Loss of civil rights, inheritance, property, etc. Such loss of civil rights occurs after a person has committed treason or felony and received a sentence of death for his crime.

Attest. To bear witness and testify under oath or signature.

Autopsy. Examination and dissection of a dead body to discover the cause of death.

Bailiff. A sheriff's assistant who serves processes and the officer who has charge of prisoners and guards the jurors in court.

Bailment. Provision of bail for an arrested person.

Bench warrant. Order issued by a judge or law court for the arrest of a person charged with contempt of court or a criminal offense.

Bunco game. Act or trick contrived to gain the confidence of the victim, who is then defrauded. This form of theft is handled by a special investigative unit in most police departments.

Cadaver. Corpse; the body of a person who has been dead over a period of time.

Causa causanas. Immediate cause and the last link in the change of causative factors (Black's Law Dictionary).

Caveat emptor. Under this particular rule, it is incumbent upon the buyer to examine the goods and determine any malfunctions or defects. Often termed as "let the buyer beware" or "take care."

Certiorari. Review; the higher court issuing a writ directing the lower jurisdiction to forward all records and proceedings for *review*, or trial, of issues in question.

Change of venue. A suit that is initiated in one county or district and is changed to another county or district for trial purposes has had change of venue. A good example of change of venue in a criminal case would be the Angela Davis trial and John Linley Frazier trial transferred from its county of initial jurisdiction to the County of Santa Clara.

Chattel. Item, article, or piece of property that is somewhat personal and transferable.

Cold blood. Crime not committed in a fit of anger; this is a term utilized in cases relating to homicides in which there is an absence of emotion or violent passion: "The crime was executed in cold blood."

Collusion. Secret agreement for fraudulent or illegal purposes; conspiracy.

Commitment. Consignment to state prison; commitment by means of a court order or warrant of a person to a particular facility for incarceration.

Common law. Unwritten law of the county based on custom, usage, and decisions of law courts, as contrasted with *statute law*. Common-law marriage is not solemnized by religious or civil ceremony but effected by an agreement to live together as husband and wife; cohabitation.

Coroner. County officer whose function is to inquire into the circumstances and causes of any violent or sudden death (with suspicion) occurring within her jurisdiction. Often referred to as "the coroner's inquest."

Corporal punishment. A punishment that is physical, as distinguished from punishment by a fine.

Corpse. Dead body, commonly of a human being.

Corpus delicti. Substance of the crime; the essential elements of a violation of law—*not* a dead human body.

Corroborating evidence. Further confirming evidence; evidence that seconds or confirms initial evidence.

Deadly weapon. Weapon designed for the destruction of life or inflicting a severe injury.

Debauchery. Excessive hedonistic pleasure; usually in the sense of sexual immorality or the unlawful excessive indulgence of lust in the form of sexual activity.

Deliberately. Intentionally, willfully, with premeditation—"in cold blood."

Demurrer. Plea for the dismissal of a lawsuit on the grounds that even if the statements of the opposition are true, they do not sustain the claim because they are insufficient or otherwise legally defective.

Dictum. A formal statement made by the judge; a judge's statement or opinion on some legal point other than the principal issue of the case. Such a statement usually is utilized as illustration or argument.

Domicile. Customary or permanent dwelling place, home, residence. Taken in a legal frame of reference, domicile refers to "one's official or legal residence."

Duress. Coercion or compulsion, as confession signed under duress.

Emancipation. Rendered free or set at liberty by his parents, guardian, or master, as "a child emancipated from his parents." trusted to one's care.

Eminent domain. Government's power to take private property for public use.

Entrapment. Deceiving or tricking a person into committing a crime not contemplated by the individual. Entrapment does not imply the mere act of a police officer furnishing a person the opportunity to violate the law, where the criminal intent was already present.

Evidence. Represents any question of fact; the procurement of facts to substantiate the violation; the gathering of facts that would constitute sufficient evidence to prosecute.

Exparte. Action in behalf of one party only.

Ex post facto law. Retroactive laws. Under the Constitution of the United States, the states cannot pass any *ex post facto* laws.

Extortion. The use of coercion, force, or fear to obtain property from others.

Extradition. The fleeing of a felon to another state and the surrender of a felon by the state where he is found to a receiving state for prosecution of the crime.

Facsimile. *Exact* copy of the original.

False arrest. Unlawful physical restraint upon another's liberty. Such restrictions could occur in prisons, jails, or other maximum-security facilities.

Felonious. Malicious intent to commit a crime; an important element here is intent.

Habeas corpus. In Latin, *habeas corpus* means "you have the body." *Habeas corpus* is a term accorded to a variety of writs. These writs serve as instruments for bringing the accused party immediately before the court or judge. In law, a writ or order requiring that a prisoner be brought before a court at a stated time and place to decide the legality of his detention or imprisonment. In other words, the right of *habeas corpus* safeguards one against illegal detention or imprisonment.

Holograph. An instrument, usually a deed or will, written entirely by a person without the benefit of an attorney or any kind of legal advice. It is written in his own hand and is accepted by courts throughout the land as his last testament.

Indictment. An accusation or charge in writing by a grand jury; specifically, a formal writing; an accusation; a charging of one or more persons with the commission of a crime, presented by a grand jury to the court when the jury has found, upon examining the prosecutor's statement of the charge (bill of indictment), that there is a valid case.

Infanticide. The murder of an infant immediately after birth. The actual birth of the infant distinguishes this particular act from "procuring abortion." Abortion is the destruction of the fetus in the womb.

Information. In law, *information* is an accusation of criminal offense, not by indictment of a grand jury but by a public officer such as the district attorney. It is an accusation in the nature of an indictment, differing from the grand jury indictment in that it is presented by a competent public officer in his oath of office.

Injunction. Writ or order from a court prohibiting a person or a group from carrying out a given action, or ordering a given action to be done. An injunction enjoins, binds, or commands a person to refrain from or to commit a particular act.

Inquest. Judicial inquiry, especially when held before a jury, as a coroner's investigation of a death. The coroner's inquest investigates the manner of death and is authorized to bring forth a verdict of such an inquiry.

Insanity. Legally there are numerous tests of insanity, such as the Duran and the M'Naughton Rules. It is a state of illness or derangement and, specifically in law, any form or degree of mental derangement or unsoundness, permanent or temporary, that makes a person incapable of what is regarded legally as normal, rational conduct or judgment. Such a state, legally, prevents a man from comprehending the nature and the consequences of his acts and from distinguishing between right and wrong conduct.

Intent. A state of mind. A formulation of a design or a resolve to do a particular act. Some criminal laws specify that there be a concurrent act and intent to commit said act.

Juridical days. Days in which courts are in session.

Jurisdiction. 1. Territorial range of authority; "jurisdiction of the court." 2. The administration of justice; authority or legal power to hear and decide cases. The power to adjudicate or exercise any judicial power over a person within the jurisdiction (1) of the court.

Jurisprudence. The science of philosophy of law or system of laws; a part or division of a law.

Jurist. An expert in law; a scholar or writer in the field of law.

Jury. In legal terms, a group of people sworn to hear the evidence and inquire into the facts in a law case and to arrive at a decision in accordance with their findings. "The right to be judged by a competent jury of his peers."

Kleptomaniac. One who continues to involve himself in thefts of items because of an irresistible, persistent, and abnormal impulse or tendency to steal.

Maladministration. Insufficient or corrupt conduct of public affairs.

Malfeasance. Misconduct in handling public affairs, as, for instance, when an official is found guilty of taking graft.

Malice aforethought. The intention to commit an unlawful act; a deliberate intention and plan to commit a violation of law—as in murder, for example.

Malicious. Spitefully and maliciously causing the injury of someone; intentionally mischievous or harmful.

Malign. Slander; an evil deception causing harm to one's reputation.

Malum in se (plural: **Mala in se**). Wrong in itself; and offense against conscience; the very nature of the act is illegal based upon principles of natural, moral, and public law (*Black's Law Dictionary*).

Malum prohibitum. An act expressly prohibited by law. The act need not be considered immoral, but by the very nature of the fact that the law forbids such an act it is *malum prohibitum*.

Mens rea. "State of mind"; criminal intent.

Motive. Refers to any impulse, emotion, or desire that moves one to action (e.g., "Greed was his only *motive* for stealing." "His *motive* for murdering his grandfather was for the inheritance."). Motive is an inner drive, impulse, or intention that causes a person to do something or act in a certain way. In order to allay any confusion, the distinguishing factor between motive and intent is that *motive* is, as previously stated, an inner drive, impulse, emotion, etc. that moves one to action to obtain a definite reward or result; *intent*, in contrast, is the desire to use a particular "tool" to create, effect, or produce such a result.

Murder. Unlawful and malicious or premeditated killing of one human being by another. A murder can also be viewed as such when in the course of committing a felony such as rape or robbery, a human being is killed by another. The killing of a person unlawfully with malice.

Nolo contendere. Noncontested issue. (Latin: "I will not contest it.") A plea in a criminal action that may have the same legal ramifications as the plea of guilty insofar as all proceedings on the indictment, and on which the defendant may be sentenced by the court. It may not be used as an admission elsewhere, such as in a civil case whereby the victim attempts to obtain civil remedy for any losses sustained (for example, an automobile accident case, in which restitution for damages is sought).

Precedent. A previous decision by a court that may serve as an example or authority for a similar case.

Presentment. A statement made by a grand jury of a crime that they observed on their own, without a bill of indictment having been laid before them.

Prima facie. From the first disclosure or at first sight. "We will put on a prima facie case."

Recidivist. Person who continues to commit criminal acts—a habitual criminal (repeater).

Stare recisis. Upholding precedence; resting upon the principle that any law by which government seeks to govern its people should be unfluctuating, definite, and of common knowledge. Laws cannot be changed unless changed by competent authority.

Subpoena. Order by the court compelling a person to appear in court (as witnesses). The subpoena (*subpeona duces tecum*) may also require the party to bring with them all documents, records, and evidence that may be in their possession.

Substantive law. Codified law; that particular part of law that creates and defines and regulates rights, as opposed to remedial law, which prescribes a particular method of obtaining redress for their violations.

Summons. An official order to appear in court; a writ, directed to a public servant, usually a sheriff, to notify the person named that an action had been taken against him in court and to require him to appear on the date and time named in the writ in order to answer the complaint and the action in question.

Tort. A wrongful act, injury, or damage (not involving a breach of contract) for which a civil action can be brought.

Transcript. Official description of a court hearing; proceedings in court are recorded by an official court reporter, thereby making the proceedings available to anyone interested in a judgment or other pertinent information in court.

Trauma. Injury or wound violently produced and the condition of neurosis resulting from such a wound. Psychiatrically speaking, an emotional experience, or shock, which has a lasting psychic effect.

Trial. The act or process of trying, testing, or putting to proof; a formal examination of the facts of a case by a court of law to decide the validity of a charge or claim.

Venue. Specific place in which a case is tried; the place in which the court has jurisdiction of the case. The county or locality in which the cause of action occurs or where the crime is committed and the locality in which a jury is drawn and the case is tried. Venue is that part of a declaration in an action that designates the county in which the trial is to occur. "Change of venue," in law, is the substitution of another place of trial, as when the jury or court is likely to be prejudiced.

Writ of certiorari. A writ utilized by a high court directing the lower court to send all the available information (records) of a proceeding in order that it be reviewed by the higher court. All cases on appeals usually involve the writ of certiorari.

Writ of execution. A writ issued to confiscate property to satisfy a civil judgment.

Writ of habeas corpus. Any person responsible for the confinement of another individual may be required by order of the court to immediately present the person before the court in order that the judge can ascertain the legal reasons for such a confinement. If the court is of the opinion that such a confinement is illegal, the judge orders the person so confined to be released. Such a writ may be directed to police officers, prison officials, sheriff (responsible for jail incarceration), or, with unusual circumstances, a private citizen. Such a writ orders the person responsible for the confinement of another to present the prisoner before the court immediately and assigns a time and place for such adhering.

INDEX OF
LEGAL CASES

INDEX